To my favourite musiac.
Anthony,
Christmas, 2000

Fiddler on the March

Fiddler

A Biography of
Lieutenant Colonel Sir Vivian Dunn
KCVO OBE FRAM Royal Marines

on the March

Derek Oakley MBE

Foreword by HRH The Prince Philip KG KT
Captain General Royal Marines

Royal Marines Historical Society

Dedicated to the memory of
my beloved wife Pam
who sang in a wartime Wrens' choir
under FVD's baton at the Royal Albert Hall

Published 2000 by the Royal Marines Historical Society
in association with Eastney Collection
60 Mayford Road, London SW12 8SN

Designed and composed in Monotype Photina by Peter Moore
Printed in Spain by Bookprint S.L., Barcelona

ISBN 0 9536163 0 4

Contents

BUCKINGHAM PALACE.

I am delighted that Derek Oakley has written this biography. Vivian Dunn was a remarkable man and his life was one long success story. He was obviously talented beyond the ordinary, but, unlike so many, he made the very most of it. His contribution to military music alone is impressive enough, but that, together with his dedication to the Royal Marines Band Service, singles him out as someone who stamped his personality on his contemporaries and successors.

I had the pleasure of first meeting him when he was Director of Music of the Royal Yacht Band during The Queen's Tour of the Commonwealth in 1953-54. The Tour started in SS 'Gothic' and then we transferred to the newly completed Royal Yacht 'Britannia' in Malta for the passage home. Under his direction, the Royal Yacht Band provided wonderful entertainment onboard and performed with outstanding success at every opportunity ashore. He established a standard and a tradition for quality, which the whole Royal Marines Band Service retains to this day.

His subsequent appointments continued to bring us into contact and it was a pleasure to witness his achievements and his growing stature and reputation in the musical world as a whole. There was a very apt phrase in his obituary. "When he raised his baton, it was like a call to arms".

Introduction

The title of this book, suggested in jest by his friend and accountant, aptly conveys the unique transition from the first violins of the symphony orchestra to the martial music of the military band.

Histories of families serving in all branches of the Services abound, and many renowned names come to mind. The tradition of family service is synonymous with the glorious British history of the sea, of regiments and corps, and in these days in the air, too.

Where the history of military music in families is concerned, the Army takes pride of place through such names as Godfrey, Winterbottom, Miller, Ricketts, O'Donnell and Dunn – fathers and sons, brothers, uncles and nephews abound. Two generations were not uncommon, but the Dunns may be said to be unique in extending in unbroken service in succession to three generations, through grandfather, father and son, the last into the Royal Marines.

Francis Vivian Dunn was probably the greatest of them all, certainly the only military musician ever to be knighted and have such a profound influence on military music throughout the three Services. From the time he was born within the sound of his father's bandroom in India in 1908, until conducting his last performance in 1994, he could proudly boast of being involved with military music in all ten decades of the twentieth century.

He was the last of his line and always claimed that he had been born under a lucky star through having a wonderful father and mother who allowed, and indeed encouraged, him to indulge his passion for music. His was the good fortune to inherit a pedigree in the family profession which allowed him exceptional opportunities for musical education and study.

Brought up to a classical education, playing in the Henry Wood Promenade Concerts and being a founder member of the BBC Symphony Orchestra by the time he was 22 years old, he changed course and astounded the military pundits by applying and being accepted for the position of Director of Music of the Portsmouth Divisional Band of the Royal Marines. This gamble was a precedent which was not popular with the military musicians of his time, but proved to be one of those inspirational decisions that subsequently bore more fruit than anyone could ever have expected.

In retirement, he continued to work unceasingly in pursuit of musical perfection, conducting major orchestras and lecturing throughout the country. He also conducted many youth orchestras and bands in the United Kingdom and travelled widely in the United States becoming heavily involved with University and College wind bands.

Vivian Dunn's service to four Sovereigns, as first ever Principal Director of Music of the Royal Marines, and the transformation he effected of an old-fashioned band service into arguably the finest in the world, coupled with his excellent compositions and arrangements, are the bare threads of this extraordinary story. The first serviceman to become Master of the Worshipful Company of Musicians, amongst the many honours bestowed on him were an EMI Gold Disc and the Silver Statuette of the American Academy of Wind and Percussion Arts.

This book is being published at the same time as a series of early recordings made by the orchestra of the Portsmouth Division Royal Marines, under Captain F Vivian Dunn, are being released on CDs under the title *Concert Classics*. The initiative of issuing digitally enhanced reproductions of these old recordings comes from Major Paddy Dunn and John Ambler, and the series is a Royal Marines Historical Society Production.

Derek Oakley
Hayling Island, Hampshire
October 1999

Acknowledgements

So many people have contributed to this biography that some names will inevitably be left out, for which I apologise. Many *are* mentioned in the text, but all have been invaluable in providing me with a more intimate insight into a brilliant musician and friend, whom I had the privilege of knowing for over fifty years.

Having been invited to write Lieutenant Colonel Vivian Dunn's biography by his family, I must first pay tribute to the late John Trendell, who had started on some very comprehensive research but sadly died before he had put anything but a few notes on paper. The support from Vivian and Mike's three children, Major Paddy Dunn, Mrs Leonie Lithgow and Mrs Rosemary Foster and their families has been substantial and willingly forthcoming. They have given me complete access to the very extensive Dunn archives and photograph collection whilst adding the human and family touches so important in getting to the heart of one's subject.

I would also like to single out John Ambler, the UK Chairman of the International Military Music Society for providing me with considerable factual information as well as the comprehensive index of compositions, recordings and arrangements. Thanks to both Major Gordon Turner and Alastair Mitchell, for their appreciations of the military and orchestral compositions of Vivian Dunn, appraisals which I, as a non-musician, was certainly not qualified to make.

Others I would like to thank for their help and contributions include Drum Major Charles Bowden, Lieut Colin Bowden, Colonel John Coke, Mrs Freda Connah, Colin Dean, Mrs Brian Dunn, Robert Farnon, Capt Terry Freestone, Miss Sidonie Goossens, Capt Doug Haigh, Lt Col Graham Hoskins, Lt Cdr David Hough, Capt Tommy Lambert, Lt Col Jim Mason, Roy Morgan, Lieut Roy Nash, Lt Col Paul Neville, Capt Robin Patteson-Knight, Maj Richard Powell, Michael Rice, Dudley Ruel, Lt Cdr Jack Shepherd, Capt Wally Shillitto, Capt Peter Sumner, Alan Toze, Stuart Upton, Lt Col Richard Waterer, Capt Ted Whealing, Lieut Ray Woodfield and Dr Al Wright; Major Alastair Donald, Anthony Perrett and Miss Elspeth Scott have kindly commented on the text before publication and many others have provided snippets and anecdotes.

Extracts from various sources have been freely granted by the Royal Marines Band Service journal *The Blue Band*, the Royal Marines journal *The Globe & Laurel* and the IMMS journal *Band International*; the Royal Marines Museum and the Royal Marines School of Music have provided archive material.

Most of the photographs have come from Vivian Dunn's private family collection and many have no indication of their source. Credit is due to the following, their heirs or successors:

> Lambert Weston, Folkestone; Stage Photo Co.; London News Agency (Photos) Ltd.; Wright & Logan, Southsea; Portsmouth Newspapers Ltd.; Kirk & Son, Cowes; Adco Photo Service; *Luton News*; E. Philipps, Southampton; Dominion Press, London; Central Press Photos, London; Basil Kidd, Deal; Norman Cavell, Deal; Media Colour Services Ltd., Midhurst; Doug Mckenzie, London; Lewis Photos, London; *The Times*, London (Royal Tour Pool Photos); *The Hobart Mercury*, Tasmania; Cowderoy and Moss Ltd., London; Chapman & Day, Deal.

CHAPTER I

Opus One - Born into the Bandroom

CHRISTMAS WAS APPROACHING in the garrison region of Jubbulpore in the Central Provinces of India. The scenery in the countryside around the city was breathtaking. Surrounding the city there were numerous small lakes, shaded by trees and interspersed with craggy gorges. Situated almost in the centre of India, 600 miles from Bombay and 200 miles from Alahabad, Jubbulpore had been garrisoned by units of the British army since the early days of the century and it was a much sought-after posting.

The 2nd Battalion of the 60th Rifles, The King's Royal Rifle Corps, had arrived in Jubbulpore on 20th January 1907, having been in India since landing in Bombay from South Africa on 31st December 1900. Here they found rather more luxuriant and peaceful surroundings than the Regiment had experienced in their prolonged fighting during the Boer War.

It was into these peaceful surroundings that Francis Vivian Dunn was born on Christmas Eve, 1908, thus just escaping being christened Noel. His father was William James Dunn, known as 'Paddy' throughout his life, who had enlisted in the 1st Bn Duke of Wellington's Regiment in 1889, and began the pupil's course at Kneller Hall in 1898 followed by the Student Bandmaster's course in 1903. He was then appointed the Bandmaster of the 2nd Battalion KRRC on 13th November 1906 when he had a magnificent band built to 80 strong and enjoyed an enviable reputation due to his industry and innovative ideas. Mr Dunn had even been invited to score the National Anthem for the visiting Amir of Afghanistan, a tune which had been passed down by ear for generations – this was arranged with entirely satisfactory results for the Band Fund. Regimental reports on Bandmaster Dunn for the period from 1906-1910 indicate 'Great zeal, nothing to be desired. Exemplary, steady and reliable. Indefatigable. A great acquisition.' He remained with the Battalion for 21 years and subsequently became Director of Music of the Royal Horse Guards (The Blues) from 1927-1935. He was appointed MVO in the New Year's Honours 1935 on his retirement.

Not only was W J Dunn a fine musician and conductor, but he was also a redoubtable character. He was the only Bandmaster in the British Army to be awarded the Military Cross in World War I for gallantry on the field of battle on 25th January 1915. He told his son in later years that, strictly speaking, as the band had been left behind when the battalion went to France, he should not have been there at all! He was so keen to join his battalion that, with the connivance of the Adjutant and RSM, he dressed as a rifleman and secretly joined a draft. His CO was furious and threatened him with court-martial. Not knowing what to do with him, it was discovered that the 2nd Infantry Brigade Ammunition Column was without a commander, so Dunn filled the gap. He was responsible for saving an ammunition column and was ordered to take small arms ammunition to the 3rd Infantry Battalion who were in the front line under heavy fire. For this action he was awarded the MC, one of the very few Warrant Officers to be awarded this medal and certainly the only Bandmaster. He was severely wounded and fell from his horse during the Battle of Neuve Chapelle in March 1915. After being evacuated to England and a period of convalescence he was appointed to take charge of the Rifle Brigade bands at their Depot in Winchester.

He wrote a few marches *Bravest of the Brave*, *Brabazon* and *United Empire* being three of the best and a couple of fanfares *Dunns* and *Dunns No 2*. In addition to his widely appreciated musical ability he was a great innovator and a good businessman with a keen eye on enhancing the reputation and popularity of his band. He was the first to establish what was known as the 'Silver Band' – all the brass instruments were silver plated – as well as the long model 'Aida' trumpets. In conjunction with the silver bugles, the Band of the 60th Rifles at 140 paces to the minute was an unforgettable sight on parade. At the Paris Exhibition of 1912 he acquired an electric instrument with a keyboard of an octave and a half of well-tuned bells, called a Unaphone. It had a magical effect when playing slow melodies accompanied by the band. At its first appearance at an

Beatrice Maud with her first born son Vivian at his christening

officers' mess guest night it was played by Vivian's mother. When the commanding officer learnt that it had not yet been paid for, he passed a menu round for donations which promptly secured the purchase. The Unaphone is preserved in the Museum at Kneller Hall.

Vivian's mother, Beatrice Maud Dunn, whom he described as 'a beautiful woman', was the one who had the greatest influence on his early life and musical education. She came from a military background and her father Captain Francis Stone, an officer in the Rifle Brigade (the 95th), had married Frances Scutt in Gibraltar, which might have led to some confusion during conversations! Their marriage certificate shows that one of the witnesses was illiterate and signed with 'her mark'. Beatrice encouraged and taught Vivian in the musical arts especially the classics. She was an accomplished pianist with an outstanding sense of perfect pitch, an organist and harpist who was also a talented artist in her own right. Prior to her marriage she had played a number of pianoforte concertos which her future husband had conducted.

However music in the family went back a further generation to his grandfather, Thomas Dunn, a Band Sergeant of the 1st Battalion, the 33rd Regiment of Foot (The Duke of Wellington's Regiment) and whose wife was Spanish. Thomas, who served from 1863 to 1886, seeing active service in the Abyssinian campaign of 1867-68, had three sons who were all given a thorough musical education. He was a strict disciplinarian and expected great things of his offspring.

He married a beautiful Spanish girl while serving in Gibraltar; and there is a family story that when she was in her sixties, Vivian was presented to her at a very tender age to have a filial kiss bestowed on him. The sight of the old lady dressed all in black with a white lace cap and a silver knobbed cane was too much for him and he burst out howling *fortissimo*; to be quickly despatched from the scene by his father. He claimed it was not the most enjoyable incident in his young life at that time. He never knew whether he was forgiven for this black mark.

Thomas's eldest son, also Thomas, died at an early age whilst serving as a Corporal with the 'Dukies' in Malta. He had always been referred to as 'a bit of a character' and was returned to his regiment from the Royal Military School of Music, Kneller Hall, for some unspecified reason!

Augustus Joseph Dunn, the second son, was also a fine musician and conductor, having joined the Royal Field Artillery in 1886. A legend in his time when Bandmaster of the 2nd Battalion The Royal Irish Fusiliers (1897-1910), his confidential reports record 'His tact leaves nothing to be desired – Perfectly satisfied, admirable service – Great efficiency – Exemplary'. Although he had been offered the appointment as Director of Music, The Coldstream Guards, an appointment he refused, he became Bandmaster of the Royal Artillery (Mounted Band) in 1918, retiring prematurely in 1920 due to ill health.

Augustus was a fine clarinettist, but it was his ability as a pianist and organist that gave him a complete insight into his profession. On one occasion he had the misfortune to break an arm, but he was invoked to continue practising the piano with one hand until the use of the other was restored. Such keyboard ability was rare in the Army at that time. He was reported to have been quite outstanding as a bandmaster, one of the smartest and most accomplished in the Army. His compositions included *Quatre Bras*, a quick step which was published by Rudall Carte, and

L'Affaire d'Amour for which he won the composition silver medal at Kneller Hall in 1906. He had a fine ear and was a perfectionist in everything he did, demanding the same from his band. The combination of his father's Irish and his mother's Spanish blood gave him a true artistic temperament. He was devoted to his band and his regiment and his sterling qualities were never more aptly demonstrated than when he was taken prisoner of war in South Africa. He became dangerously ill and was only saved by the devotion of his Band Sergeant, who managed to obtain some gruel to keep him going. His experiences in the South African War, allied with his being invalided home with enteric fever, were undoubtedly responsible for his untimely death in middle age in 1923.

During their simultaneous careers there was great rivalry between the two brothers A J and W J, and at times the friction led to them hardly speaking to each other. One such incident was in 1911 when W J successfully obtained an engagement at the White City Exhibition, which both had sought after. They shared volatile temperaments and outstanding musical reputations with the concert-going public of that era. Their brilliant personalities clearly demonstrated the axiom that 'a band is only as good as its Bandmaster makes it!' Perhaps it was the Irish blood in them that occasionally fomented, but they both found their profession all-rewarding and their life's work, in which they stood supreme, absorbing.

A young musician in the making. Vivian with his toy drum in 1911 when his father was Bandmaster of the 2nd Bn KRRC, stationed at Shorncliffe.

Thus Vivian inherited a tradition in military music unbroken in the family since 1845.

W J's first family home in England in 1910 was at Shorncliffe in Kent, and maybe the young Vivian's first 'taste' of royal occasions came when his father's battalion lined the route of the funeral procession for King Edward VII on 20th May. Vivian recalled that when the family returned to England, his father used to sit him on a high stool whilst he meticulously rehearsed the classics for hours at a time. The child was only three, so it was not surprising that it rubbed off on him and stood him in such

Bandmaster Dunn with the Band of the 2nd KRRC at Colchester in 1905

good stead throughout most of the century. The family remained at Shorncliffe until 1913. War came the following year and five years later, after occupation duties in the Rhineland, the 2nd Bn KRRC was posted to Victoria Barracks in Portsmouth. When his father moved to the Rifle Depot at Winchester in 1916, the family remained there for some years. The family's connections with the Green Jackets stretched even further back to his maternal grandfather, Francis Stone, and an uncle, Captain Edward Scutt, in the KRRC (60th Rifles). Vivian recalls an early staple diet of 140 paces to the minute in march tempo!

Vivian's brother Geoffrey Brian was born in 1916 and was soon inculcated in musical ways. Like his brother he became a violinist and conductor. He was known as 'Chiffer' from his school days at Kingston Grammar school leaving there in 1933 to go to the Royal Academy of Music. He then spent six years mainly studying the violin and conducting for which he was awarded the Manns Memorial prize. While he was there he discovered that there was another Geoffrey Dunn at the Academy and so assumed his second name of Brian.

RIGHT:
Bandmaster W J Dunn, Vivian's father, the only Bandmaster to be awarded the MC in the Great War

FAR RIGHT:
The first signs of a nautical career when at Winchester in 1916

Vivian's early schooling began at a kindergarten run by Madame Mollet, a French refugee. Her assistant Miss Gore-Brown, a formidable apparition remembered for an ample bosom and a high neck lace dress with huge leg-of-mutton sleeves, is portrayed as having been something of an ogress, but was probably very kind, doing her best with a somewhat reluctant pupil.

On Saturday mornings, he regularly came under the influence of a charming singing teacher, a Miss Graham, who had a studio above Teague & King's music shop in the Piazza, near Winchester Cathedral. He studied further under the rather irascible Dr Prendergast, the Cathedral organist, and was soon accepted as a probationer in the choir of St Maurice's church, directly in the Piazza by the Buttercross. Sadly, the proving ground for this excellent choir was demolished by a flying bomb in 1944.

In 1917 Vivian was sent to Peter Symonds School in Winchester, which he recalled with much happiness. Two contemporaries with whom he became particularly friendly in later years were Horatio Murray who joined the Cameronians and subsequently became GOC, Scottish Command as General Sir Horatio Murray KCB; and Joe Cox, whom he met again when he was an Air Vice Marshal in Colombo. Cox had been one of Douglas Bader's flying instructors.

During the year a severe bout of influenza caused voice strain which resulted in him leaving the cathedral choir, but the experience had instilled in him a love of church music. Vivian wrote about this incident 'Due to this change in fortune, perhaps posterity was saved from just another pushed-up baritone being foisted on the long suffering public!' Nevertheless he later affirmed his view that every conductor should have a thorough grounding in the art of solo and choral singing and the phrasing that equates in instrumental playing. He felt that Sir Henry Wood's *The Gentle Art of Singing* sums it all up.

Three years later, in 1920, Vivian went to St Helen's College in Southsea, Hampshire, where he again seems to have been very happy. For once this was a static period in the Dunn family's constantly moving existence, typical of service life in those days.

CHAPTER 2

Accelerando - Student Days

EARLY IN 1922, his father's regiment was sent to Cologne in the Rhine Army of Occupation. The family took up residence at Kleingedankstrasse 10, and his formal education continued privately with a former Bonn University student, Herr Helmut Klein, who had been discharged from the German army. He was an excellent teacher with whom Vivian immediately got on well. German became his principal subject, in addition to the three Rs. His brother Geoffrey, eight years his junior, went to a British Army Junior School at the nearby *Zugwegkaserne* (barracks) for his early education which included pianoforte tuition too.

At this time Vivian was introduced to the violin by a venerable teacher, Herr Fritz Alt, a former violinist at the Cologne Opera House. His father, W J, was very strict about the number of hours he should practise and it was his decision that the violin should become his son's principal instrument. Vivian's days became more than fully occupied, and his progress was such that he was accepted as a student at the *Konservatorium der Musik* in the Wolfstrasse at the age of 15. He was very much younger than most of his contemporaries.

Herr Hermann Zitzmann was his new professor and he took a keen interest in his eager English pupil and taught him well. Herr Zitzmann was the viola player in the Eldering String Quartet and the principal viola in the Gurzenich Orchestra, the conductor of which was the celebrated Hermann Abendroth, the Principal of the *Konservatorium*. He was a leading authority on Brahms, Wagner, Strauss and Mahler. Under his direction, the student orchestra was invited to attend the Quartet rehearsals and *der Junger Englander* benefited from the whole new world of music this opened up to him. Whilst attending the *Konservatorium* Vivian boarded with a German family at Volksgartenstrasse 36, a general practitioner and his wife and four children, the eldest, Arthur, being his own age. It was here that he was helped considerably by the Schmidt children to become fluent in German, although they were given strict instructions that this was only to be for the first three months. After that time, any incorrect request in German was never granted, although this was soon overcome with the surreptitious help of one of the younger daughters. He kept up a correspondence with the family until the outbreak of World War 2 and in 1946 was grieved to see their house had been destroyed by bombing.

His mother was his staunchest ally and, being so fond of cricket and football, would always tell him when the coast was clear so that he could go out and play. There were even occasions when she played his piano exercises and pieces to cover for him. His father never let on whether or not he knew. Vivian also got on well with all his student colleagues who marvelled at the young Englishman who spoke such excellent German.

Vivian later appreciated his father's insistence that he should attend the Opera. Although inflation of the German mark was rampant, he obtained a season ticket at minimal cost in the front row of the stalls immediately behind the conductor, Otto Klemperer. This experience riveted his attention on the conductor and the orchestra, rather than on the stage, though the singers and chorus made a lasting impression on this young student.

It was during this period that Vivian had his first taste of wearing uniform and no doubt some of the glamour rubbed off on him. He joined the 1st Cologne Troop of the Boy Scouts and came under the influence of a magnificent Scoutmaster, Captain Evelyn Rockley Gibson MC, of the Royal Artillery and an Old Sherburnian. Known to the boys as 'Gibbo', he was the manager of the Cologne branch of Lloyds Bank. He was an outstanding leader and his inspiring examples of conduct, ethics and belief in the code of honour remained with Vivian for the rest of his life. He also owned a Model T Ford, and gave the boys venturesome trips in it to Scout camps.

In 1925, the family returned to England and settled in Farnborough, Hampshire. Such had been his progress in Germany, that Vivian was accepted into the Royal Academy of Music at the age of 16, an experience he found to be the most rewarding of his student life as there were

Sir Henry Wood with his Queen's Hall Orchestra in 1928 rehearsing for the Promenade Concerts. Vivian can be seen in the first violins to the left of the conductor.

unrivalled opportunities for progress as an orchestral violinist. In addition, he was able to study as an embryo conductor under the great Sir Henry Wood, who later picked the young man out from the senior orchestra to play in his Queen's Hall Orchestra at the Promenade Concerts in 1928. This great conductor, who knew no superior as an orchestral trainer and master of the classics, was renowned by his players as a champion of new works by British composers and invariably included contemporary compositions in his programmes.

In those days the Proms season stretched over eight weeks, with three-hour rehearsals every morning from Monday to Saturday, and followed the pattern: Monday – Wagner; Tuesday – Mozart and Haydn; Wednesday – Bach and Handel; Thursday – Tchaikowsky, Brahms, Strauss, British composers and contemporary works; Friday – Beethoven, including all nine symphonies; whilst Saturday was regarded as 'Pops'. There were concertos for all instruments and accompanying singers in arias became their staple diet. This was a veritable saturation in everything that an aspiring conductor could wish for. It was all free for this young student and he was able to soak up the atmosphere and experience whilst being paid as a professional member of the orchestra in the first violin section.

His violin professor was Charles Woodhouse, a fine all-round musician in addition to being the leader of the orchestra, from whom he learned much. Harmony and composition were studied under B Walton O'Donnell, who had been Director of Music of both the bands of the

Portsmouth Division Royal Marines Light Infantry(until July 1923) and the Royal Marines Depot at Deal until he prematurely retired in 1927. He was another truly wonderful musician with illuminating, original ideas who also gave excellent harmony lectures. At his invitation, Vivian was given the opportunity to see him rehearse and broadcast with the Wireless Military Band of the recently formed British Broadcasting Company on many occasions. This was a fine band, formed from the cream of the professional wind players in London and O'Donnell's performances were legendary.

In the 1920s all the young students were interested in the dance bands which abounded in the metropolis. One day Woodhouse sent for the young student and said 'I don't believe you have been practising'. Vivian had to admit that he was right and owned up to the fact that he was spending his evenings – and half the night – playing the violin and saxophone in Jack Hylton's Kit Cat orchestra at the Kit Cat night club. He was earning about £25 a week, but it had meant staying up until 2am and then finding his way home. Woodhouse continued 'Thank you for telling me. I believe you have a choice; either you continue in the dance band world and probably make quite a lot of money – or you will only ever be half trained musically. Apart from wearing yourself out with the late hours, you will have to give up the Academy.' Vivian's mind was made up for him. Although he was a good violinist, he was not the greatest saxophone player in the world! It was soon after this that the offer came from Sir Henry Wood and his place in the first violins earned him £8.14s a week.

As a member of the Conductor's Class he was directed by Ernest Read, and amongst his contemporaries was Maurice Miles, who subsequently succeeded Read and was a fine conductor of several municipal orchestras and the BBC. Another, Douglas Hopkins, became Director of Music and organist of Canterbury Cathedral, while William Chalmers Burns became Professor of Music at Newcastle and Glasgow Universities. Friendships abounded and included the brilliant pianist Myers Foggin and Gwynne Edwards, a fine viola player, who later became director of the Chamber Music Class at the Academy.

A close friend was Kathleen Murray, later to achieve fame as Kay Cavendish for her marvellously popular BBC programmes. Yet another superb pianist was Phyllis Grover and Vivian was fortunate to enjoy many tennis occasions with both these ladies who were of pre-war Wimbledon standard. There were many more friends such as the organist Douglas Hawkridge and Edward Power Briggs, who emigrated to the United States to become a virtuoso recording artist. With this abundant talent around him, Vivian was determined to make a successful career in the music world.

The conducting students were encouraged to widen their experience with amateur choral, operatic and orchestral societies which abounded in areas around London before the war. Vivian conducted one in Kingston, close to where the family now lived in Teddington, and even played at the local Empire to improve his violin sight-reading!

Vivian also joined the Opera Class, which rehearsed twice a week at the Academy. In 1929 the students of this class gave performances at the new Scala Theatre in Tottenham Court Road of *Rigoletto, La Bohème* and *Merrie England* in the course of a single July week. They were accompanied by the RAM Opera Orchestra under Julius Harrison. This was a busy week as Vivian was chosen as one of the two assistant conductors, along with Maurice Miles. He also sang the small part of the Usher in *Rigoletto* on the Wednesday and the part of a Lord in *Merrie England* later in the week.

He soon realised that to improve his all round ability he needed to conduct operatic, choral and symphonic works. It was hard work trying to persuade distinguished conductors that he should be given an opportunity, but he persisted with very encouraging results. He was even taken on as the Chorus Master and *répétiteur* in the Opera Class, such was his determination.

Sir John McEwen, Principal of the Royal Academy of Music, approved Vivian's submission to stage two small operas, *La Serva Padrona* by Pergolesi and Debussy's *L'Enfant Prodigue* with members of the Opera Class under the direction of Winifred Baines. Irene Morden and Bernard Cannon were the principals, both of whom subsequently appeared in successful Ivor Novello shows of the 1930s and 1940s. He was supported by the illustrious Griller Quartet (Sidney Griller, Jack O'Brien, Philip Burton and Colin Hampton) along with the famous clarinettist Reginald Kell and the fine brass band composer, Gilbert Vintner, who played the bassoon. This array of talent voluntarily supported Vivian in his project at the Duke's Theatre, assisted by Julius Harrison, the Director of Opera. Two years working with him demonstrated what a wealth of music he absorbed during this period. He was prepared to work hard, to learn and he had the ambition to succeed. It left an indelible memory on the young musician as the opportunities were exceptional. Relishing in continuous hard work in the Chamber Music Class, Vivian recalled playing the whole of the Beethoven and Haydn quartets, the operas *Meistersingers, Madame Butterfly* and *Carmen*, all in one week!

Widening his conducting skills still further, his father 'Paddy' Dunn, along with Walton O'Donnell, who was to have such an influence on his career, invited Vivian to rehearse his Academy examination pieces by conducting the Blues (Royal Horse Guards) Band. Thus his military music experience was taking shape.

Sir Henry Wood, known to all as 'Timber', rehearsed the senior orchestra twice weekly for three hours on Tuesdays and Fridays, a model of the art of conducting and orchestral training. What more could a young man want? This gave Vivian the unrivalled opportunity for playing under the finest conductors of the day, Wood, Beecham, Boult, Sargent, Barbirolli and the visitors Klemperer, Malko and Bruno Walter. He was able to absorb the classical repertoire – Elgar, Vaughan Williams, Holst, Stravinsky, Ravel and so on. He saw, at first hand, the playing of the world's best soloists, Kreisler, Casals, Rachmaninoff, Myra Hess and the renowned Russian bass Chaliapine. He knew intimately those who formed the next generation of soloists: Aubrey Brain, the great horn player; Leon Goossens, probably the world's greatest oboe player; the Goossens sisters, Marie and Sidonie, the harpists; and Arthur Catterall – the list is endless.

Sidonie relates that as far as meeting people, the string section were 'in a different world' from the harpists, but they were always hoping for a sign of recognition from 'a certain tall, handsome violinist'. She does remember being offered a lift in Vivian's car after a party at a friend's house. In her hurry she got into the back seat and sat down on his bowler hat! She says she was shocked to silence and never knew when he found out. She must have created a deep impression on the young Vivian because, many years later when he was the Master of the Worshipful Company of Musicians, he invited the by then celebrated Sidonie Goossens to be his guest of honour.

Lest it seems that it was all work and no play, Vivian enjoyed some wonderful friendships. There was the Bearne family, whom he had originally

Vivian (far right) with the Bearne and Randall families with whom he played tennis regularly during the day and Charlestoned all night – about 1929.

met in Germany, in which there were three boys of comparable age, Sidney, Colin and Guy, all excellent athletes. Then there was the Randall family, four beautiful daughters, Aileen, Betty, Christine and Doreen. This eightsome is reported to have 'Charlestoned' hundreds of miles and played a lot of tennis. Mr and Mrs Randall were charming and tolerant of the mountains of teas and suppers consumed by such ravenous teenagers! These were enduring friendships, and coincidentally Guy Bearne was also knighted after a career in the RAF. There is no doubt that Vivian appreciated how fortune had favoured him in these formative years and took full advantage of his opportunities.

In 1930 came the founding of the BBC Symphony Orchestra under Dr Adrian Boult. This was an entirely new concept in the form of a permanent orchestra with players under contract to play exclusively for the BBC and not permitted to accept outside engagements. Many of the finest principals were immediately enlisted, and the final orchestra contained almost every player of note throughout the country. However, the rank-and-file aspirants had to undergo searching auditions before selection. Their reward was to sit behind and alongside a brilliant group of experienced musicians. Vivian had already had two seasons with the Promenade Concerts and his name was submitted for consideration as a violinist by Mr Woodhouse.

He was summoned to Savoy Hill, the BBC Headquarters, and was ushered into Studio No 1. To his surprise he found a screen confronting him, behind which a somewhat sepulchral voice said 'Good Morning, Mr Dunn, what have you brought for us?' The newcomer said that he had brought the Brahms *Violin Concerto*, which he had been studying. 'Excellent', came the reply, 'Please begin in your own time until you hear the bell.' A hand then firmly descended on an old-fashioned counter-type bell mechanism!

After playing for about a page and a half, the bell sounded and the voice asked him if he had brought anything else? 'How about the *Partita* from the *Sixth Sonata in* E by Bach?' 'Very good' continued the voice, 'please continue.' After another page and a half, the bell interrupted and the sepulchral tones said 'Thank you, now turn to the desk and play from Figure 16.' The young violinist was confronted by a mass of difficult passages and, taking his life in his hands, proceeded with enthusiasm. When the final bell sounded, the voice said 'Good Morning, Mr Dunn' in tones that clearly indicated 'Don't ring us, we'll ring you!' A second, similar nerve jangling session took place a few days later. They were referred to by the students as 'The Spanish Inquisition'.

Days of waiting intervened before the BBC letter arrived appointing Vivian a member of the first violin section at a salary of £11 14s for a 36-hour week. This was a goodly sum in those days for a young musician and meant a permanent engagement in the finest orchestra of the era. They started rehearsing at the end of July and played their first concert at the Queen's Hall on 22nd October 1930. Many of their rehearsals were carried out in what was known as the 'Pickle Factory' under Waterloo Bridge.

Before the creation of the BBC Symphony Orchestra, there had existed what was called 'the deputy system', which allowed players who had been offered more lucrative work elsewhere to send a deputy to play in the orchestra engaging them. Vivian had often played in the Royal Philharmonic, the London Symphony and the National Symphony Orchestras under these terms. It was with the latter orchestra that he first played in the Royal Albert Hall, which he described as a vast echoing arena before the modern acoustic improvements of today. Indeed, this notorious echo was only discovered at the opening ceremony when the Bishop of London's 'Amen' reverberated round the building. It has been said that the

Royal Albert Hall is the only place where a British composer can be sure of hearing his work twice!

Vivian often recounted the story of the celebrated German conductor who had been engaged for a special concert and insisted on having six rehearsals. All went well at the first, but the appearance of different players at subsequent rehearsals did not please him; on enquiring the reason he was told that this was 'the deputy system'. Finally, at the last rehearsal there was only one player who had attended them all, the principal double bass. In broken English the conductor congratulated him and said 'I vish him somezing extra in his pay'. This was greeted with some laughter and again enquiring why, a voice came forth 'You needn't worry, he ain't coming to the concert!'

At one particular concert in 1930 Sir Edward Elgar came to conduct his own *The Dream of Gerontius* with Heddle Nash, Margaret Balfour and the great Australian bass, Harold Williams. Vivian claimed that, compared with the full time professional conductors, Sir Edward could not be described as a virtuoso of the art. However, it was the very presence of this great patrician figure that inspired the players. He subsequently wrote:

> 'I would like you to try and picture the curtained area immediately leading from the artists' room on to the platform. It was here that I first met Elgar when he was waiting to commence a rehearsal and I, one of the back desk 1st violin players, also waited for the senior players to pass through. Just picture this young violinist and embryo conductor of twenty years of age politely bidding Sir Edward "Good Morning" and saying what a thrill it was to play under him and perform his music. He replied in his courtly manner "Thank you, I'm glad you like it, and what a fine orchestra." '

Vivian claims that particular night at the Queen's Hall playing *The Dream of Gerontius* was his greatest ever musical experience. Soloists, chorus and orchestra reached heights of inspiration through the composer himself, communicating this transcendency to the musical forces and audience alike. A night to be cherished and never to be forgotten.

This was a very happy time for the young musician, who was most assiduous in preparing himself by practising all the scores beforehand. He was determined never to be caught out or found wanting in any of the difficult passages – he claimed he never was. He looked back upon this period of his development and recalled how significant it was. He later wrote:

> 'No matter how deep is the individual study of an embryo conductor, there is nothing like the experience of interpretation and the creation of music to cap it in a great orchestra.'

CHAPTER 3

Overture to a Military Career

IN AUGUST 1931, during the Promenade season, the 22 year old Vivian Dunn applied for the appointment of Director of Music of the Portsmouth Division, Royal Marines. This was a public appointment and had been advertised in the national press. Before applying he spoke to his father and asked, 'Do you think it would be right for me to apply?' The latter answered 'Well, yes, by all means, but I can't help you or be seen to help you'. The appointment had become vacant when Captain R P O'Donnell, the brother of B Walton O'Donnell, transferred to the Royal Air Force as Director of Music of the RAF Central Band. He subsequently rose to the top to become the Organising Director of Music of the Royal Air Force in the rank of Wing Commander.

Vivian was particularly attracted to this job as, apart from his military music background, he knew that the orchestral potential of the Royal Marines Divisional bands would enable him to use his undoubted talents in this sphere. The Portsmouth Band, along with those at Chatham and Plymouth maintained fine orchestras and excellent concert bands. Indeed, Rudolph O'Donnell, himself an accomplished cellist, had trained the orchestra during his ten years at the helm, to a very high standard. Incidentally, when O'Donnell transferred to the RAF, he became the first ever military musician to serve as Bandmaster or Director of Music in all three arms of the Services.

There were about 50 applicants for the job, but none could match the credentials of Vivian Dunn, who bore testimonials from Sir Henry Wood, Sir John McEwen (Principal of the Royal Academy of Music), Sir Adrian Boult and B Walton O'Donnell. Receiving his summons to the interview,

Vivian Dunn went to explain to Sir Henry Wood who merely gave him the day off and wished him luck. He travelled down to Portsmouth and was invited to conduct the orchestra in Brahms *Symphony No 1*, a fortunate choice as he had previously played it under a variety of conductors. Then they changed to a military band, concert formation. The piece they had chosen was *Songs of the Gael* by B Walton O'Donnell – an even more fortunate choice as Vivian had studied harmony and composition under him. Although no records of the interviewing board can be found it is believed to have included Colonel Commandant Richard Foster (of Chatham Division), Lieutenant Colonel Thomas Hunton and also Captain Robert Neville. It is presumed that the senior Royal Marines Director of Music, Major P S G O'Donnell was also present. Vivian was then invited over to the officers' mess by the Commandant who talked to him about his general interests, including sport. When he said that he was not a bad cricketer and that he played squash, tennis, golf and racquets, he felt he had made an impression. His smart London suit and his obvious enthusiasm came over well. He knew he was being 'summed up' as a potential Royal Marines officer as well as a musical director.

Perhaps his sporting activities counted more in his favour than he thought. He had not realised at his interview that his predecessor, Rudolph O'Donnell had also been an outstanding sportsman, a Royal Marines Corps cricketer of note and an excellent goalkeeper at both soccer and hockey, at which he had represented the Royal Navy and the Combined Services.

Three days later Vivian received a telegram from the Admiralty, confirming his appointment and was told to report as soon as possible. He was overjoyed. His appointment, at the age of 22 years and 9 months, on 1st September 1931 was unique in several respects. No younger Director of Music has ever been appointed in the Royal Marines. He was also the last civilian musician to be recruited for such a post in any of the three services. He was commissioned as a direct entry Lieutenant. It is not certain at what stage the famous moustache first appeared but it was not apparent in the photographs of his Academy days. The story goes that, when the family lived in Teddington, his mother kept Borzoi dogs, one of which bit him on the upper lip leaving a scar. He grew a moustache to hide the scar but it gave the resulting growth a slightly crooked parting. It may also have been encouraged by his ambition to follow a military career.

The appointment coincided with the naval mutiny of the Atlantic Fleet at Invergordon. Many historians believe that the foundations for this mutiny were laid three years earlier in the Mediterranean Fleet, when the infamous Bandmaster Barnacle incident took place. Whilst HMS *Royal Oak*'s Royal Marines band was playing for an evening social function, the Admiral walked across to the Bandmaster and swore at him. Subsequent courts-martial shook the otherwise peaceful navy.

There was no doubt that the announcement of Vivian Dunn's appointment was received by both Army music and the old Royal Naval School of Music with astonishment and animosity. The contention was that he had never actually served in a military band and therefore did not know anything about it; and to be granted a direct commission instead of serving in the ranks was an appalling blunder on the part of the Royal Marines that must end in disaster. It was not, in fact, a precedent, as in 1907 Charles Hoby had been appointed direct to the Chatham Division from civilian life, although he had previously served as a bandmaster in the Indian Army and South Africa. Vivian often quoted that he had been born literally within the sound of his father's band room in India and something of the military musical traditions must have rubbed off on him.

There were three other factors that had been entirely discounted by those who harboured such ill feeling. A previous appointment from the army had ended unfortunately through the incumbent becoming over familiar with his band ranks which had resulted in a severe falling in standards. There was also a failure to recognise that throughout his entire life Vivian had lived in the midst of military music and knew the repertoire thoroughly. Perhaps most important of all, in ten years of intense study he had gained more all-round knowledge in music than other candidates who had not had such fortunate opportunities.

His contemporaries were Major P S G O'Donnell, the third brother, at Chatham and Captain F J Ricketts at Plymouth, both of whom were considerably older and were very talented musicians. Neither of them bore the young Dunn any animosity – rather the opposite. They gave him great support and understanding. It is perhaps not coincidental that Vivian's father W J Dunn had been a contemporary of Ricketts when they were fellow students at Kneller Hall in the early part of the century. Vivian later wrote how much he owed to the three O'Donnell brothers, paragons as Directors of Music, to Major F J Ricketts, a remarkably fine man and composer under the *nom de plume* Kenneth J Alford, and to Lieutenant Colonel George Miller MVO MBE of the Grenadier Guards, son of Major George Miller MVO, Royal Marines Light Infantry. The last named, he was sure, knew there was a similarity in their early careers as choristers, Miller at St George's Chapel, Windsor and later a student in Berlin. They had also both followed in the footsteps of famous fathers.

A word here about the organisation of music in the Royal Marines at that time. Each of the three headquarters, Chatham, Portsmouth and Plymouth had a Divisional band. They recruited differently from the Royal Naval School of Music, which had been formed at Eastney, Southsea in 1903, and which provided bands for the Royal Navy at sea in all ships of cruiser size and above. The Divisional bands recruited musicians direct from civilian life and their standard was undoubtedly higher. They also stayed together for longer periods and performed in large bands, anything from 35 to 50 for the Divisional bands, compared with 15 to 25 for those of the RN School of Music.

The Portsmouth Band, up to 1923 the Royal Marine Artillery Band, with its distinctive cap badge dating from King Edward VII's reign, had the privilege of providing a band for the Royal Yacht when required. Vivian recalled that when he took over they had a fine orchestra and an excellent concert band, but 'they were not too hot on parade and did not relish the idea of being sharpened up!' He soon realised that the many Royal, ceremonial and private occasions at which the band was required to perform, demanded 'meticulous effort and strict attention to the musical detail!'

* * * * *

When Vivian crossed the threshold of Eastney Barracks, Southsea on 3rd September 1931, after being released from his contract with the BBC, he was met by the Assistant Adjutant, Captain Derek Shepherd, later to become a lifelong friend. He was taken to his quarters in the Officers' mess, nowadays the Royal Marines Museum, and introduced to the MOA (Marine Officer's Attendant) who had been assigned to him, the genial and upright Marine Fred Wheeler. Wheeler was a remarkable man with a great sense of humour, a fund of service lore, who kept the newcomer spick and span. The two enjoyed a great rapport, while Mrs Wheeler, who was Maltese, did his weekly washing.

Derek Shepherd took Vivian down to the splendid firm of Trayler and Sons, military tailors, in Portsmouth High Street to be kitted out. Armed with his Admiralty uniform grant of £105, he was provided with a gold laced full dress tunic, frock coat, greatcoat, two suits of blues, mess dress, overalls, Sam Browne belt, helmet, sword, cap, gloves, shirts and ties – everything required, all properly tailored and complete with appropriate name inscribed on his tin uniform cases. The outfit was completed with patent leather Wellingtons, parade boots and shoes, which the estimable Wheeler boned to perfection. Mr Trayler observed, as the bill was paid on the spot, 'what a great pleasure it was to make it for you, 6ft 2in and the figure to go with it!' The firm was sadly blitzed in 1941, with much money owed to it by Royal Marines officers who had not paid their bills! Vivian's philosophy was that a smart, well dressed appearance may do nothing to make one a better musician or conductor, but there was nothing, sartorially speaking, like being in tune and playing all the right notes.

At first the musicians in the band did not know quite what to make of this young, immaculately turned out musician and tried to take him for a ride or put one over on him from time to time. It therefore came as a bit of a shock to find that their new Director was up to all the dodges and tricks that military musicians the world over get up to and often get away with. From the outset he made it abundantly clear that there would be no nonsense and that everything would be thoroughly rehearsed and meticulously prepared, demanding their best efforts at all times. He expected their discipline and smartness on parade to match the standard of their music in concert, whether it be orchestral or military band. There is no doubt that, when Vivian Dunn first took over, the standard of the Portsmouth Band was excellent as an orchestra and in the concert hall, but needed smartening up in their drill and deportment.

The majority of the musicians were fine men who quickly saw the merit of Lieutenant Dunn's approach and gave their best in support of the name and reputation of the band and the proud Corps to which they belonged. They sat firmly on the dodgers, the small minority of what he called 'reluctant dragons', those who suffered from inflated egos and whose attitude was eternally cast in the 'what's in it for me?' mould.

Dunn admired the quality of his first rate instrumentalists and good all-rounders as double-handed players of string and wind instruments. Notably there was the splendid Drum Major Jack Dacombe, a fine figure of a man renowned throughout the Corps, not only for his prowess in heading the band, but also as the Royal Navy quarter mile champion and a member of the 1924 Olympic team. He was also an excellent trombonist who later joined the BBC Variety Orchestra under Charles Shadwell. Vivian was also supported by Band Sergeants Crabtree and Hamilton and the indefatigable librarian, Corporal C R Webb. Every band needed such important and reliable back-up staff. One of his young recruits was 14 year old Clive Pafford who had Saturday morning violin lessons under the maestro, and who subsequently became a member of the Bournemouth Symphony Orchestra.

But life was not all music. Vivian was soon accepted by his fellow members in the officers' mess and joined in Mess life to the full. Sport was a regular feature of afternoon activities and his love of cricket figured largely in the 1932 season. His first match for the Divisional side saw him scoring 88 against Havant on their ground. The opponents were a formidable club side and included Johnny Parker who was currently playing for Hampshire. In due course Vivian was selected for a place in the Corps side. One of his musicians, Musician Mallard was a particularly good batsman who made many hundreds for the Divisional and Corps sides. He was a likeable man, but was 'a dead loss as a clarinet player after losing all his teeth and the replacements never fitting properly!' Mallard seemed quite happy playing cricket throughout the summer and being the band practice room sweeper, when he was in barracks.

Arriving at the end of the summer, Vivian found the season's concerts of the band were nearly over, but he made his first of many visits to Brighton that year. The band played on the West Pier where Mr Scholey was the manager. Although they travelled and played throughout the country it was to Brighton that the band went regularly. Right up until 1937 the Portsmouth Division Royal Marines orchestra performed on the West Pier for three fortnightly seasons, giving three 90 minute concerts a day! Coincidentally his father, W J Dunn, who had retired in 1935, was engaged at the Palace Pier for two seasons with his own civilian orchestra. History does not relate whether they were ever in competition but there was one unique occasion in 1936 when father and his two sons, Vivian and 'Chiffer', all conducted at one of W J's concerts on the Pier. In 1938-39 the Royal Marines moved to the Palace Pier, but somehow he felt it did not have the same atmosphere as the West Pier.

ABOVE:
On being commissioned as Lieutenant Royal Marines, Director of Music, 1931.

RIGHT:
Band concerts on piers were popular in the 1930s. The Band of Portsmouth Division entertain a damp crowd.

Piers in the thirties provided the mecca of seaside entertainment with Service bands, orchestras, concert parties and shows, and Vivian particularly enjoyed conducting at South Parade Pier in Southsea on Sunday afternoons. His first public appearance in Southsea was in October 1931 when he conducted two concerts on the Pier, afternoon and evening. The local press reported:

> 'A large audience in the afternoon showed their appreciation of the fine playing of the orchestra, the masterly efforts of the youthful conductor and his well chosen programme, by the number of encores they asked for.'

In those days crowds flocked to hear the military bands at seaside resorts, mostly hearing a different regimental band each week, but there was always a special spot for the 'home town' band and its handsome, smart and effervescent Director of Music. And he was still only in his twenties.

Another great feature of Southsea life in those days was the weekly Church Parade at Eastney, when up to 1,000 marines would march to St Andrew's Church behind the Corps of Drums and the band. In the church, Lieutenant Dunn would conduct the orchestra in appropriate pre-service music and then lead the congregation in the hymns. After the service, the band would march back to the main parade ground to be inspected and finally dismissed. Many hundreds of locals turned out in their Sunday best to witness this weekly extravaganza. After the parade, the officers and SNCOs would repair to their messes for pre-prandial drinks and roast Sunday lunch. This was all part of the social life of the thirties and continued into the 1950s, even during the war, though necessarily in a lower key.

On 29th October 1931, Vivian Dunn was elected an Associate of the Royal Academy of Music. This was his first acknowledged step up the musical ladder. His first major ceremonial occasion came on 3rd December 1931 when HRH Prince George, afterwards the Duke of Kent, presented new Colours to the Portsmouth Division, Royal Marines. This involved a considerable amount of preparation in ceremonial and drill on parade with the band playing an all important part. In order to prepare himself for this, immediately after his appointment he joined up with the September 1931 batch of Royal Marines officers undergoing the Second Lieutenant's Course 'A' which consisted mainly of drill in the afternoons. Such a sight as a Director of Music, dressed in a Marine's tunic but with a broad red stripe down his trousers, was unheard of, and many faces were to be seen overlooking the parade with amazement.

One of those witnessing this parade was a young impressionable fourteen year old, Charles Bowden. The son of a Royal Marine, he was the Drum Major of the Royal Marines Volunteer Cadet Corps Band. He writes:

> 'Just eighteen days before my fifteenth birthday I stood at a window in the Band and Drums room in Eastney Barracks. On the parade ground, which had been lashed by wind and rain in the morning, the delayed ceremony was at last taking place at 2.15 in the afternoon. As I watched the intricacies of the parade and listened to the music, I had no idea that I was watching two officers who would have a tremendous influence on my life.
>
> The Colour Officer was Lieutenant Ralph Garrett who, ten years later, led the party of Royal Marines, including myself, in the escape in an abandoned landing craft, from Crete to North Africa. The other was Lieutenant F V Dunn, whom I subsequently met when I was the Drum Major of the Deal Band in 1950 when he became the Principal

> Director of Music. That was the beginning of an eighteen-year working relationship and forty-five year friendship.'

From the start he was determined to show off his new 'command' as much as he could, such was his pride and perhaps, ego. Musically, he was in his element, but he was also keen that the band should take a wide sporting interest. During his first winter in charge, he not only organised a soccer match between the Portsmouth Divisional Band and those he had just left, the BBC Symphony Orchestra, but he also captained the side. *The Portsmouth News* Musical Reporter commented:

> 'This was not the usual and accurate game played by our beloved cup-tie teams, but football as she is played by musicians, whose artistic souls admit to no such thing as science, and who, while hardly transforming the noble game into an art at least enthuse as heartily over the latest open goal as over the latest opus. Invoking shadows of Beethoven and Alex James, these musicos, ranging from Marine buglers to leaders of the symphony, scampered over the Eastney turf and put up as fine an exhibition of keenness and clean football as would be seen on many grounds. Early in the first half the fiddles began to assert advantage over the wind. It was left to a thrustful bugle who scored the Marines' first goal that completely beat the principal BBC oboe, who was beginning to think himself a kettledrum by virtue of his lack of work!'

The famous leader of the BBC Symphony Orchestra Arthur Catterall refereed this match. Enough to add that the fraternal game ended in a very satisfactory two-all draw.

One of the duties and privileges of the Portsmouth Division Band was that it provided the band for the Royal Yacht *Victoria & Albert* when the Royal Family embarked. This privilege had been first granted in 1904 by King Edward VII to the Royal Marine Artillery Band. As this commitment involved a section of the band, some 20 musicians, to be absent from Portsmouth for about four months each year, the complement was increased to 50 musicians in order to provide a viable combination ashore. Whilst serving with the Royal Yacht, the musicians were authorised to wear a special gilt cap badge consisting of a bursting grenade surrounded by laurel leaves. This badge continued to be worn when the title was changed to the 'Band of HM Royal Marines (Portsmouth Division)' in

1923, and it still provided the band for Royal Yacht duties. In his impetuous way Vivian looked forward to going to sea, but not without some apprehension at performing personally for the monarch and his family.

The new Director of Music's introduction to the Royal Household came with his first trip in the Royal Yacht in July 1932. It was here that he made the acquaintance of Lord Louis Mountbatten. This friendship with 'Dickie' Mountbatten was to last until the end of his life, and had a considerable influence on the restructuring of the Royal Marines Band Service in years to come.

One incident he recalled of his early service in the Royal Yacht. In 1934, the Admiralty introduced the *English Hymnal* for prayers in place of the old *Hymns Ancient and Modern*. At one Sunday morning service, the padre announced the first hymn as No.165 and after the King had turned it up in his beautiful gold-bound ivory prayer book, he looked puzzled. Obviously thinking he had misheard it as No.265, he then turned to that page. Finding neither of the hymns ones that he knew, he stood silently by as the Royal Marines orchestra played it. This happened again with the other two hymns and he looked very cross. After the service, the Admiral was sent for and asked what was the matter with the hymns that morning. 'I couldn't find my place.' The Admiral did not know the answer so he sent for the young Dunn to explain. In anticipation of the summons Vivian had checked and found, as he suspected, that the hymn numbers were different in both books. The King had brought his usual prayer book with him, not having been given a copy of the new one. He was furious and commented 'Here am I, Defender of the Faith, and I wasn't even consulted!'

There was another short cruise in the Royal Yacht *Victoria & Albert* in July 1933, but it was generally a year of consolidation with his band. In his spare time Vivian had established his place as an opening batsman in the Eastney cricket side, as well as playing on the wing at hockey. He felt it was imperative that his musicians should keep fit and encouraged them to play sport whenever they could.

In 1932 the city of Portsmouth was concerned that they did not have their own symphony orchestra, as did the other south coast towns of Bournemouth and Eastbourne, although there were regular Municipal Concerts. At these, such musical organisations as the Portsmouth Chamber Music

The Royal Yacht Victoria & Albert

Society, St Simon's Orchestra and the Portsmouth Elizabethan and Bach Society made regular appearances, as had Captain R P O'Donnell and his Royal Marines Orchestra. Vivian was delighted to continue this tradition and widen his scope and influence. As a result of a scathing article in the local paper entitled *'Is Portsmouth a Musical City?'* the city council looked into the matter and thus the City of Portsmouth Symphony Orchestra was founded the following year and the youthful Lieutenant Dunn was invited to be the conductor.

Their first concert was held on 22nd February with three more to follow that year. The Lord Mayor, Alderman Sir Harold Pink and his Lady Mayoress attended what was described as an outstanding concert before an audience of 1,200 people 'some enthusiastic, some just curious'. However during the season there was one major *faux pas*, which illustrated the naiveté of the Portsmouth musical audience and temporarily distracted Vivian and the orchestra. It was whilst playing as a finale Tchaikovsky's *Fifth Symphony*, which apparently had never been performed in the city before, that there was an unexpected burst of clapping. The audience was obviously not prepared for the telling pause before the final triumphant entry of the main theme. Perhaps Vivian held the pause too long, but the local paper described it as 'musically unforgivable', with no blame attributed to the conductor.

The third concert of the season was broadcast by the BBC direct from the Portsmouth Guildhall. It gave the city an uplift as they felt that they were now the equals of Bournemouth and Eastbourne – musically at least. The concert was described as 'remarkable' as it featured for the first time a violincello soloist, Antonia Butler, in Saint-Saens' *Concerto in A Minor*; she was the first of many acclaimed soloists Vivian brought to the city.

* * * * *

Being a bachelor and living in the barracks, Vivian had much spare time. He had only started tinkering with the idea of composing, but greatly admired his opposite number in Plymouth, Captain Frederick J Ricketts, who had already written a host of successful military marches under the pseudonym Kenneth Alford and was being hailed as the British answer to the American John Philip Sousa.

Vivian decided to investigate Alford's successful formula by studying his march scores, but to his surprise he discovered that even the estimable firm of Boosey & Hawkes did not publish a short score of these marches. So he sat down during his quiet evenings to write out in his own fair hand about a dozen marches in short score. It was only by doing this that he realised exactly what was in the instrumentation, sitting there with all the band parts on the table. He decided to write an original march of his own, but nothing significant came to his mind. Probably his first to be played was *Eastney* composed in 1939, which he dedicated to the Colonel Commandant of the Division, Colonel (later General Sir Thomas) Hunton. Strangely enough this was only recorded for the first time in 1998 by the Central Band of the Royal British Legion, conducted by Captain Ted Whealing, who had served under Vivian at Deal in the 1960s.

He was so much better at making arrangements for both the orchestra and the military band, which took up much of his time. He was also able to try these out with the orchestra at periodic matinées musicales and soirées. These would be performed for the officers and their ladies and guests. They were very pleasant social occasions when light classical music was played and soloists from the orchestra were able to display their individual skills. It was all part of routine service life. However his choice of music was not to everyone's liking. A concert in the officers' mess at Eastney was described as 'a little too modern for some tastes, but for the more enlightened the whole programme was delightful. The following evening produced an equally successful dance in the officers' mess.' Also that year at a concert in the Globe Theatre, the full Divisional orchestra 'gave a superb interpretation of modern symphonic rhythmic music. These concerts by our own orchestra are undoubtedly the finest shows presented by the Divisional Entertainment Scheme and anyone who is fond of a really good musical programme should not miss them under any circumstances. At this concert the male voice choir acquitted themselves exceptionally well.' One young admirer, the wife of an RM officer subsequently wrote: 'He never failed to include an item or two in the programme for his "low-brow" friends!' Already FVD had begun to use his wide musical background to benefit his audiences.

Vivian set an example in all things he did. His dress sense was immaculate and with his extra earnings from private engagements, he was able to kit himself out with the best and most expensive clothes. He bought two pairs of brogues from Lobbs. He kept them in an immaculate condition through the expert ministrations of a succession of MOAs and they lasted until the late '70s. The brown pair obtained the patina of well-matured mahogany.

In 1934 Commander the Lord Louis Mountbatten offered *The Preobrajensky March* to the Royal Marines for adoption as its official Slow March. At this time the Corps did not have an official Regimental Slow March. Lord Louis had been presented with the original score of this march of the Preobrajensky Guards, a prestigious regiment of Czarist Russia, by one of his kinsmen, King Alfonso XIII of Spain. One of the last colonels of the regiment had been a great uncle of Mountbatten. Vivian Dunn was asked to make an arrangement of it suitable for military band. He found that the score was very tattered and not easy to decipher. However he managed to arrange it for full military band both in concert and on parade. A committee was covened by the Adjutant General, Sir Richard Foster and met in the Eastney band room to hear the Portsmouth Division Band play it. The committee members were musical laymen and on a first hearing the march did not commend itself easily; for instance the trio was in the minor key. The committee therefore did not recommend its adoption and Mountbatten's offer was politely turned own.

However this did highlight the fact that no regimental slow march existed to complement *A Life on the Ocean Wave*, the Regimental Quick March. General Foster ordered that the Directors of Music of the three Divisions and the Musical Director of the Royal Naval School of Music should submit original compositions for audition later that year.

Another committee, headed by General Foster himself, met in the Eastney band room and on the parade to assess the merits of five competing compositions. One came from Mr B Walton O'Donnell, the conductor of the BBC Wireless Military Band and a former Director of Music of the RM Depot Band at Deal, who had also been approached. The other compositions were by Major P S G O'Donnell, Captain F J Ricketts, Captain Samuel Fairfield and Lieutenant F V Dunn.

When trying to compose his march, Vivian used to slow march on the tennis courts in front of the Eastney officers' mess, where he lived as a bachelor in No 4 passage. He tried to think up something original preferably with a nautical theme, but nothing seemed to emerge. However the traditional folk tune *Early One Morning* kept recurring, almost to the exclusion of everything else and although it had no connection with the sea, he found it such a fine smooth-flowing melody, easy to play and easy to march to, he felt that it would be effective as a slow march. After much deliberation he thought 'here goes', and got on with it. He decided on an original introduction of four bars, followed by the sixteen bars of the main tune, *Early One Morning*, repeated. Then came the second subject, powerfully played in the bass and with a repeat of eight bars. A *da capo* to the main tune.

At the audition all five compositions were played. None registered any kind of approval with the committee, who undoubtedly faced a difficult task. No definite conclusion was reached from the compositions offered nor was any recommendation made. However the committee did express a liking for the old English air *Early One Morning* which Vivian had included as the Trio of his march. But that was all.

He did not let his love of choral music diminish and made his mark on the Portsmouth scene by becoming involved with the Portsmouth Choral Union which had been formed in 1933. In 1934 he conducted their Music Festival. At the same time he had the pleasure of conducting the newly formed City of Portsmouth Symphony Orchestra regularly and persuaded a number of his musicians to join it, where they could widen their musical knowledge and improve their skills.

* * * * *

About this time the London Battalion was being formed, as the Royal Marines had been invited to perform London Duties the following year for the first time in their history. It also celebrated King George v's Silver Jubilee and there was a requirement for a slow march to precede the Regimental March to dismount the Old Guard at St James's Palace. The dismounting guard had to advance in slow time before breaking into quick time. The sixteen paces of the tune *Early One Morning* exactly fitted this requirement. Vivian's march was played for the first dismounting and on every occasion subsequently, the watching crowd appreciated the tunefulness and even hummed it.

Through its use in the London Battalion, the march grew in popularity both with the Royal Marines and the general public so that it became accepted as a traditional slow march. However it was still not officially adopted. A few years later Vivian decided to rewrite the march with a new introduction, using *Early One Morning* as the first subject and adding a further second subject. He gave it the title *The Globe & Laurel* and it became very popular during the war years and afterwards. However it was not until 1954, when several of the junior officers of the 1938 London Battalion, Campbell Hardy, Malcolm Cartwright-Taylor, Ian Riches and 'Busty' Fellowes had reached much higher rank, that Fellowes recommended that it should be officially adopted as the Regimental Slow March. It was irreverently known as *'The Whore's Lament'*! One can only surmise on the coincidence that this recommendation was made following General Fellowes previous appointment as Commandant of the Royal Marines School of Music, where Vivian had been the Principal Director of Music!

The matter of the Regimental Slow March cannot be left there as, ten years later in the Corps Tercentenary year, Vivian Dunn's rearrangement, 30 years after his original, saw *The Preobrajensky March* supersede *The Globe & Laurel*. But more of that later.

Coincidentally Captain Ricketts' submission was also subsequently rewritten and became his most famous slow march *By Land and Sea*. Whilst it was considered too long for use with troops on a ceremonial parade, it was magnificent for a band troop where full justice could be done to it. Ricketts remarked to Dunn, 'You hit upon a very apt idea – why didn't I think of it?' Neither the O'Donnell nor the Fairfield marches were ever heard of again!

Back to 1934. Later that year on 29th November, another Royal occasion presented itself when the Portsmouth Band was selected to play at the wedding of the Duke of Kent and Princess Marina of Greece and Denmark. The band formed part of the street lining party in the Mall and were positioned appropriately abreast the Duke of York Steps. At the conclusion of the ceremonial part of the celebrations, the band marched from Wellington Barracks to Victoria Station before returning to Portsmouth. The story goes that it was on this occasion, as the band passed the Army & Navy Stores in Victoria Street, that Drum Major Jack Dacombe was seen to throw his staff (mace) to the level of the second floor of the building.

There were regular Royal Marines band and orchestral concerts at which Vivian would invite members and students of the Academy to appear as soloists. This kept him in touch with the London musical scene, besides showing them what the military music world had to offer. It also kept the orchestra up to the highest standard and introduced Portsmouth audiences to the musicians of the future. One such, on the 6th February 1935, was the solo pianist Myers Foggin, later to be appointed the Principal of Trinity College of Music. He was to become a very great friend of the Dunn family, being nearly a twin of Vivian, just one day older.

In 1935, the young Vivian Dunn had his first taste of organising a big occasion. During the King's Birthday Parade on Southsea Common in June he found himself responsible for conducting the Massed Bands, consisting of his own Portsmouth Divisional Band, three RN School of Music bands from the C-in-C Portsmouth, HMS *Victory* and *Excellent*, and three Army bands, the Royal Artillery Portsmouth, the Yorks & Lancs and the Rifle Brigade. The complexity of this occasion stood him in good stead for the future, especially after the war when he was responsible for the Royal Marines ceremonies of Beating Retreat on Horse Guards Parade and other great ceremonial events. The young 26 year old found that he was nearly a decade younger than any of the Bandmasters on parade that day, and he rose to the occasion grandly.

Although he took no personal role in the London Battalion ceremonial, he ensured that when the Royal Marines mounted guard on Buckingham Palace, St James's Palace and at the Tower of London for the first time, only his best trained musicians were included in the composite band which went to London under Major P S G O'Donnell and, of course, his slow march *The Globe & Laurel* saw daylight. Drum Major Jack Dacombe from Portsmouth shared his duties with Drum Major Bill Day from Chatham.

In that year there were many concerts to celebrate the Silver Jubilee of King George v and Queen Mary. There was a full month's cruise with the Royal Family in the Royal Yacht that year, taking up much of August. Vivian was awarded his first medal, the King's Silver Jubilee Medal, an honour for his service to the monarch.

Tours around the country took this extremely handsome young Director of Music to many parts of Britain. Stories abound of the many young ladies who instantly fell in love with this Adonis. Vivian was renowned for his immaculate turnout and, in full dress uniform, conducting his band in concert halls everywhere, he set young female hearts fluttering. He was well aware of these attentions and would flirt from time to time. On a visit to Bristol he met and fell in love with Eileen King, who had been to see his concert; they were engaged briefly, but Eileen's formidable mother with her excessive possessiveness, and Vivian's constant travels were obviously too much of a strain on their courtship.

There was plenty of social life in the Portsmouth area and it was at one of the many dances in the city that he met, among many other young ladies, Rita Tinn, the pretty red-headed daughter of the Portsmouth Football Club manager, Jack Tinn. They became friends and appear to have danced many a happy hour together. She remembers well a group of Royal Marines officers, including 'Blondie' Hasler, who were in constant demand at all the social functions particularly the Christmas and Summer Balls in the officers' mess. It appears that all the young ladies used to swoon over the tall, handsome director of music. Rita Tinn later joined the WRNS and was drafted to the orderly room in the Royal Marines Barracks at Eastney. She is now Lady Mallalieu, having later married the author and politician J P W Mallalieu.

* * * * *

1936 started on a sad note when King George v died on 20th January. Hurried preparations were made for the band to take part in the funeral of the monarch who had granted them their distinctive cap badge and Royal Yacht shoulder flash. This took place on 28th January. On 27th May the band were invited to play at Southampton for the departure of the super-liner RMS *Queen Mary* on her maiden voyage to Cherbourg and New York. Vivian jumped at the chance of going on board the ship before she sailed. The band played on the vessel's 'quarterdeck' (sterndeck) and the music was broadcast live on the National Programme, the band being taken off by lighter at Spithead. This was the beginning of a long association with Southampton, Cunard and other great shipping lines, lasting to the present day, when the band was often invited to play for important sailings. In July the band had two London engagements playing on the bandstands in Hyde Park and Regent's Park. In those days most parks in the country had their own bandstands, and it was a traditional and pleasant summer relaxation to sit and listen to the strains of a military band concert.

One major ceremonial event at Eastney Barracks in 1936 was when King Edward VIII, during his short reign, paid his only visit to the Corps to inspect Portsmouth Division; indeed it was the first time that a reigning monarch had been on the parade at Eastney. This was another chance for Vivian to renew his acquaintanceship with Lord Mountbatten, who accompanied the King, along with Admiral of the Fleet Lord Keyes, of Zeebrugge fame, and who was Honorary Colonel Commandant of Portsmouth Division.

One concert of note occurred on 19th September 1936 when Captain W J Dunn conducted his own band at the Palace Pier bandstand. For the first (and last) time he was assisted by his two sons, Lieutenant F Vivian Dunn and Mr G Brian Dunn, just 18 years old, who had only recently been awarded the silver medal for conducting whilst a student at the Royal Academy of Music. *The Brighton Herald* suggested that this was a unique occasion and believed it to be the only time a father and two sons had ever conducted in the same concert. The music played was mainly that of Albert Ketelbey, a great friend of the family. So popular was this concert that the threesome returned for a second concert the following Sunday. *The Sussex Daily News* reporting on the second occasion wrote:

> 'As guest conductors the two "boys" enjoyed a well-deserved popularity, and their father may be justly proud of their ability. A glance at the following programme will show that all three certainly worked for their laurels: – Second Suite to *The Wand of Youth* by Elgar (Lieutenant F Vivian Dunn); Overture to *The Merry Wives of Windsor* by Nicolai (Mr Brian Dunn); Overture *Russlan and Ludmilla* by Glinka (Capt W J Dunn); *Slavonic Rhapsodie No 2* by Friedmann (Lt Dunn);

ABOVE:
W J Dunn, his wife and two sons, 'Chiffer' (left) and Vivian on Brighton Pier prior to them conducting a concert together in September 1936

RIGHT:
Captain W J Dunn MVO MC, Director of Music the Royal Horse Guards (The Blues) 1935

> Schubert's *Marche Militaire* (Brian Dunn) and the wonderful descriptive overture written around the great French Revolution by Litolf, *Robespierre* (Capt Dunn).
>
> Unfortunately for the music-lovers of the town the season's engagement of Captain Dunn's orchestra on the Palace Pier bandstand terminates on Sunday, when a special farewell concert will be given, but it is to be hoped that Brighton is not seeing the last of this famous combination.'

Sadly this was to be the case.

The following year, 1937, was a year of mixed fortunes that began, happily, with the coronation of King George VI and Queen Elizabeth. There was plenty of ceremonial work to be done with even more official functions than usual, which included the Coronation ceremony itself, where the Portsmouth Band marched in the procession, and then went on a two months Royal Yacht cruise. But the 12th May, joyous to so many, turned out to be a sad day for Vivian as his beloved father passed away at his home in Bushey Park Gardens, Hampton that evening at the comparatively young age of 62. He managed to steal away from the coronation celebrations to be at his father's bedside. His father had been his mentor and taskmaster throughout his early life. He owed so much of his own success to the perseverance of his father in giving him the finest musical upbringing that any aspiring musician could hope for. Indeed it was more than could be expected. The name of Captain W J Dunn MVO MC is commemorated in the Royal Green Jackets Museum in Winchester where there is a cup won by the 2 KRRC Band in 1924 against 324 competing bands at the Ostend International Music Contest. A Gold Medal was presented to Bandmaster Dunn and a Silver Medal to each member of the band.

One memorable event of Coronation Year was a Searchlight Tattoo at Fratton Park, the home of Portsmouth Football Club. Once again Vivian and Rita Tinn met up, serving on the same organising committee. His love of football led him to watch his home team on numerous occasions, and Fratton Park was the venue of many fund raising displays and concerts in the pre-war years.

Vivian Dunn appeared at his first Royal Tournament at Olympia in July 1937 which was the Royal Navy's year to organise. A composite massed band was formed including musicians from all three Divisional bands in equal numbers. This would appear to be the first time that Divisional bands had appeared at the Royal Tournament, though RNSM bands had occasionally accompanied the appearance of the King's Squad drill displays previously. It is interesting to note that his father, as Lieutenant W J Dunn, Director of Music of the Royal Horse Guards, had conducted the resident band at the Royal Tournament only three years earlier, his farewell appearance there. It was in this year that Vivian was awarded the Coronation Medal.

* * * * *

Later on in 1937 he met a local beauty Margery Halliday at a dance at the Assembly Rooms near Clarence Pier in Southsea. Margery Kathleen was born in 1913 in Portsmouth, the second child of James and Grace Halliday who lived at 9 Clarence Parade. Her father ran a highly successful chain of tobacconists, called Harveys, along the south coast. She attended Holy Cross Convent in Portsmouth and later went to the High School. She was a shy child and got teased about her Christian name (it being unfashionable even in those days), until one kind friend made use of her two initials M.K. and called her Mike, which stuck for the rest of her life. She recalls that her earliest memory of the Royal Marines Band was standing at the roadside watching them march from Church Parade and plaintively remarking to her father 'Daddy, I wish you had a nice red stripe down your trousers!'

Margery 'Mike' Halliday during her modelling days in London

Mike was tall, slim, blonde and graceful with a beautiful complexion. She was a natural dancer, although her great love was skating and a considerable amount of her teens was spent with her cousin, Alan Dawson, at Southampton Ice Rink improving their ice-dance routines. On leaving school she took a secretarial course with the intention of working in an office. However, on a shopping trip to London, she was gazing in the window of Margaret Marks, a fashionable Knightsbridge clothes shop, when she was spotted by the owner and there and then was offered a job as a house mannequin. In those days clients would sit comfortably sipping their tea while the mannequins modelled the gowns. She spent a happy year there before returning to work as her father's secretary.

From the time she was 18 years old she enjoyed a hectic social life with her two friends Toni Adams and Sheila Waller, the daughter of a Royal Marines colonel. It became the girls' goal to attend every social function, party and dance to such an extent that they christened themselves 'The Three Must-get-theres'! She recounts that the best parties were those given by young Royal Marines and Naval officers. This pattern of life went on throughout the 1930s. She had been taken to one particular dance by another Royal Marines officer, 'Bertie' Lumsden. Unfortunately Lumsden

Officers of Portsmouth Division in Full Dress, including Lt Col A R Chater, Capts K Hunt, Mercer, S G Paine and Lt F V Dunn (back right)

had lost his driving licence and Mike drove him round in her very smart white Jaguar. He then made the mistake of introducing her to Vivian, a great chum, who was also a member of this social scene and they met each other in the mêlée of a Paul Jones dance. They soon hit it off and became engaged. Mike had previously been engaged to a Naval Officer, who looked not unlike Vivian, but he left her for someone else. Mike was distraught and shortly afterwards smashed her car into a tree, badly injuring her mouth and front teeth.

It was also the year in which Vivian wrote an arrangement of a folk song, which would later become one of the most played marches in the Royal Marines. Major A N Williams RM had been serving as Staff Officer (Intelligence) on the staff of the C-in-C South Atlantic at Simonstown, and was appointed as Brigade Major at Eastney Barracks. Whilst in South Africa he had become very fond of a trekking song used at the turn of the century by the Boer commandos. He suggested to the Portsmouth Director of Music one day that it might make a military march. And so it was that Vivian sat down and wrote an arrangement of *Sarie Marais*, little knowing at the time that it would become so popular. Of course the name of Commandos had not yet been coined for any connotation with the British forces, but he was later to rearrange this when it was officially adopted as the march of the Royal Marines Commandos in 1952.

The Portsmouth Divisional Band had undergone many changes in personnel in the seven years since Dunn took over. Many of the older musicians had gone to pension and new auditions were held regularly as the Divisional bands enlisted musicians straight from civilian life. It was not always easy to attract the solo instrumentalists required to make up a balanced band. He became so desperate in 1938 that he approached the Royal Naval School of Music for 'cello and euphonium players. This move was against all the previous dictates of recruiting into the Divisional bands as the two branches of such a similar service were so very far apart in their methods and terms of service at this time. Perhaps this was an indication of Dunn's forward thinking which was to see the amalgamation of the Divisional bands with the RN School of Music in 1950.

There were no set fees for private or semi-official engagements in those days, and it appears that Directors of Music were free to agree their own terms for band concerts and other engagements. For instance in 1938 the full band of 53 musicians of the Portsmouth Division was booked for the Anglo/German Cultural Week, where they were to be paid a fee of £400, a tour which does not appear to have come to fruition, presumably because of the political situation. However it is noted that for a concert at Portsmouth Guildhall on 9th March that year, each of the 29 musicians was paid 10s 6d, but there is no mention of what the Director of Music or the Bandmaster was paid. The Band Fund would also have profited from this excursion, and no doubt the 15s paid to Hurdle's Garage, Eastney to cover the cost of transporting the instruments back from the Guildhall was taken out of the total.

His freelance engagements had also become more frequent, although he insisted that they were to improve his musical knowledge and technique, rather than to increase his personal income. One such was when he joined the composer Albert Ketelbey in conducting the City of Portsmouth Orchestra on 12th February 1938 at the Kingsway Hall in London in a selection of the composer's works. They were in turn joined by the Kingsway Hall Choral Society of 100 voices in a programme consisting entirely of Ketelbey's works. This was the second family concert with Albert Ketelbey, as W J and his Royal Horse Guards Band had played with him exactly three years earlier, a programme which was broadcast on the wireless.

On 9th April 1938 a telephone call came through to Vivian from Lord Louis Mountbatten asking him if the Royal Marines could supply a band to lead the procession at the funeral of his elder brother George, Marquess of Milford Haven at Bray parish church. This was classed as a royal occasion and attended by King George VI and HRH The Duke of Kent. The next day, by first post, came a letter from Adsdean in Sussex, Mountbatten's home at that time, saying 'Thank you; it meant so much to me.' This expression of thanks in his own handwriting further cemented the friendly relations between the two men. Vivian realised that in the eyes of Lord Louis, the Royal Marines would always turn up trumps. He remembered that day very well as in later years wrote:

> 'I was making a final recce at Bray Parish Church when a voice asked me "Is everything all right?" I turned to see who had spoken. It was Lord Mountbatten. "Everything is ready, sir." On the day of his brother's funeral, I realised that it is only in England that such a scene could take place with the King walking in the procession of family mourners. What so impressed my mind was that the very next day, written from Adsdean, was that nice letter from Lord Mountbatten.'

* * * * *

On a very happy note, the marriage of Francis Vivian Dunn and Margery Kathleen (Mike) Halliday took place at St Andrew's Church, Eastney on the 30th April 1938 – early enough not to interfere with his cricket season! It was a great occasion and they made a very handsome pair. It was very much a full dress occasion with the bride looking radiant in a shimmering ivory satin dress with a long fan-shaped pleated train. Her bridesmaids were Toni Adams and Sheila Waller. Vivian was as immaculate as ever. Captain Kit Boothby was best man and, as seems appropriate, Vivian chose all the music except two pieces *Crimond* and during the signing of the register, *Ave Maria*, both the choice of his bride. Mike later said that when the orchestra played it, there was 'not a dry eye in the house'! After the blessing the Walford Davis setting of *God Be in My Head* was sung kneeling, a setting that was played over half a century later at Vivian's Memorial service. They left the church to the bridal march from *Lohengrin*. The reception was held at the Royal Beach Hotel, Southsea, and they departed for their honeymoon in Paris, Venice and then Scotland. Vivian was not as well as he should have been on this memorable day, as his stag night very nearly went wrong. This was held in the officers' mess at

ABOVE:
Vivian and Mike at St Andrew's Church, Eastney on 30th April 1938

RIGHT:
Boy buglers draw the happy couple from St Andrew's church

Eastney where his old chum, Bertie Lumsden, urged on by fellow officers, rolled the bridegroom up in the mess carpet when he all but suffocated. His best man, Kit Boothby was orderly officer and not present to assist him. The effects were noticeable the following day when a doctor had to be called on the wedding night to help him with his breathing.

There was the customary Royal Cruise in the autumn to Cowes and then Scotland, where there was a much more relaxed atmosphere aboard the Royal Yacht *Victoria & Albert* than there was on official visits. Cowes week was always a special occasion when the band were extremely busy and Vivian made a large number of contacts that he was to appreciate in years to come. It was a time when Vivian came to know the Royal Family very closely. He was meticulous in arranging musical programmes for dinner, interspersing royal favourites with arrangements he had made of new

King George V and Queen Mary with the officers of the Royal Yacht Victoria & Albert

popular music from films and London musical shows. In 1938, after he had played a medley from Noel Gay's hit musical *Me & My Girl*, he was invited to teach them all the steps of *The Lambeth Walk*. One of his great attributes was to try to keep one step ahead of the Royal Family in anticipating requests.

For many years Vivian had been involved with the Portsmouth Bach Society as a guest conductor. The Society had been formed in 1923 as the Portsmouth Bach and Elizabethan Society. In 1938 he was honoured by being offered the conductorship of it, and although there was a wartime break in the Society's activities, he reformed it in 1946 and gave regular concerts, with the Society often being accompanied by the Royal Marines Orchestra. This was one of many 'outside' activities which kept him closely in contact with the orchestral scene.

After returning from their honeymoon Vivian and Mike lived in a small flat on Clarence Parade, Southsea. Vivian's MOA, Marine Weare would arrive at the flat each morning and bring them their tea in bed before getting Vivian ready for parade. Despite her years of preparing herself for probable service life, Mike found that life as a young officer's wife was rather intimidating. When she made a formal call on the wives of senior

Lt Dunn with the Dance Orchestra

officers in her best dress, be-hatted and be-gloved, she fervently hoped that no one would be in. Life was extremely formal and great store was put on precedence and hierarchy. She recalls one Ladies' Night at Eastney in the officers' mess when she joined the ladies after dinner in the powder room. She was lining up in the usual way when a bossy Major's wife took it upon herself to reorganise the queue by sending the junior officers' wives to the back while she stepped aside for the colonel's wife saying 'please go first, you are senior to me!' From then on Mike was determined that she would never be guilty of such snobbish behaviour.

Not long after this Vivian was on a band engagement in London accompanied as always by his MOA. He sent a telegram to Mike 'RETURNING SUNDAY STOP WEARE BACK TUESDAY STOP'. The Post Office clerk took it upon himself to make a minor adjustment to the punctuation, thus the cable that Mike received read 'RETURNING SUNDAY STOP WE ARE BACK TUESDAY STOP'. This caused great confusion!

At the end of two months of marriage Mike, as the daughter of a successful businessman, presented her carefully kept household accounts to her husband so that they might discuss their budget. Vivian looked at the figures in astonishment and asked what they were for. When Mike explained they were to show where their money was spent, he put them aside, remarking on their neatness, and never looked at them again. Indeed he seldom looked at any other accounts, bank statements or tax demands for that matter for the rest of his life. Other people dealt with that, not FVD.

The final cruise ever to be undertaken by the Royal Yacht *Victoria & Albert* took place in August 1939, only weeks before the outbreak of World War 2. The last programme played by the band under Lieutenant F V Dunn was on the 8th August before they disembarked at Portsmouth.

The year culminated with the New Year's Honour's List gazetting Lieutenant Francis Vivian Dunn to be appointed a Member of the 5th Class of the Royal Victorian Order. This was awarded in recognition of his duties with the Royal Family aboard the Royal Yacht. A signal honour for such a junior officer.

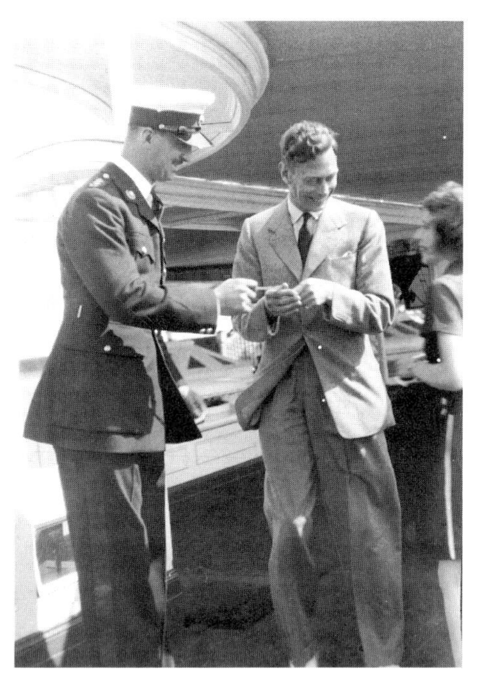

Vivian with King George VI and Princess Elizabeth in HMY Victoria & Albert *in 1938*

CHAPTER 4

A Change of Tempo - Wartime

ALTHOUGH VIVIAN AND MIKE had moved into a flat near the sea front at Southsea, he still maintained his cabin in the barracks so that his many uniforms, and constant changing, could be carefully cleaned, pressed and monitored by his MOA.

It was in August 1939 that Mike announced that she was pregnant and Vivian was absolutely delighted though a little apprehensive about his forthcoming fatherhood. Work took priority over everything and the threat of war and an uncertain future hung over their heads.

Vivian was promoted to Captain two days before the outbreak of war, having served the requisite eight years as a Lieutenant as did all regular officers at that time. He claimed that he was in the officers' mess at Eastney on the Sunday morning when war was declared. He often recounted the legendary tale of the Duty Officer who arrived breathless in the ante-room and said to the Colonel. 'Sir, war has been declared. What shall I do?' The Colonel is reputed to have looked up from his paper and replied 'Close the White Gates!'

When the war came Mike's father suggested that they might like to move to Hambledon, near Petersfield about 12 miles north of Portsmouth, where he had rented a lovely house called Combe Down. Living in the country was a much safer proposition as Portsmouth, being a major naval port was always under the threat of enemy bombing; indeed small air raids had started soon after war was declared. This meant a longer journey to work every day but Vivian enjoyed driving and was able to go over the day's musical programme in his head.

Early in 1940 a reception was held at Portsmouth Guildhall for the crews of HMS *Ajax*, *Exeter* and *Achilles* after their successful action against the *Graf Spee* the previous December. Vivian sat down and wrote a new march for the occasion. When few people attending recognised the tune, he explained that it was written in three days and he had entitled it *Heroes of the River Plate.* Although some hand-written stanzas of the march were printed in the *News Chronicle* the following day with Vivian's signature under them, no manuscript has ever been found.

It was on the 13th April 1940 that their first daughter, Leonie, was born in a local nursing home. On the night before the birth Mike woke Vivian to say the baby was on the way. She then had to sit and wait for over an hour whilst he bathed, shaved, dressed and chose the right tie!

Leonie's appearance into the world pleased Vivian though he was rather taken aback by the new born's as yet unfocussed eyes, which he claimed to be crossed, and he was only partly reassured by Dr Angus Munro (a family friend) that this was normal in new born babies. Leonie's entrance into this world was a tremendous joy to them both, and Grandfather Halliday (known to the grandchildren as 'Pop' – Grandmother Halliday being known as 'Mop'!) visited them regularly.

The outbreak of war heralded a new era for the band. Whilst the bands of the Royal Naval School of Music were embarked in some 80 seagoing ships with around 2,000 musicians at sea, the Divisional bands remained based in their respective barracks. However they travelled the length and breadth of the country, playing concerts in canteens, naval and military establishments, broadcasting and performing on many ceremonial occasions. They helped to give the people of Great Britain a much-needed boost to their morale and in many ways it was a busier time than ever.

It was not long after the war had started that Vivian's brother, Geoffrey ('Chiffer') joined the Corps. Although a musician in his own right, he gained a temporary commission as a general duties officer. As we have seen Chiffer had become a student at the Royal Academy of Music in 1933, after some early teaching on the pianoforte from the old family friend, Myers Foggin. He was still at the Academy when war broke out and enlisted in the Royal Marines for hostilities only on 1st December 1939. He served in MNBDO 1 (Mobile Naval Base Defence Organisation No1) from 1943 to 1944 seeing action in north-west Europe. Towards the end of his service in 1945, as an acting temporary major, he became Head of the Theatre and Music Section of BAOR in Germany and the success of his work was the first indication of his gifts as an administrator in the musical field. Whilst in Berlin he met and married a charming ex-WRNS Officer, Constance Schofield, who was also in the Control Commission. He was subsequently elected an ARAM in 1948 and became an FRAM in 1964. He involved himself in all forms of serious music, travelling extensively up and down the country. His last appointment before he died in 1967 was as Orchestral Director of the new BBC Orchestra in Bristol. We shall see how he applied for the appointment of Director of Music of Plymouth Division later.

Capt Geoffrey 'Chiffer' Dunn RM is married to Constance Schofield in 1945

War with Germany meant that there was a need for interpreters in the services. Vivian's schooling in Germany in the 1930s had given him more than a working knowledge of the language, indeed he was a qualified interpreter in both French and German. He volunteered his services as an interpreter and was quickly called upon by the Naval Headquarters in Portsmouth. He spoke little of this after the war, considering his cipher work an essential part of the war effort and one of the ways in which he could contribute to the more active side of hostilities. His musical duties in pursuit of morale raising concerts kept him and his band extremely busy, but his interpreter skills were called upon regularly when he was in Portsmouth.

One particular incident Vivian recalled was a visit to the Royal Artillery camp at Blandford in 1940. To make all the necessary arrangements for a concert and parade, he called on the Commanding Officer, who at one point said that he had a 'tame musician' there. He asked the Adjutant to bring the man in. When he arrived in a dreadfully ill fitting denim suit and an equally disastrous cap, he saluted in a most unpractised manner.

'This is Gunner Fenby', said the Colonel. Vivian recognised him immediately and said 'Do you realise who this man is? He is Eric Fenby, Frederick Delius' amanuensis and something should be done to transfer him to where his talent can be put to good use.' It was not long before Fenby was commissioned into the Army Educational Corps. Before the war Fenby had selflessly devoted himself to writing down many of Delius' works when the composer became blind. Later he became a professor at the Royal Academy of Music and was responsible for teaching many Royal Marines musicians.

It was in 1940 that Captain F V Dunn and the Orchestra of the Royal Marines, Portsmouth Division, made their first recordings and because of the threat of bombing, the band moved into the chapel in Highland Road, near Eastney Barracks in Southsea. The first was *Amporita Roca*, with *La Belle Pense Op 98* on the reverse side. These were quickly followed that year by two further 78rpm records.* Exactly where these 78s were recorded is not clear, but the band made five more in 1941 and a further three in 1942, all orchestral recordings.

The bombing of Portsmouth brought its own hazards. Living at Hambledon, the Dunn family spent many happy off-duty hours in the countryside. On one particular occasion, as they drove along the leafy lanes with Leonie safely ensconced in her carrycot, they were suddenly overtaken by two fighter planes in a dogfight. Vivian pulled the car off the road and close to a ditch putting the carrycot under a hedge. Leonie claims that looking up at the hedge from underneath was her earliest memory – though her parents disputed this saying she was too young to remember.

Combe Down was a happy place where Mike kept chickens and ducks to ensure the family were well supplied with eggs. She enjoyed working in the vegetable garden with the gardener Mr Briggs. Mike and Vivian entertained freely and many of the bachelor officers with whom Vivian had been friendly during his days living in the mess at Eastney, came out to the house at weekends for a rest. Among them were Leonie's godfather, Leon Fraser, Bertie Lumsden, Gerry Ross and 'Blondie' Hasler. Vivian had joined the Hampshire Hogs Cricket Club and would often field a side at Broadhalfpenny Down to indulge his passion for the game.

---

* listed in full in Appendix E.

Vivian with Leonie at (left) Combe Down, and (right) Sandown, I.O.W.

Alan Gibson, who joined the Corps as a Hostilities Only marine had been an enthusiastic, but indifferent performer on the flute. He made the acquaintance of the principal flautist in the band at Eastney and was auditioned by Captain Dunn and subsequently invited to sign on for twelve years. He protested that the war was going to be over by Christmas and decided not to sign on. After Gibson was commissioned a few years later, he happened upon Vivian in the officers' mess, who greeted him with 'You're Gibson, aren't you? You refused to join the band back in 1940. Well, I'll tell you now; I only wanted you because I'd found out you could type!'

Another young wartime Royal Marines officer who later became Head of BBC Light Entertainment, Con Mahoney, recalls Vivian at Eastney in 1940 as:

> 'A well-uniformed officer, not exactly military – but distinctive. He struck me, at a distance, as I was just a Second Lieutenant, as untouchable; but in his years of Knighthood as a kindly modest person. At Broadcasting House he mixed well and gave his services and advice in a generous manner. I seem to remember he had a rearward twitch when 'at ease', as he pulled the cloth of his tunic down at the vent.'

* * * * *

Musician Albert Marland

Mossley Pianist Broadcast Own Composition

Mossley's pianist, Bert Marland, of Henry Hall's Dance Band fame, now a member of the orchestra of the Royal Marines (Portsmouth Division) recently had one of his own compositions featured in a General Forces programme broadcast by the orchestra.

A large audience of marines, sailors and Wrens gave the work a terrific ovation. Admiral Sir. Chas. J. C. Little, C.B.E., K.C.B., Commander-in-Chief, Portsmouth Command, was in the audience and joined in the congratulations showered on Marland after the performance.

The idea for "American Prelude," as the piece is called, came to Marland—who is son of Alderman Edward Marland, of the Butchers' Arms, Stockport-road, Mossley—at Christmas. He put his ideas to the conductor of the Royal Marines Orchestra, Capt. Vivian Dunn, who put his office at Marland's disposal and told him to "go ahead."

The work was completed in six days.

Marland frequently broadcasts in the weekly " Mediterranean Merry-Go-Round." He shortly expects a second composition to be broadcast.

Joining Henry Hall's Band as pianist and arranger in August, 1937, Bert Marland broadcast frequently and toured widely with the band. He was broadcasting from Berlin shortly before the outbreak of war.

He first learned to play the piano while living with his parents at the Rising Sun Hotel, Stalybridge—his home address is now Leigham-avenue, Streatham — and for several years, from the age of 12, he was pianist at the Royal Pavilion, Mossley.

He became a student at Manchester Royal College of Music in 1924. After passing the entrance examination, one of the professors described his playing as "revealing musical promise of a distinctly high order."

As solo pianist in the band of the White Star liner Homeric during a winter cruise two years later, he met many world-famous celebrities and travelled thousands of miles.

In New York he met and played for Irving Berlin, and whilst in a cabaret in Alexandria he met Pearl White, a famous film star.

In 1926, Mr. Marland signed a 12-months contract with Jack Hylton—who has close associations with Stalybridge—and played at the Kit-Kat Club and the Piccadilly Hotel, London. He went to Berlin with Percival Mackey's Band in 1928.

Later, with his own band, he appeared at many of London's principal hotels and also took part in a C. B. Cochran revue.

He volunteered for the Royal Navy about two and a-half years ago and afterwards transferred to the Marines. He now arranges musical items for the Navy section of " Mediterranean Merry-Go-Round." Last year he composed a " Rhapsody for Freedom," which he dedicated to the Forces.

Vivian was always seeking outstanding young musicians whom he could engage in his band who were doing their war service. He felt it a waste of a young man's musical talent if he was employed in a mundane military role, because there was plenty of important work to be done behind the scenes, much of it by Royal Marines bandsmen. Not only could a young musician play a morale-boosting part in the war effort, but he could also enhance his musical career. It is not absolutely clear how Vivian discovered that Albert Marland, a celebrated pianist and arranger, had volunteered for the Royal Navy and been called up to be trained as a signalman; or even whether they had previously met. They had parallel musical careers, although Vivian was at the Royal Academy in London while Albert was at the Manchester Royal Academy of Music from 1924. As we have already seen, Vivian's continued interest in modern music had resulted in his playing in Jack Hylton's Kit Cat Club Band. Bert Marland had played the piano at the club about the same time.

Since then he had become one of the most well known pianists, arrangers and night club players in the country and was contracted for Henry Hall's BBC Dance Orchestra in the thirties. Scarcely a programme was performed without one of Bert's arrangements or compositions being played. Marland had had his own dance orchestras and bands, composed film scores and performed as a double act with another pianist, Harry Tait. On the death of Bert Marland in 1977, Vivian wrote:

> 'I regarded it as a fortunate day when I first met him and was subsequently able to arrange his transfer to me and thus prevent a terrible waste of talent in a situation to which he had been sent and at a time when he was very unhappy ...
>
> I recall that during the blitz on Portsmouth I used to arrange for him to come out to my family to rest at Hambledon where we lived and continue his work in relative peace. Our children were very young at the time, but years after they spoke with great affection of his playing nursery rhymes and children's music to them. They adored Uncle Bert.'

Musician Marland became an integral part of the Portsmouth Divisional Band until the end of the war when he went back to his piano playing in famous orchestras, clubs and concerts, often as the soloist in classical works. Marland was not the only professional musician conscript to join the band but undoubtedly the most talented and the one with whom Vivian had the greatest affinity. The renowned cellist Sydney Wright, who came from the Hallé Orchestra, was another wartime Marine who played in the Portsmouth Divisional Band.

Patrick Dunn, their second child, was born in the middle of a snowstorm in January 1942. Vivian was very proud to have a son to bear the family name, naming him after his father and quickly dubbing him 'Paddy'. This happy event was another ray of sunshine in that dark cheerless winter. Paddy was born at Combe Down, and no doubt the event was celebrated in the famous *Bat & Ball* pub at Hambledon, just up the road.

One of the morale boosting features in war-torn Portsmouth in which the Divisional Band played a significant part, was the regular concerts at the King's Theatre and, before it was bombed, the Guildhall. The move was prompted when Mr Leonard Glanville joined the City Council and had talks with Vivian with a view to organising concerts on a bigger scale. The city librarian Mr H Sargent was the executive brain behind the enterprise. On 18th January 1942, '1,728 stalwarts braved a cold and slushy winter's day to attend the first concert at the King's Theatre. The experiment was such a success that 11 more concerts followed before the spring.' The Royal Marines orchestra was the backbone of these concerts and in addition to professional artists, many service personnel were given the opportunity of appearing. These concerts continued until 1945 and developed into one of the major wartime amenities of Portsmouth and Southsea.

In his book *The Portsmouth Letters*, Admiral Sir William James, who was then the Commander-in-Chief, Portsmouth recalls one concert on 12th July 1942:

> 'Mark Hambourg was the star – Captain Dunn the Director of Music at Eastney, has done a tremendous service for the people of Portsmouth. It used to be said that Portsmouth people would not go to hear good music. Now the King's Theatre is packed every Sunday, and all due to Dunn's initiative and enthusiasm.'

This concert with Mark Hambourg brings to mind another a few years later at the King's Theatre, Southsea when Mark's daughter, Michel, played Grieg's *Piano Concerto*, with Vivian Dunn conducting the Southern Philharmonic Orchestra. Yet another example of how he encouraged top class musicians and orchestras to play in Portsmouth.

One of the major engagements of 1942 was the *'Battle For Freedom'* concert held at the King's Hall, Belle Vue, Manchester on 18th June. Presented by the *Daily Express* it had an all-star cast produced by Flt Lt Ralph Reader. In addition to the Portsmouth Divisional Band, were the Band of the Coldstream Guards and the Hallé Orchestra with the music under the direction of Dr Malcolm Sargent. Others in the cast included Lieutenant Laurence Olivier RNVR, Lieutenant Esmond Knight RNVR, Wilfred Pickles, Gladys Ripley and Alan Wheatley. This was typical of many concerts around the British Isles that were put on for Service Charities.

More recordings were made by the Portsmouth Divisional orchestra during 1942, mostly popular light classics, like the *Skater's Waltz, Dance of the Comedians* and *Perpetuum Mobile.*

Later in October 1942, King George VI paid a visit to Portsmouth and attended a large Youth gathering in the Guildhall Square at which the band was in attendance. Admiral James wrote:

> 'I asked His Majesty if I could present Captain Dunn, the Marine Bandmaster, who had done so much for music in Portsmouth. His Majesty asked what other bands there were, and I slipped in that Dunn's is the only one that could play the big concertos with men like Mark Hambourg and Pouishnoff, and that the "big shots" now came to Portsmouth as a result.'

These concerts continued throughout the war when the band was available. Vivian made the most of these opportunities for enlarging the band's orchestral repertoire and, in doing so, improving the standard of his musicians. His London contacts with some of the greatest soloists of the period, meant that Portsmouth enjoyed music of a rare quality almost every week. There is no doubt that Vivian used Marland's name to boost the high profile of his band and in most programmes his name can be found as the soloist and arranger. They were sell-outs and did much to enhance the prestige of the Royal Marines Band – and of course, his own reputation.

It was during the war that Vivian became more embroiled in regular broadcasting. The Overseas Recorded Broadcasting Service came into being in 1942 to provide recorded entertainment for broadcast to Allied Personnel throughout the world. All recordings were made by Service

A concert in Luton for the Electrolux 'Rest Week', 4th July 1943

personnel, guided by the ORBS organisation, which also consisted of servicemen. Initially the records were made on unprocessed acetate discs, but owing to their vulnerability a halt was called to the project until shellac and vinyl-shellac records as used by the commercial companies, such as HMV, were used.

Vivian took his band to the Abbey Road Studios (HMV), the Drury Lane Theatre (headquarters of ENSA) and the Fortune Theatre where they had mobile recording equipment. As one of the leading military bands and one that Vivian had kept in the London musical limelight, the Portsmouth Band was in at the beginning of this enterprise. Although the producers suggested what should be played, Vivian had more than his say in the programmes that were recorded. The music was always light orchestral with dances, marches, musical comedy selections and solo items, complemented by the leading vocalists of the day, including Frances Day and Anne Shelton, together with the comedians Jack Warner and Jewell & Warris. ORBS was finally wound down in 1948, but many of these recordings have recently been released on compact disc as a Royal Marines Historical Society charity project in support of the Royal Marines Band Benevolent Fund.

However there was one very unusual recording session which was the result of a request from Harold Robin, a brilliant technician who was responsible for the transmission of black propaganda broadcasts in Germany, which he had begun on 5th February 1943. Captain Dunn and his Portsmouth Band were summoned to London. Whether they were chosen because of Vivian's grounding in German music and its sounds is not known, but Roy Morgan, one of his trumpet players in the orchestra who later became Bandmaster of the Portsmouth Divisional Band recalls the occasion:

> 'The band assembled at the Albert Hall for a recording session; apparently it had been decided to intercept radio transmissions to German submarines and give them false information. An 'ideal' way was to interrupt a genuine broadcast – a military band broadcast – so we were lined up for the job. The skill, apparently, was to copy exactly the quality of the sound of a broadcast received by the submarines. The empty Albert Hall was suggested to supply the 'echo' noise of the reception and we thumped out German marches in true German style. But to no avail – the quality of the music was too good and the reception was also too good. We battled away for hours and suddenly, as musicians do when pushed to the limit, made a loud and discordant noise. Captain Dunn with a brow of thunder stopped the band and set to quell the mutiny. However the producer, the expert on noises, crashed out of his cubby-hole with "Great, great lads! You've done it". And who led the laughter? – Captain Dunn!'

He spent many happy and worthwhile hours working on broadcasts with his band and on one occasion these included the entire London cast of Ivor Novello's *The Dancing Years*. There were many such occasions, but as an example a memorable date was 12th September 1943, when the *Radio Times* announced that they were broadcasting an ENSA concert from the Royal Albert Hall entitled *'Seascape'* in aid of King George's Fund For Sailors. The Massed Orchestras of the Royal Marines, along with the Bugles and Drums accompanied a choir of Naval Ratings and WRNS, all under the direction of Captain F Vivian Dunn. The cast that day was legendary: Lt Cdr Ralph Richardson, Edith Evans, Robert Speaight, Dennis Noble, Heddle Nash, Nancy Evans, Gracie Fields and Evelyn Laye were on parade. On the rostrum, besides Vivian and Captain Tommy Francis (of the Chatham Band), Constant Lambert conducted one of his own suites and dancers from the Vic Wells Ballet performed with choreography by Robert Helpmann. This is just one example of the wide scope of concerts given by Royal Marines bands during the war in aid of morale boosting and service funds. The following day the *Manchester Guardian* described it as a 'spectacular concert devised and produced by Basil Dean ... the whole show, besides being flawlessly managed, had an artistic quality unusually high for an occasion of this sort.'

One thing that disturbed the peace of a Sunday at Combe Down in 1944 was when a small bomb landed in the manure heap at the bottom of the garden. It exploded, shattering the dining room windows and hurling manure all over the Sunday lunch. This was too close for comfort and Mike and the children were packed off to Yeovil to stay with Vivian's mother for the rest of the summer until things quietened down. The children found Granny Dunn with her maxim of 'children should be seen and not heard' rather tedious after the carefree atmosphere Mike had created at Hambledon. They all found the summer rather strained and thankfully they returned to Combe Down at the start of the winter. This proved a long hard winter with plenty of snow and Vivian found the drifts too deep to drive over Portsdown Hill into Eastney on occasions.

Another bomb incident occurred when the band were doing one of their many broadcasts in Abbey Road Studios. Roy Morgan recalls:

> 'The days at St John's Wood were very long and hard; there must have been hours of broadcasts produced for the Forces networks. Lieutenant Commander Kim Peacock was the announcer/presenter and band entertainer. About a dozen of us younger chaps used to finish up in his flat in Piccadilly every night, where he took it upon himself to entertain us (much to Captain Dunn's horror). Next morning Kim Peacock would turn up late for the next recording session, and when told off by Vivian, would point at the band and say "Look at them with bleary eyes and white faces – blame them!" Vivian would then give the brass section hell for the next 15 minutes! On one occasion, we were returning from a lunch break when a flying bomb practically demolished the pub we had just left. Our only casualty was the Librarian, L/Cpl 'Tanky' Webb, a rather pompous sort of chap. His wound was a slashed backside, which suggested he was running away from trouble.'

It was not long after this that there was a rehearsal of the Combined Services Massed Bands at the Albert Hall. Along with the Portsmouth Divisional Band were the RAF Uxbridge and a Guards band. The Guards

Director of Music took the first session of conducting, followed by the RAF man. Then it was the turn of Vivian who had chosen music that was not beloved of the Guards Band and they didn't have the necessary scores. The Librarian at the time was Moze Redding, as 'Tanky' Webb still had a sore backside. Vivian looked around and bellowed out 'Redding! Where the hell's Redding?' to which an anonymous voice from the assembled bands shouted out 'In Berkshire!' Everyone collapsed with laughter including Vivian and they all had a good rehearsal as a result of this breaking of the tension.

Another Massed Bands story, this time on parade, showed a side of Vivian which was as delightful as it was unexpected to his musicians. The bands had been waiting around for ages and the musicians were not at all happy. Then there erupted some screaming by Sergeants Major and some yelling by Directors of Music to get their bands ready for the 'off'. At last there was silence, at which moment someone broke wind with the loudest fart they had ever heard. The assembled ranks dissolved into laughter and all tension disappeared. Jack Miles, one of the percussionists, heard Vivian say quite loudly 'If that was a musician and not a horse, I'd make him a Sergeant at once!'

* * * * *

In 1944 Henry Hall, probably the most famous of the dance band leaders of the era, brought his BBC Dance Band down to give a concert in the Globe Theatre at Eastney Barracks. This had been arranged with the cooperation of Bert Marland. Unfortunately the piano in the theatre was out of tune and 'quite ghastly'. With much apprehension, Vivian ordered that the grand piano from the bandroom in the barracks should be moved. Even more anxiety was manifested when a group of hefty and inexperienced marines arrived from the Duty Company to move it. However all was accomplished without disaster and Marland gave a marvellous performance. Vivian recalled afterwards that he could not bear the thought of Bert playing 'on that old tin can'.

We have already seen much evidence of Vivian's interest in choral music, and his association with a number of civilian societies. During the war, some of these were forced to cease operating, mainly due to the menfolk being away. However there are numerous stories of his involvement with, and his efforts to improve, local Portsmouth Societies. One such was the

Airspeed Works Choir, mostly made up of ladies. Their pianist was Dudley Ruel and there was an occasion in the middle of the war when they sang with the Royal Marines Band at a charity concert at the King's Theatre. There were selections from *Die Fledermaus* and Verdi, and Weber's *Invitation to the Waltz*. Vivian was in his element; for the rehearsals he used Ruel and then on the performance day he brought over some of his band to accompany them. After that, he invited Ruel over to Eastney to play with the orchestra when another of his pianists, Paddy Burke, was away.

Towards the end of the war, a temporary Royal Marines officer, Captain Eric (Mike) Mitchell, joined Eastney and, as he had a musical background, found himself as the unofficial Entertainments Officer for the band. He raised groups of singers, including WRNS, forming them into choirs. Not only did Dudley Ruel play for them, but Vivian polished them up before charity performances. One such was a WRNS concert in Oxford, including items by the Oxford String Players. About fifty all told, including Vivian, 'Mike' and Dudley, travelled rather uncomfortably in 3-tonners. Pam Oakley recalls singing in it and there being more performers than there were audience!

Mike Mitchell went into the musical business after the war, having married the mezzo-soprano Constance Shacklock in 1947. He became a *répétiteur*, teaching opera singers and choirs; he died in 1965 aged 56.

A long lasting friend whom he met during the war was Robert Farnon who was the Director of the Canadian Army Band of the Allied Expeditionary Force. Farnon has since written a large number of suites and popular light music, together with several film and later television scores. Much of his light music is almost compulsory in such programmes up to the present day. The two kept up with each other, subsequently became firm family friends and Bob Farnon was often invited to the School of Music at Deal after the war to conduct orchestral concerts.

During the summer of 1944, whilst living at Combe Down, Vivian made an arrangement for unison voices and military band which he called *O England My Country* from Gustav Holst's original composition, with words by G K Menzies. Nothing much was heard of it again until the early 1960s, when it was included in all practices and rehearsals for Beating Retreat, sung by the Massed Bands. Mysteriously, after the final rehearsal, it was withdrawn and disappeared from the repertoire, although the score and parts for military band and unison voices are held in the Central Musical Library of the Royal Marines Band Service.

It was in 1944, that the Director of Music of Plymouth Division, Major F J Ricketts, was forced to retire due to ill health. He had reached the retiring age of 60 in 1941 and had been re-employed, and then promoted to Major in 1942. Ricketts sat on the board that was to select his successor, and here we see the first glimpse of things to come. There were more than 80 applicants for the post as might be expected of one of the most prestigious appointments within the three services. The selection board chose Bandmaster (WO1) Charles Nalden of the Royal Artillery (Portsmouth) Band as their first choice, but added that, should Nalden not be appointed, then Commissioned Bandmaster R H Stoner RM, Port Bandmaster on the Staff of Commander-in-Chief Portsmouth, should be offered the vacancy as 'he was quite outstanding and would be a most suitable selection for the appointment'. This latter recommendation was taken up by the General Officer Commanding the Royal Marines (now Commandant General) and Stoner became the first and last officer from the old Royal Naval School of Music to command a Divisional band.

Nalden was deeply distressed at not getting this job, but he did have a consoling letter from Major Ricketts saying how much Nalden had impressed him during the two days of his auditioning, which he felt could hardly be improved upon. Ricketts expressed his deepest sympathy in missing the appointment by so narrow a margin and hoped Nalden would not meet such misfortune in his next appointment. Nalden was a tremendous admirer of Kenneth Alford's compositions. It was ironic that, when *Vanguard* sailed for the Royal Tour to South Africa, his Royal Artillery (Portsmouth) Band was instructed to take up position shortly after dawn on the bitterly cold morning of 1st February 1947 on a desolate stretch of Portsmouth's foreshore and told to 'blow like hell until the *Vanguard* was out of sight'. They were also detailed to play when *Vanguard* returned to Portsmouth later in the year.

It can be presumed that Vivian had no say on the selection board for the Plymouth appointment as his younger brother Geoffrey ('Chiffer') was one of the candidates, and reached the final short list of ten.

It can be speculated that Vivian, who counted Ricketts as one of his close friends and had undoubtedly spoken to him of the right person for this appointment, had looked far enough into the future to see the way ahead. Promotion to Director of Music through the non-commissioned ranks is now the normal avenue of promotion, but was not so in those days. The appointment of Dick Stoner, who had come up through the ranks, subsequently led to a much higher calibre of musicians joining the Royal Marines, knowing that they had the unlimited opportunity for such exalted posts in the future.

The output and variety of music that Vivian and his Portsmouth Band played during the war was phenomenal by any standards. Bath was a particularly favourite venue, where they played regularly at The Pavilion. After a visit on 30th May 1944, where the stars were Evelyn Laye and Bert Marland, the orchestra returned at the end of July to play a series of concerts in the Parade Gardens. In three days they performed eight concerts, providing eleven hours of orchestral music and an evening of dance music. In all that time they did not repeat any of their items. Vivian drove his band hard and they felt that they were playing a significant part in Britain's war effort. It is interesting to note that the dance at the Pump Room in Bath designated 'Uniform or Evening Dress essential – no single tickets issued'!

Vivian judged his audiences well, providing them with what they wanted – many patriotic arrangements, usually by Bert Marland, coupled with a few of his own, and only a minimum from the military band repertoire, but they always included a comprehensive dance band selection.

No wonder a few eyebrows were raised one evening at Eastney during an officers' mess guest night to welcome back 45 Commando from the Normandy campaign. After a sober and traditional selection of light music played from the Minstrel's Gallery during dinner, a small group of musicians came down to the mess room for 'extras' as usual. Wartime Commando officers were not used to such highbrow airs and solos and became restless. Between numbers, an anonymous voice called for something rather more lively. Vivian did not require second bidding, and despite the frowns of older pre-war regular officers, he let the orchestra rip as a dance band, led by the magical piano playing of Bert Marland who opened up with Glenn Miller's *In The Mood.* The evening was a tremendous success and the Commandos were loath to let the band go. Only the President ended the session by replacing the stoppers in the port decanters.

As we have seen, major concerts and pageants in aid of war charities abounded during the war years, and another which must be mentioned was held at the Royal Albert Hall just before the end of the war in Europe on 6th April 1945. Written by Edward Neil and produced by Squadron Leader Ralph Reader, *'Heart of Oak'* was a pageant of the Royal and Merchant Navies. Vivian selected and arranged all the music. He gathered a symphony orchestra from the best that the three Royal Marines Divisions and the RNSM could muster. With a naval chorus of ratings and Wrens from HMS *Collingwood*, there was gathered together a fine collection of actors and singers. Once again Lieutenant Frederick Harvey RNVR sang while Lieutenant Alec Guinness RNVR played Nelson. Narrators included Leslie Mitchell, Frank Phillips, Nicholas Parsons and Beatrix Lehmann, while on 'parade' that day were the likes of Tessie O'Shea, Ernest Jay, Wally Patch and Balliol Holloway. One budding young actor who took part in the show, John Stratton, recalled that during a break in the not inconsiderable rehearsals for the show, the musicians let off steam by playing football in the Albert Hall arena using a load of old rag.

There were many more concerts such as this one. No wonder Vivian had so many contacts in London at the end of the war, contacts which he later used to tremendous effect for the good of the Royal Marines Band Service.

In August 1945 the Band of the HM Royal Marines Portsmouth travelled to Holland to play ostensibly to the Royal Netherlands Navy and the Royal Marines Commandos. However Vivian called on the *Burgomeester* of Rotterdam and requested the band should give concerts to the wonderful Dutch people. In no time at all a platform was set up on the steps of the *Bourse* and the band gave four lunchtime concerts, which were greeted with enormous enthusiasm in this war torn city. Vivian also met Prince Bernhard at a formal parade, an occasion which recalled an earlier wartime meeting with HM Queen Juliana in England. Vivian, always an opportunist to show off his band, then took the band to The Hague where they gave another concert in the Wittenburg Hotel.

Whilst he was in Holland V-J Day was declared and that night Vivian was taken on a tour of many Dutch naval ships in the harbour which were all celebrating in style. He vaguely remembered the paddle steamer *Gracie Fields*, a mine clearance vessel, but the evening became less clear the further the *schnapps* flowed.

* * * * *

Eastmey Barracks, showing the wartime air raid shelters

Almost as soon as the war finished the family decided to move back to Southsea. The move from Combe Down was traumatic in more senses than one. Vivian had collected a number of 12-inch discs of recordings he had made for the Overseas Recorded Broadcast Service which were packed, along with most of the other family belongings into two furniture vans. Vivian had loaded most of his own uniforms into his car as he was going into the barracks later. When they had loaded the first van, one of the removers asked Mike 'Do you mind if we smoke while we are working?' She said she didn't mind if that was the usual thing. The family then drove down to Southsea and waited outside the house for the vans to arrive. Suddenly a man in a funny old mac and a bowler hat appeared and said ' 'Ave you 'eard?' 'Heard what?' 'Well, there's been a fire on board one of the vans and it's been burnt out!' In that van was the collection of ORBS cardboard boxes which, if they hadn't been destroyed, had melted. Over half his recordings ceased to exist. Luckily he had kept some in his office in the barracks. Many of the manuscripts of Vivian's early compositions and arrangements were also destroyed in this fire. Mike complained that while she had lost all her clothes in the tragedy, relatively few of Vivian's things seem to have disappeared! Most of his uniforms, music, violin and two pianos had been in the first van and remained unscathed. Whilst insurance money could so easily replace clothes and material things, the manuscripts and ORBS recordings were irreplaceable.

It was in early 1945 that Vivian rewrote and revised the slow march *The Globe & Laurel*, later to be officially adopted as the Regimental Slow March. It can be presumed that this is the version that is played today. In October he also arranged *Song of the Sea* (Kunneke) for choir and orchestra, and in addition produced a military band version.

19 December 1939. King George VI and Queen Elizabeth with Captain F V Dunn at Eastney.

Their third child, Rosemary, was born at 50 Craneswater Park, opposite the Canoe Lake in Southsea in September 1945, at the time that Leonie had started kindergarten in Whitwell Road, subsequently going on to Seacourt, an elementary school on Eastern Parade, where she was later joined by Paddy. There were plenty of family outings now that the war had finished and regular trips across the ferry to Hayling Island where the sand was so thick and deep the children sank up to their shins in it.

Regular concerts at the King's Theatre in Southsea continued to be given by the orchestra of the Royal Marines mainly on Sunday afternoons. In late 1945 they were taken up by the newly constituted Southern Philharmonic Orchestra under the baton of Herbert Menges.

Since Major F J Ricketts' retirement through ill health in 1944, no further promotion to Major had been made within the Band Service officers, but Dunn had assumed the mantle of the Corps' Senior Director of Music. On 15th May 1946 Vivian was promoted to, firstly Temporary, then the following day Local, Major, his substantive rank being confirmed on 1st September, seven years after being made a Captain, and 15 years to the day since he joined.

The orchestra in the band room at Eastney just after the war

One of the first major ceremonial events to be held at Eastney Barracks after the war was at Beating Retreat on 3rd June 1946. The performance was held as a final rehearsal for the Victory Parade and celebrations in London immediately following. As Senior Director of Music Vivian had selected 130 musicians from the Divisional bands at Chatham, Portsmouth and Plymouth as well as the Royal Naval School of Music. In addition there were 180 troops on parade representing all branches including tradesmen and Royal Marines Engineers. The salute was taken by the Commander-in-Chief, Admiral Sir Geoffrey Layton. They travelled to London on the Thursday, and after rehearsals the next day came the national triumphal march through London on the Saturday. They stayed in London and the band Beat Retreat at the Cock Pit in Hyde Park on the following Thursday.

The Royal Yacht *Victoria & Albert* had been decommissioned in 1937 and, although there were plans for a new one, *Britannia*, this had not been built in 1947. King George VI and Queen Elizabeth had decided to carry out their first major overseas tour since the war to South Africa, and the new battleship HMS *Vanguard* was earmarked to convey them there. The upgraded Royal Yacht Band of 40 musicians and 20 buglers (later reduced

HMS Vanguard, 1947

ABOVE: *flying the Royal Standard*
RIGHT: *Beating Retreat. Vivian Dunn stands behind the King and Queen and the two Princesses.*
BELOW: *the Dance Band in improvised staging*

to 14) embarked on 3rd December 1946 for a shake down cruise to Gibraltar returning on the 20th, while the ship's RNSM Band was disembarked to Eastney. By the time the ship sailed for South Africa, Vivian had added three pipers, all Royal Marines, who played the bagpipes presented to the Corps to commemorate the association of the 2nd Battalion the Argyll and Sutherland Highlanders. The battalion had fought alongside the Royal Marines survivors of the ill-fated HMS *Prince of* Wales and *Repulse* in Malaya in 1941. Indeed one of the pipers, Marine Evans, had been a prisoner of war of the Japanese.

HMS *Vanguard* had been refitted for the Royal party and their entourage during the autumn and winter of 1946, and left Portsmouth on a grey and misty 1st February 1947. Vivian recounted that, on the embarkation of the Royal Family, 'The weather was foul, the King was in a filthy temper, and all the Princesses were interested in were the *Vanguard*'s guns.' They soon met rough weather in the Channel that lasted until they had passed Madeira. This was to be a tremendously exciting and exacting tour, but the fun had only just started when they approached the equator ten days later, the first time the Portsmouth Band had ventured into the southern hemisphere. The ship's commemorative brochure recounts:

> '*10th February 1947*. Immediately after the initiation of the two princesses, who had been let off lightly, a fresh contingent of bears now entered the bath and the clerk called for Major Vivian Dunn Royal Marines. The victim having been produced, the Clerk continued:
>
> "We now indict Major Vivian Dunn
> For having had a lengthy run;
> As Director of Music, Royal Marines,
> And yet, incredible though it seems,
> He's never yet once Crossed The Line –
> A really dreadful, horrible crime.
> We order him soused, and a bath and a shave,
> Bears – deal unmercifully with this knave." '

This *Crossing The Line* ceremony was later broadcast by the BBC and his children were able to hear their father on the wireless for the first time.

During the passage south the orchestra was playing for a wardroom guest night dinner on board. The music got slower and slower and the overworked band did not seem to be giving its young conductor the support

Vivian about to be initiated in the Crossing The Line ceremony aboard HMS Vanguard, *10th February 1947*

he should have. Vivian jumped up from his meal and began conducting the orchestra to the amazement of all. It was reported that the music 'greatly improved'.

Whilst in South Africa, the King heard a local group singing a local folk tune *N'kosi Sikelele* to which he took a particular liking. When he arrived back on board he asked his young director of music if he knew it. Vivian pleaded ignorance but immediately got hold of the BBC correspondent, Frank Gillard, and his sound engineer who had luckily recorded it and had it 'in the can'. Vivian sat down that afternoon to make an arrangement, and played it at dinner that night. The King expressed surprise and pleasure at this rendering, especially as Vivian had denied all knowledge of the piece only a few hours earlier!

There was another side to Vivian's character which was seldom seen in public. It portrayed considerable compassion and kindness. Colin Bowden recalls being one of the four Boy Buglers to go on this tour. Whilst holding the great man in awe, it was the Director of Music's insistence that these young lads should see something of the hinterland so he arranged for them to spend four days with a friend of his on a farm near Stellenbosch. At the end of the tour the four were marched into his office by the Drum Major and congratulated on their general behaviour and presence. Vivian then presented them with a large box of *Black Magic* chocolates – a small gesture but not forgotten.

Yet another story of the tour was when Vivian had accepted a series of *orchestral* engagements in and around the up-country city of Johannesburg, taking the appropriate instruments. On arrival the Town Clerk informed him that the citizens were expecting the band to lead a big ceremonial parade the next morning where the salute would be taken by the Commander-in-Chief of the South Africa Station. The military band instruments had been left miles away in HMS *Vanguard*, but someone remembered a set of band instruments which had lain dormant in the basement of the Town Hall for many years, having been bought during the war and never used. A hasty inspection was made of the dusty instruments and it was found they were reasonably serviceable, many still in their original cellophane wrappings. What was missing was a bass drum, so the Town Clerk arranged to borrow one from the South African Light Horse! Vivian set the band to give them a quick polish, checked their tuning and the band gave yet another immaculate performance as though nothing untoward had happened.

It was around this time that Vivian had started to write more marches. Before the Royal Tour to South Africa, he had composed two new quick marches; firstly the march *Royal Vanguard* to commemorate the tour, which he also arranged for the orchestra; and whilst on passage he penned *The Springbok March*, an arrangement based on Afrikaans songs. Prior to the tour he had visited South Africa House in London to do some research and made a re-acquaintance with the Boer marching song, *Sarie Marais*. He borrowed, or was given, a book *Volksangbundel vir Suid Afrika* from the embassy library, but it was never returned. A note in the book in his handwriting indicates that he selected *Vanaand gaan die volkies koring sny* (16 bars) *Aai, aai, die witborskraai* (8 bars), *Sarie Marais* (40 bars) and *Dis te ver om te ry* (24 bars) for his arrangement.

His love of folk music, coupled with a request by HM The Queen, led him to a further arrangement that year. Hebridean folk tunes were the foundation of his *Westering Home*, a slow march which has been used for half a century to accompany the Royal Navy's mast manning displays. It was not without complications as the copyright of *Westering Home* was open to question. It would appear that the tune is partly traditional and partly the original composition of Sir Hugh Roberton who had arranged it for the Glasgow Orpheus Choir. When this was pointed out to him Vivian remembered meeting Hugh Roberton and their subsequent friendship. Indeed Vivian expressed his respect and admiration for the latter's work and fully accepted his authorship of the tune. However Vivian pointed out that his arrangement for military band had been specially requested by HM Queen Elizabeth, The Queen Mother. His own hand-written list shows:

> Title – Scottish Airs Slow March *'Westering Home'* and *'A'e Fond Kiss'*
> Composer – Roberton and Traditional
> Publisher – Curwen (with permission), MSS
> Written in 1947

Many years later, in 1970, he was being interviewed by Roy Plomley as one of his castaways on *Desert Island Discs*, Vivian summed up one of the most memorable experiences in his life when asked about the tradition of the Sunset Ceremony. He said:

> 'One of the most marvellous moments that I can recall was after leaving South Africa on completion of the Royal Tour at the beginning of May, HMS *Vanguard* was turned, and on the wonderfully calm sea, the band Beat Retreat on the quarterdeck exactly as the flaming orb sank over the horizon. It's often said that this tune *Sunset* makes strong men weep.'

Soon after the *Vanguard's* return Vivian and Mike were invited to the Royal Garden Party, where Mike was introduced to HM The Queen. In the King's Birthday Honours announced the following day Vivian was promoted in the Royal Victorian Order to Fourth Class. Although this honour still carried the initials MVO, it was a higher class than any that his predecessors had been granted.

There was a typical piece of Dunn showmanship when the King's Birthday Parade was held on Southsea Common. There was a total of 1,200 on parade which included Wrens for the first time, 150 of them. As they had no march past of their own, Vivian decided that, after *Heart of Oak* for the sailors, *A Life on the Ocean Wave* for the Marines and sundry regimental marches for the soldiers, that the Wrens should have *All The Nice Girls Love a Sailor*, which he had specially arranged for the occasion. This caused the biggest cheer of the day.

Returning home from the South African tour, there was the first post-war Eastney Barracks Tattoo to organise in which the newly re-designated Portsmouth Group Band took a very prominent part. In the following year, 1948, it was repeated on a much larger scale with Massed Bands from the Depot at Deal and the bands of HMS *Pembroke*, *Excellent*, *Victory* and *Daedalus*. Over 35,000 came to see the show, including the Duke of Edinburgh and Earl Mountbatten, whilst two coach loads came all the way from Manchester – the shape of things to come. Unfortunately the weather on one night broke half way through and the rain washed out any thoughts of completing the finale. For this Tattoo Vivian made a special arrangement of Ravel's haunting *Bolero*, which was a particular favourite of his wife. He had first played it at a South Parade Pier concert in 1934, where it was received as an exciting and exacting orchestral work. This tune was to haunt him for the rest of his life.

Despite being away from England for several months, there was another trip abroad that year, this time to Paris with the Guard and Regimental Colour from Portsmouth Group to take part in ceremonies arranged by the British Embassy. Vivian, always striving to match the occasion with something suitable, entranced the French by alternating British and French marches on their way up the Champs Élysées.

* * * * *

In January 1948 Vivian found himself having to face the music, when he was called to account for an overdue bill from Boosey & Hawkes. He was invited to comment to the Major General Royal Marines, and explained that the bill had been occasioned by the purchase of new instruments and appurtenances for the Royal Tour. He said that the Band Fund had not enough to cover the cost because of the loss of earnings forced on them by being away in HMS *Vanguard* for so long. He was told to go to London to sort out a settlement with the firm. Once there he agreed that £200 would be paid immediately with the balance to be forwarded at the earliest opportunity. It was the custom in those days for officers to make a small monthly subscription to the Band Fund. Vivian claimed that these amounts had not been received for 1947 and when they had, he would complete the deal with a further payment of £200.

Already the first two children were being taught the rudiments of music, indeed there was little escape from it. Leonie and Paddy were 'dragooned' into learning the piano. Leonie remembers sitting on her father's knee and placing her small hands over his being taught how to find Middle C. One day she was taken to the Royal Marines band room, aged eight, to play some elementary pieces with the orchestra. One such was *A Selection of*

ABOVE:
Leonie, Mike, Rosey and Paddy

RIGHT:
Paddy with trumpet

Country Pieces for the Piano by Walter Carroll. The band had been hoodwinked into expecting that a distinguished pianist was about to appear. No doubt the band were astonished to see this small figure march in with her father. Corporal Leale led the applause for the young pianist, but what they said afterwards in the wet canteen has never been disclosed. This is probably the nearest equivalent to William J Dunn, sitting Vivian on a stool in the band room at Shorncliffe all those years before.

During these early days Leonie and Paddy had a temporary, unpaid nanny, 'Yetta' (Loretta) Wright, who was the daughter of the renowned composer of light music, Horatio Nichols (Lawrence Wright), known as the Daddy of Tin Pan Alley, and who lived in Southsea. She subsequently married a Royal Marines officer, Peter Williams, who was the OC of Officers' Training Wing when Paddy joined the Corps in 1964 – another coincidence.

Paddy rebelled against the piano lessons and scales that his hapless teacher forced on him. He claims that was the reason he subsequently took up the trumpet. He enjoyed his time as a brass player and made some progress in both the military and dance band fields, especially in the realms of jazz playing. He also played in the school orchestra, but by the time he joined Boosey & Hawkes in the early 1960s, he came to realise that he had reached his musical ceiling. After the family had moved to Deal Paddy was coached at the School of Music by that powerhouse of a trumpet player, Band Sergeant A V 'Taff' Lewis, who was a leading light in the *Oceanaires* Dance Band and who later joined Edmundo Ros. Walter

Hargreaves, one of the first and foremost of the RMSM's professors, also tried to develop Paddy's technique and golden tone. He added that Taff Lewis's teaching method on his young pupil had ruined any chance Paddy might have had of being a good trumpet player. Vivian, too, played his part in developing Paddy's double and triple tonguing, but it was all to no avail. He drove his young son hard but his offspring fell far short of the mark achieved by members of the Royal Marines Band Service. Looking back, Paddy says that his father's praise for his musical efforts was a little thin to say the least, but the master had only one standard – hard work and nothing but the best.

Like the rest of the family Rosey was coaxed early into learning to play the piano. The children grew up in Southsea although they were subsequently packed off to boarding school. The holidays and weekends home were great fun. They remember visits to Fratton Park to watch Portsmouth play football, picnics on Hayling Island and especially the children's parties in the officers' mess at Eastney. These were grand occasions, particularly the Christmas party, when a small section of the band was always present to play for them. Sport, which played a great part in Vivian's life, was soon taken up by the children. Easter Monday at the Cowdray Park point-to-point meeting, where the Royal Marines had a tent, was always a memorable event, as were the two-day Mead Cup and Corps cricket matches at Eastney, where Vivian, even if he was not selected, always made his presence felt. Those were the days when the band would play on the boundary edge at important matches at tea-times and sometimes during the match itself. The regular beat of the bass drum often interfered with the rhythm of the bowler approaching the crease and many a dropped catch was blamed on a sudden staccato blast on the trumpet!

His elder daughter Leonie writes about this period:

> 'Life with a father as a musician was by no means easy. When in the throes of a composition we had to endure the same musical phrases played all day and well into the night, over and over again, very loudly, on the piano. If we asked him a question there would be an immensely long pause and then, instead of an answer, would come "pom-pom-tiddle-tiddle-tum" (in the key of the current composition), and we had to start all over again as he hadn't heard us in the first place! At the dining table he would frequently drum with his fingers as he put in the rhythm section of the arrangement

or suddenly beat time in the air or begin whistling or humming the next musical phrase to be committed to paper. He would read and memorise scores in the evening though the radio or television might be on in the same room, the dog barking, or the telephone ringing. His concentration was absolute.

My mother believed that she should not come between my father and his career, and therefore unselfishly did not travel with him, but nevertheless was always in attendance at every local or London-based concert giving support and encouragement. She arranged and hosted numerous luncheon, dinner and cocktail parties for him.

In the whole of their married life, I only remember one quarrel between them, and that was over the weighing of some drinking chocolate powder brought back from the South African tour. They were an extremely loving and close couple.'

There is no doubt that Vivian found it a great sadness that none of his children took up music as a career. None of them had developed the natural talent of their father. The first thing he looked at on their school reports was progress in music. The children admitted that they were, at best, mediocre and far short of the high standards expected of them by their father. Leonie had inherited an artistic ability from Granny Dunn and could draw and paint well, but Vivian was solely concerned that they should concentrate on music and her paints were often confiscated until she had come to grips with her music. As we have seen, Leonie played the piano and Paddy the trumpet, whilst Rosey took up the clarinet, but none of them furthered their musical careers.

Although this may sound as if Vivian was an overtly strict parent, nothing could be further from the truth. He was a kind and loving father, always happy to play with the children (as long as it was cricket!). He was an excellent storyteller and had a knack of lighting bonfires during their frequent picnics. One day Paddy had been particularly naughty all day and was sent to his father on his arrival home 'to be dealt with'. Vivian discovered that his son's misdemeanours were nothing more than normal childish behaviour and had a quiet talk with him. He then told Paddy to yell as hard as he could while he gave six of the best to the armchair! Thus justice was 'heard' to be done and it was many years before Mike learned the true story.

Vivian had captained the Royal Marines Barracks cricket team from time to time during the war and immediately afterwards, but band concerts around the country, mostly at weekends, took him away so often that he never did command a regular place. He was an inspiring sight striding to the wicket to open the batting, with his six foot plus upright frame, immaculately clad in the cleanest of cream trousers and shirt, the whitest of pads and a bat which had always been meticulously oiled and scraped after each match, almost certainly by his MOA. After taking middle and leg guard, he was no respecter of any opposition bowling, often smiting the new ball back over the unsuspecting bowler's head in the first over, with the straightest of lofted drives. His impetuosity to keep the boundary fielders in action frequently let him down but his fielding was agile and tidy, usually patrolling the cover field. He was known to turn his arm over occasionally as a regulation 'military medium' bowler.

He maintained his fitness with regular squash and tennis, the convenience of the officers' mess lawns providing some excellent surfaces worthy of Royal Marines representative matches. He also played the occasional game of golf. The family went to Shanklin in the Isle of Wight for their summer holidays in 1947 and 1948 where Vivian could let his hair down out of sight of his usual working environment. He could enjoy his children and he let them dive off his shoulders into the sea. He was an expert at building sandcastles and dug huge holes deep enough for the children to stand upright in. However, work was never far away, and it was a source of amusement to others on the beach to see him sitting in bathing trunks, sun hat on head, pipe in mouth, writing music. In fact much of his work in those two summers was written on the beach!

There had never been any rules and regulations laid down for the payment of musicians for private engagements and Divisional Directors of Music were free to negotiate terms for their services. There were no scales of payment according to rank, and Directors of Music were able to take a substantial cut. The Admiralty asked the Commandant General to advise on a scale of fees for both military band and orchestral engagements. This was passed to the Commandant of the School of Music for discussion at the Directors of Music's annual conference. As a result, an Admiralty Fleet Order (AFO 3174/47) was issued on 5th September 1947, setting out the four categories of engagements. Although no amounts were specified, nor the percentage payments by rank or appointment, it laid down that charges were to be made at Musician's Union rates! This became standard in the three Services.

* * * * *

Vivian maintained his close links with London and the Royal Academy of Music. In 1947 he endowed the annual 'Vivian Dunn Prize for Orchestral Playing', a prize that exists to this day. The following year he was invited to be one of the adjudicators for the John Solomon music prize on 24th March 1948. Before that he and his band had twice broadcast on the BBC Light Programme. These broadcasts were made at the Camden Theatre, Mornington Crescent. On the second occasion they made an early start as balance tests had to be carried out by 9am. His programmes were always biased towards the classics, and the programme on the 15th January included works by Beethoven, Delibes, Bach, Rossini and his favourite Elgar.

This was shortly followed by another memorable occasion, the unveiling of the Franklin D Roosevelt statue in Grosvenor Square, London, opposite the United States Embassy on 12th April 1948, the third anniversary of the former President's death. The President had sadly not lived to see the end of the war. 430 Royal Marines were on parade that day. There was a Royal Naval School of Music Band under Captain H Kenward who accompanied the Royal Guard and a Memorial Guard of the King's Squad from Lympstone parading the King's Colour of Chatham Group. In a covered stand nearby were the Massed Bands of Chatham and Portsmouth Group, under Major Vivian Dunn, with the choir of St Paul's Cathedral.

The ceremony was attended by Mrs Eleanor Roosevelt, Her Majesty Queen Mary, HM King George VI and Queen Elizabeth, The Princesses Elizabeth and Margaret with the former's newly-wed husband, Prince Philip. The Archbishop of Canterbury conducted the service. The Massed Bands and choir provided the accompanying music. As soon as King George had delivered his address, Vivian Dunn raised his baton and conducted the Massed Bands and choir in his own, new arrangement of *The Battle Hymn of the Republic*, often described as the finest arrangement he ever made. The crowd joined in, tentatively at first, then fully throated, singing this vital, optimistic American tune. It was one of his proudest moments.

The following day saw a complete change as he continued his involvement with the Portsmouth musical scene, when he conducted the Portsmouth Bach Society in Brahms' *Requiem Mass* at St Mary's Church. This was a very big undertaking for such a small Society. Although all went well at the performance, during the rehearsal that afternoon Vivian discovered that not only did the acoustics cause problems, but the organ was tuned to the old high pitch making it necessary for him to alter the composition of the orchestra. Portsmouth's music critic was obviously more attuned to the serious scene than the pre-war journalists as he commented that 'Miss Brice's solo was marred by over-weight woodwind and there sometimes seemed a lack of a steady bass line in the orchestra'. What Vivian's reaction was to reading this can only be imagined. The Society had been 'rested' for seven years during the war but Vivian had helped to revive it afterwards and they had played their first concert on 1st November 1946 at St Mary's Church, followed a fortnight later by one in St Anne's Church in the Dockyard in aid of the church restoration fund.

St George's Day, 23rd April 1948 was to be commemorated for the first time as 'Corps Remembrance Day' and a particularly large ceremonial parade took place at Eastney, with a march past, a Drumhead Service, an afternoon concert and a Commemoration Ball at South Parade Pier in the evening. During the interval there was a display by the full band and bugles of the Divisional band. Such was the force with which Vivian drove himself in his meticulous and detailed planning for such events that everything was made to look so very smooth on the actual day.

The following week saw Vivian and his band in yet another State occasion. On 26th April, the 25th wedding anniversary of the King and Queen when, along with a Guard of Honour, they played during the state drive to St Paul's Cathedral. Later in the day they played at a King George's Fund for Sailors rally in Trafalgar Square. To show how busy the bands were, the previous day had been rehearsals of the Massed Bands for their Royal Tournament display, in which there would be counter marching merging four small bands into one large one, a manoeuvre not undertaken by the RNSM before.

The 100th Portsmouth City Municipal Concert took place on Sunday 9th May when Vivian conducted several items being played by the Southern Philharmonic Orchestra at the King's Theatre, Southsea. He had secured Michel Hambourg to play Grieg's *Piano Concerto* and Dennis

Portsmouth Band, supplemented by musicians from Plymouth Division Band play at a KGFS rally in Trafalgar Square following the parade for the King and Queen's Silver Jubilee celebrations, 26th April 1948

Noble, the famous tenor to sing Verdi's *Credo* from *Othello*. Over 1,500 people attended. Vivian had, of course, conducted the very first concert on 18th January 1942, then at the Guildhall, and the Royal Marines orchestra had played in more than half of them. At the reception afterwards, Herbert Menges paid tribute to the spadework done by Vivian and, of course, Wing Commander R P O'Donnell, Vivian's predecessor and well known to older Portsmouth audiences, who had occasionally brought his RAF orchestra to play during the war. As a result of this concert, the *Portsmouth Evening News* carried a headline 'Musical Portsmouth Needs a 3,000-Seat Hall – Concerts Here To Stay'.

Whilst accolades were being received for the public high profile events, things were not going quite so well at the officers' mess at Eastney. Following the appearance of the Royal Marines dance orchestra at a mess dance the night before, the Mess President wrote to the Commanding Officer as he had received several complaints that the dance band were too noisy, and the Band Sergeant could not conduct – neither should he announce 'Take your partners for the two-step'. It was further suggested that advice should be sought from the leader of the *Oceanaires*, or an outside orchestra would be hired in future. Although Vivian was informed of this letter, his response was not recorded!

Later that year whilst living at 'Cranesmere' in Southsea, Vivian penned a march specially dedicated to the Royal Naval Association, of which he later became a Vice President. For this composition he used the naval bugle calls 'Alert' and 'Carry On', coupled with references to *A Life on the Ocean Wave*. He entitled this march *Under the White Ensign*, and it remains in the repertoire to this day. The themes of the march are original but, as in so many works with a nautical flavour, well-known sea songs and tunes are woven into it. Then came the march *Camberley*, which was dedicated to the Commandant, Staff and Students of the Army Staff College. This was written as a result of a request from Lieutenant Colonel Douglas Drysdale for the band and Corps of Drums to Beat Retreat at the Camberley Cocktail Party on 24th August. Sadly the march did not prove a lasting success but he subsequently transcribed this march for solo cornet and small orchestra; as it has an Irish jig flavour, one can only presume he was harping back to his own ancestry.

One of his lasting arrangements first appeared in 1948 when he wrote a setting for buglers and military band entitled *Prelude to the Morning – a Setting of Reveille*. When it was recorded in 1950 the first batch of records bore the label *'Prelude to the Morning – a Setting of Sunset'!* It was released on a CD in 1995 and subsequently re-arranged by Captain David Cole for the *'Farewell Britannia'* recording, an appropriate choice as Vivian Dunn was the first Director of Music of the last Royal Yacht. This piece of music had laid dormant for many years until John Ambler, Chairman of the International Music Society, brought it to the notice of David Cole, then Director of Music of the Band of the C-in-C Naval Home Command, who agreed to rearrange and rehearse the piece for a visit to Portsmouth by the UK Branch of the International Military Music Society in honour of their President, Sir Vivian Dunn.

* * * * *

In June 1949 the Massed Bands of the Royal Naval School of Music and the Depot Royal Marines, were augmented by the band from ITCRM and gathered for three days at Burford, Oxfordshire, in April to prepare for their appearance at the Royal Tournament. As amalgamation followed the next year, this was the old RNSM Band's final appearance there. As the senior Director of Music in the Royal Marines, Major Dunn was summoned to take charge of the rehearsals with the aim of raising the standard. The band was 100 strong, but it was very thin toned because it was equipped with obsolescent narrow bore brass instruments. Many of the clarinets were obsolete simple key instruments and only those rated as solo clarinettists had the more usual Boehm system instruments, similar to the ones used by the Divisional bands. Likewise the horns used were sweet toned narrow bore with a very small bell, mostly dating from the early 1930s. Whilst adequate for orchestral work, they sounded very thin when playing in the military band, compared with the stronger saxophones and euphoniums.

Vivian Dunn gave the Massed Bands intensive training, harder than anything most had previously experienced. There was soon a noticeable improvement in the musicality of the band, with more light and shade in their presentation both on the move and at the halt. Realising that he could only improve the playing to a certain level, he concentrated on improving the band's strength. The RN School of Music recruited boys from the age of 14, and the average age of those on parade was much younger than most military bands which were usually made up of long service musicians. He realised that, because of their age, these young musicians could be brought up to a much higher drill standard. In the event the presentation and drill outweighed any inadequacy in the actual playing and the Royal Tournament, and later the Deal Tattoo, were a great success. The Royal Naval School of Music sampled a taste of what was to come, and Vivian Dunn became acutely aware of their shortcomings, an omen for the future.

At the final rehearsal for the Royal Tournament on the sports field at Deal, Captain Roy Harry RN, the Director of Naval PT & Sports took the salute. With him was Jack Sheppard (later Lt Cdr RN) who recalls that whilst they expected good music and got it; they expected superb marching and got that too; but what they were not prepared for was a classical variation of maze marching with some of the band at quick time and others in slow time. It was brilliantly done, and it is believed it was the first time that any military band had performed such a display. When Vivian reported 'Rehearsal completed, sir' to Captain Harry, the latter replied 'Thank you, Vivian. That was brilliant. Kneller Hall will never come back!' But back they came, and both Army and RAF bands copied this type of display as years went by.

It was a subsequent source of irritation to Vivian that only 15 of the excellent musicians in the Chatham Divisional Band, which was disbanded in 1950 on the closure of the barracks, transferred to the Corps. Twelve of the best instrumentalists decided to seek their futures elsewhere than in the Royal Naval School of Music. Eight of them transferred to the Guards bands, most to the Coldstream Guards, three to the Royal Engineers at Chatham and one to the Central Band of the Royal Air Force. The Chatham Director of Music, Captain Tommy Francis, retired from the Corps.

Up to 1948 the Royal Naval School of Music had been totally responsible for providing bands for the Royal Navy, most of them at sea. The Commandant had always been a general duty Royal Marines officer, not a musician. However a change was in the air when, early in 1944, RN School of Music bands were established at both the Infantry Training Centre, Lympstone, Devon and at the Royal Marines Depot at Deal. By 1948, they also provided a band for 3rd Commando Brigade RM.

In the Royal Marines Office in London, Colonel A G Ferguson-Warren was the Assistant Adjutant General and had recently returned from being a guest of the Japanese Government for four years, resulting in being presented with a bill from Chatham Division for the arrears in his Divisional band subscription for the years 1941 to 1945. Consequently he asked one of his young staff officers why the Corps had two kinds of bands: the RNSM being paid for wholly by the Admiralty, and the Divisional bands paid for in part by the officers of the Corps.

It was obvious that radical changes must take place and at the end of 1948, a committee under Major General J E Leech-Porter, commanding Portsmouth Division and a former Superintendent of the RN School of Music, was appointed to look into the future. It was coincidental that Major Vivian Dunn, the Portsmouth Director of Music, was a strong proponent of the amalgamation of the two arms of the Naval Band Service. Leech-Porter asked Vivian to write what he called 'a blue print'. He was frequently called into the General's office to discuss the merits of such a plan. It is certain that many of the final recommendations of the Leech-Porter committee stemmed from Vivian's ideas. It was known that the Director of Music of Plymouth Division, Captain Dick Stoner was firmly opposed to such amalgamation, an attitude which was difficult to reconcile with this particular officer's background as the first RN School of Music trained Director of Music of a divisional band. One particular aspect which advanced the amalgamation was the abandonment of every officer being required to subscribe one day's pay annually to the Divisional Band Funds.

When General Leech-Porter died in 1979, Vivian paid tribute to him for the way the former's unerring instinct for detecting what was right and wrong had steered the committee along the lines which Vivian implied that he had suggested, though none of the three Divisional band Directors of Music had been officially allowed to sit on it.

The reduction in the strength of the whole Corps forced the new Commandant General, Lieutenant General Sir Leslie Hollis to consider the recommendations of the Leech-Porter committee which had already been submitted. He promptly forwarded them to the Admiralty. Thus it was that the decision was taken in early 1950 to unite the three Divisional (recently renamed Group) bands with those of the RN School of Music to form a consolidated Royal Marines Band Service to serve the Royal Navy and Royal Marines ashore and afloat. The main element of the proposal was that the Divisional bands, renamed as Staff bands, should cease forthwith to recruit direct from civilian life, and all entry should be through the Royal Marines School of Music based at Deal. The matter was discussed in the House of Commons in March 1950, just a month after the closure of the School at Burford. The Chatham Band was disbanded that August and the official Amalgamation Day was on 1st September 1950.

One condition imposed upon the Divisional bands which Vivian initially opposed was the relinquishment of the truly valuable music libraries to a central music library at the new Royal Marines School of Music at Deal. However he could clearly see the way ahead and his next probable appointment. He therefore recommended that this might be done but only if the RNSM bands were provided with silvered instruments. This went through unopposed.

* * * * *

Although Vivian continued to compose marches, in 1949 there came a hit and a miss. *The Captain General* was inspired when King George VI, the Captain General of the Royal Marines, dined with the officers of the Corps at the Savoy in London on 19th December. A special concert arrangement of the march was performed on this historic occasion. On the other hand another quick march, *Cannatex* which was prompted by the Portsmouth Group Band's visit to the Canadian National Exhibition in Toronto in August 1949 was seldom heard again. Although this was a fine march its specific title precluded it from being played more widely, especially in the UK.

Vivian continued to transcribe modern compositions for the military band and *There's No Business Like Show Business* was heard regularly. He also wrote *The Tudor Maiden*, a Troop incorporating tunes from the Tudor era, *Greensleeves* and *The Gentle Maiden*. This was first performed publicly at the Beat Retreat ceremony on 23rd June 1950.

Two other contrasting events of 1949 were the first performance of Vivian's quick march *Pompey Chimes* before a soccer match at Fratton Park and an appearance at the Royal Command Performance. The première of his new march did not have a great reception; this might have been a captive audience for a football match but it was not in the mood for a new composition. However it proved a fascinating outing for Leonie and Paddy who accompanied their father to Fratton Park where they met and spoke with the Pompey team. Vivian mentioned to the goalkeeper, Ernie Butler, that his son played in goal. A few days later, Ernie arrived on the doorstep to present Paddy with one of his boots. It smelt horrible but hung in the young admirer's bedroom for a long time! The march was only played a few times, and slowly dropped out of the repertoire. Vivian was still in the infancy of his march compositions and had not really developed his own style. He found more satisfaction in making arrangements, many of which are still being played 50 years later.

The Royal Command performance on 7th November at the London Coliseum, which included most of the well-known variety stars of the day, saw a new side of Vivian. His views did not entirely agree with those of the producer of the show, the experienced Alec Shanks, but Vivian with the memories of those wartime spectaculars in his mind, handled him very coolly at a difficult stage of the first rehearsal. On the day before the show they had started rehearsing at ten in the morning and ended at about two the following morning. Vivian showed a very firm professional hand when he insisted that his band kept to their scheduled rehearsal time despite pressure from Shanks and some of the 'stars'. He later wrote:

> 'Before the distinguished audience the performance unfolds itself slickly and efficiently, and to those who witness it the show appears the last word in ease and finesse, the result of intense rehearsals and the genius of the producer, allied to the amazing intricacies and mechanical perfection of the modern stage. Only the performers

> and those backstage can contrast the visual result of split second timing, superb artistry, and perfect co-ordination with the apparent chaos and confusion of rehearsal. For such a performance to be staged two days of rehearsals were required. The second full day's rehearsal was only completed an hour and a half before the rise of the curtain.'

The band, in Full Dress order, provided the culminating point of the first half which was devised as a patriotic scene entitled *'Salute to the Amethyst'*. It will be remembered that HMS *Amethyst* had run the gauntlet of the Chinese shore batteries in escaping down the River Yangtse earlier in the year. After the march of the Sea Cadet Corps, Lieutenant Frederick Harvey RNVR sang the newly written tribute song while, as if by magic but achieved by skilful lighting, an almost full size model of the ship, constructed by the stage carpenters, seemed to sail straight down and into the audience. It was a moment that those present will never forget.

It is abundantly clear that Vivian Dunn had not only looked carefully at the future of music within the Royal Marines, but had established his own future. He had been promoted to Major in 1946 and now became the longest serving Director of Music in the Corps. He foresaw his future clearly as a supremo of the whole Band Service, and from that moment on, he directed all his thoughts and efforts towards it.

The appointment of Sir Malcolm Sargent as the Honorary Adviser in Music to the Royal Marines in the summer of 1949 was partly prompted by Vivian's friendship with Earl Mountbatten. How this came about is uncertain because Mountbatten was commanding the First Cruiser Squadron in the Mediterranean Fleet at the time. It is known that a parliamentary secretary, Mr Dugdale, had attended a naval function at which there was the usual 15-strong RNSM Band, and subsequently wrote to the Second Sea Lord saying that if this was the best the Royal Marines could do, he would appoint his friend Sir Malcolm Sargent to teach them, which he promptly did. There is no doubt the matter was discussed in the House of Commons. In his biography of Sir Malcolm Sargent, Charles Reid writes:

> 'Some Honourable Member having, out of the blue, asked in the House of Commons who was responsible for 'official music' in the Royal Navy and Royal Marines, the Parliamentary Secretary to the Admiralty replied that Sargent had been appointed the Royal

> Marines' Honorary Adviser in music. Another honourable (and gallant) member who happened to be a Vice-Admiral asked waggishly what 'official music' might be, a question which, the House having a sense of humour all its own, raised laughs. He was told the point at issue had no reference to the *kind* of music but the occasions on which it is played. This seemed to satisfy everybody. As has already been mentioned, the honorary advisership, which took effect in the summer of 1949, was specifically devised, on Lord Mountbatten's prompting, for Sargent and ended with Sargent's death.'

However, while the wheels were still being put in motion to implement so many radical proposals, Vivian Dunn remained at Portsmouth with his beloved band. One particularly proud moment was when he organised a concert in the Royal Naval Barracks in aid of the Queen of the Hellenes Fund for Greek Refugee Children on 29th March 1950. For a complete month beforehand he had gathered together 85 of the Royal Marines finest musicians, both from the Group Band of Portsmouth and from RN School of Music bands based in the area. These were from the Royal Naval Barracks, Portsmouth, HMS *Excellent* and HMS *St Vincent*. This was another indication of the amalgamation to come and gave rise to the comment by the *Blue Band* magazine, 'the smoothness of the co-operation between the Group Band and the School of Music bands was also a matter of congratulation.'

The concert, before an audience of 2,000 was in the Royal Naval Barracks gymnasium, which had been converted for the evening into a concert hall. Vivian had persuaded Sir Malcolm Sargent to come down to conduct the combined orchestras, accompanied by the Portsmouth Bach Society and the Emsworth & District Choral Society. Whilst Vivian had rehearsed the orchestra arduously for a month, Sargent came down and rehearsed them for a day and a half. It was Sir Malcolm's first public appearance as conductor since his appointment as the Corps Honorary Adviser in Music the previous year. Presumably to give him a taste of salt, the Commander-in-Chief, Admiral of the Fleet Sir Algernon Willis invited Sargent to dine in Nelson's cabin aboard HMS *Victory* before the concert. The soloists were Elsie Morrison (soprano) from Sadler's Wells and the baritone Laurence Holmes, and the highlight was undoubtedly the playing of Vaughan Williams' *A Sea Symphony*.

Sir Malcolm Sargent, Honorary Adviser in Music to the Royal Marines, conducts the combined orchestras at a concert in the Royal Naval Barracks, Portsmouth on 29th March 1950

It was when such visiting celebrities came to play with the Royal Marines Band and orchestra in Portsmouth that Mike played the perfect hostess. She always provided a room for famous musicians and stars. Sir Malcolm stayed with them after his concert, while Evelyn 'Boo' Laye, who was Rosey's godmother, and her actor husband Frank Lawton were regular guests. 'Boo' sat at the grand piano and played for the family. Others who came to stay during those years included Eileen Joyce, the famous pianist, Leon Goossens, the great oboist and Frederick Harvey, the renowned baritone. There were many others.

Later that year, Vivian Dunn persuaded the distinguished tenor Heddle Nash to come to Portsmouth for a performance of *The Dream of Gerontius* by Elgar at the Royal Naval Barracks on 29th November. Sir Edward had autographed Nash's score with the words 'You are Gerontius'. Once again Vivian Dunn, a Vice President of the Emsworth & District Choral Society since 1947, conducted the choir. This association was to continue for a number of years. For instance in 1951 Vivian conducted the Emsworth choir, along with the Bach Society, at a Festival of Britain concert. Later that year *The Dream of Gerontius* was sung again and in 1952 there was a further concert at which the soloist in Mozart's ***Piano Concerto in A*** was Annekate Friedlander. A report in the *Portsmouth 'News'* commented:

> '... in the concerto Major Dunn cut down the strings to the barest minimum of 11 players with admirable result as far as neatness was concerned, but the wind *(sic)* was overloud, both for piano and strings – and usually uncomfortably sharp in pitch, a failing we will charitably blame on the hot weather ...'

Vivian's reaction to this was, alas, not recorded. It is assumed that this was his final concert with the Emsworth & District Choral Society because of his move to Deal. The 1953 concert programme shows the conductor as Captain K A McLean.

It said much for Vivian's musicianship and what he had achieved with his orchestra that so many distinguished soloists and singers accepted his invitations. One renowned singer, William Herbert, when asked his opinion of the standard of the Royal Marines orchestra, said he had found it on a par with the Southern Philharmonic Orchestra, the precursor of the Bournemouth Symphony Orchestra.

Captain John Haynes recalls the occasion of an officers' mess ball at Eastney. When the band went for a break, Vivian picked up the fiddle, and John joined him on the bass, at which he was reasonably competent. He says the occasion was somewhat marred by a pianist who played 'unusual chords' – but the dancers didn't seem to notice.

Life was so busy that he regrettably had little time for his family. This was not by choice as he would dearly have loved to spend more time with them. Leonie writes:

> 'In 1950, Paddy and I were packed off to our respective boarding schools. Paddy (aged 8) having been ushered into the front door of the school by my parents, promptly walked down the drive and out of the school grounds the minute he saw them drive away, and had to be brought back again! I was somewhat more phlegmatic about mine, and in any event, being set on the Isle of Wight, there was no escape! My mother recounts that she cried all the way home from seeing us off to school, but we never knew this till many years later. Each week of our school lives (and later Rosey's) she never failed to write us a cheerful, many times funny, letter at the weekend. She also attended every Sports Day, School Play, Founders Day and exeat

> without fail. She firmly believed that her role was the home and family and no matter that our father might be away on Royal tours or with the band in some exotic (or not!) location, she was always there for us and never let us down once. When recalling past events of our youth, my father would say "I don't remember that", and we would counter with "Ah, but you were never there!"; it became the family saying.'

There were many happy family moments during the early fifties. The children, all growing up fast, were often taken to the band room during leave periods by their father and allowed to play to their hearts' content. They remember the joys of whacking the cymbals, timpani, side drums and tubular bells. Vivian smiled upon their efforts as any doting father would, ensuring that everything was shipshape by the time the band returned from leave. The children's Christmas parties were a source of great delight, when a polished linoleum slide was made down the main staircase of the officers' mess.

Church parades were a great feature of Eastney Sundays and Vivian liked to conduct the orchestra in the church where he had been married. Leonie, as the eldest, usually accompanied her father and was seated at the far end of the front row of pews in front of the clarinettists, where he could keep an eye on her. She recalls fond memories of Corporal 'Chippy' Leale leaning over and helping her find her place in the hymn book and then hurriedly handing it back before picking up his instrument and continue playing. If her father ever noticed, he never said anything. Corporal Fred Gilbert, who was Vivian's secretary, made a beautiful toy theatre for Leonie, complete with working lights, hand painted scenery and velvet safety curtain. She treasured it dearly.

As if to consolidate the way ahead, the first Massed Bands Beating Retreat on Horse Guards Parade in London took place in June 1950. This was to be in the presence of Queen Mary and it was the first time that all three Group bands had joined together with those of the Royal Naval School of Music. It did not celebrate any special occasion as it did in subsequent years and Vivian was never able to recall how or why it actually came about.

The bands gathered at Eastney on 11th June. Apart from the three Group bands, there were the Staff Band from Deal and the RNSM bands from

Beating Retreat 1950. The Massed Bands march on and execute the first counter-march.

Lympstone, the Royal Naval Barracks, Chatham, Portsmouth and Plymouth, HMS *Daedalus, Excellent, Gamecock, Ganges* and *Raleigh*. After two days sorting out the bands, totalling some 260 musicians, they started eight days of rehearsals. Whilst Vivian was responsible for the musical side, Lieutenant Bill Lang looked after the parade work. A public dress rehearsal was carried out at 6.30pm on 21st June, in cold wintry weather and before an audience of several thousands, and the following day they all moved to London.

Vivian ordered the dress rehearsal for 7.30am on the 23rd, but it was washed out after a few minutes. By evening the weather had set fair and there was a large and appreciative audience. One aspect of this parade was that all 32 Silver Bugles had been on parade together. There was a repeat performance on the Saturday, marred by even more rain. As soon as the Beat Retreat was over, the bands embussed for the White City where 55,000 people were attending the Greyhound Derby. The band performed a modified ceremony which, as the *Blue Band* put it:

> 'This performance was rendered more spectacular by the floodlights picking out the blue and white of the uniforms against the glistening wet grass, and sparkling of the brass and silver.'

This was the first of many such similar performances on Horse Guards Parade, nowadays to celebrate the birthday of the Captain General, which have become an integral part of the London spectacular scene every three or four years.

During the summer of 1951, the Portsmouth Band performed regular concerts at the Festival of Britain in London. This exhibition had set in motion the whole redevelopment of the south bank of the Thames. Whilst they were there the band became the first military band to perform at the new Royal Festival Hall. All these prestige engagements helped to keep the Royal Marines name in the minds of the British public, and the name of Dunn was always to the fore.

One London occasion that year was recalled by Captain John Stewart, at the time Adjutant of the Royal Marines Barracks at Eastney. This appointment also carried the responsibility of commanding Band & Drums Company, and as such he often accompanied the band on their engagements. One of the pleasurable jobs was playing before and during the interval of the Army v Navy rugby match at Twickenham. John was walking around the ground in the morning in plain clothes accompanying a retired Brigadier, deciding what moves the band would make. On his way off the pitch, somewhat ahead of Vivian, the Brigadier turned to Stewart and said 'Smart young fellah, your Director of Music'. It made him wonder what he thought their respective ages were, as Vivian was about 15 years the elder! Whatever Vivian did, he was always immaculately dressed, whether it be on parade, playing cricket, on the golf course, or just 'relaxing'. This dress sense, and its importance in presenting the right image, was something that he instilled in all ranks of the band, and had a considerable impact later on at Deal.

In 1951 he composed *Enthronement Fanfare* written for the enthronement of the Bishop of Winchester. After this, his composing and arranging came to a temporary halt for a couple of years, probably due to the pressure of work in preparing himself for the new challenge ahead. Writing new marches, as we have seen, was hard work to him. He aimed at perfection and was not satisfied until he felt he had achieved this. It therefore took up more of his time than for other more gifted composers, and he had not that much spare time during the early fifties.

Early in 1952, Vivian Dunn embarked with the Royal Yacht Band in the liner SS *Gothic*, as the new Royal Yacht had not yet been built, for a tour by Princess Elizabeth and Prince Philip to Australia and New Zealand. This tour was cancelled on the death of the sovereign and the band returned to England. It took place, in an extended form, after the Queen's coronation in 1953.

Whilst he had been in Portsmouth he had conducted a large number of civilian orchestras and choirs. He also encouraged his own Royal Marines musicians to join such orchestras as the City of Portsmouth Symphony Orchestra to gain more experience. Several played in the concert he conducted on 11th January 1953 at the Theatre Royal, Portsmouth, including Ken Weston, John Long, Roy Morgan, Jack Miles, Robert Horsley, Edward Leale, Alfred Joliffe and Sidney Buick. There were probably others.

Vivian always had the most devoted of MOAs who were responsible for keeping him, not only impeccably dressed, but also for maintaining his good humour. Gordon Hastie, who looked after Vivian at Eastney post-war was one of the best, as the author found out when Hastie later became his MOA at sea in the mid 1950s. Woe betide any MOA who let Vivian leave his cabin in a foul mood resulting from some sartorial mistake, as he would immediately take it out on the band. They, in turn, would make sure the MOA's life was uncomfortable for a while. Paddy found Hastie useful in another respect as he spent a lot of time in the garden teaching him the rudiments of goal keeping!

The announcement of his appointment to be the first ever Principal Director of Music Royal Marines with new and added responsibilities was made sweeter by his appointment as a Fellow of the Royal Academy of Music on 26th March 1953. This honour had only been given to one Royal Marines Director of Music before, to Lieutenant B W O'Donnell on his retirement to found the BBC Wireless Military Band in 1927. This Fellowship meant a great deal to Vivian as only a small number are granted each year. He had worked hard at his music, promoted the Royal Marines Band Service, not only in Portsmouth, but to the British public and the world at large and had served the Royal Family for 20 years.

On leaving Portsmouth, Musician R Halbert penned the following:

Farewell to 'Sir'
(*Tune:* Willikins and his Dinah)

There once was a Major who at Portsmouth did dwell
He conducted a band and marched with it as well
The parade round the barracks by the band it was led
While the Major was sleeping at home in his bed

While 'Sir' has been with us we've toured all the world
Wherever the flag of old England was unfurled
And on all of these trips we developed strange habits
One man brought home corned beef
and the others brought rabbits.

Our annual outings have been of the best
At the horse show and in Scotland we've played with much zest
And whacking great muscles we've been able to gain
By lifting the heavy gear in and out of the train.

A trip to South Africa, a very fine cruise
What better accommodation than the *Vanguard* could you choose
We were seasick then airsick when we went on a flight
And of *Vanguard* before we finished we were sick of the sight.

At Jo'burg they wanted us to march round one day
But we'd only brought fiddles, so we'd nothing to play
So 'Sir' said a prayer and then lifted his eyes
And the instruments we wanted rained down from the skies.

On a band trip to Paris we had a good lark
A visiting the night spots as soon as it was dark
And oh what a gay time in the cool of the breeze
Cherchezing la femme down the 'Champs Élysées'.

To Toronto we went for to play at the 'Ex'
And 'Sir' wrote a march which he called *Cannatex*
We played every day on a stand called a shell
And we marched in the Warriors' Day procession as well.

From there on to Quantico down south in the States
Where they threw us a party that went on very late
We ate and we drank until we could hold no more
And we rounded off our trip with a sight-seeing tour.

And now 'Sir' is leaving to go off to Deal
I'm sure at this parting regret we'll all feel
But although we have come to the parting of the way
At Massed Bands rehearsals we shall meet up one day.

Vivian left his wife Mike to reply as follows:

In replying to you we would just like to say
Our departure for Deal is a very sad day
We know we are leaving a jolly good crew
And hope that the 'Pure Drop' will keep the same brew.

Your touring the world is not right with us wives
At times we've been frightened right out of our lives
If you're seasick or airsick or make other blots
We still take a dim view of the Paris night spots.

As far as the visit to old U.S.A.
We've certain good pictures to show us that they
Could give parties that lasted until all was blue,
And how you kept upright – the Lord only knew!

But wives do not grumble as all of you know
We'll smile and we'll wave as we see you all go
We think of the nylons that will be coming through
At the Customs House jetty – it's all due to you.

And now we must bid you farewell for a while
We're afraid that we haven't quite got Halbert's style
But we hope that you'll take this all in good fun
'Au Revoir' from the Major and Mrs F.V. Dunn.

CHAPTER 5

The Main Theme - First Principal Director of Music

THE MOVE TO DEAL IN 1953 raised several important matters in Vivian Dunn's life and he wrote at length on the subject. He was obviously deeply sorry that he should be forced to sever his 21 years of fruitful active professional association with Portsmouth; whilst on the other hand he was setting off into unknown and uncharted territory in his pursuit of musical perfection in the Royal Marines. His maxim was quite clear – 'Every one of my men is a Royal Marine first and a Musician second'.

He wrote that the Portsmouth Band had, for many generations, a great tradition for maintaining a first class efficiency. Since he took over in 1931 he had carefully recruited and selected musicians of a very high quality and his band had an enviable reputation throughout the world as a musical unit. His concept that none of the other Royal Marines group or staff bands could match the quality of Portsmouth was seen by some to be narrow-minded, a misguided and selfish appreciation which left a sour taste in Plymouth and Deal. There was also a certain amount of resentment amongst some of the older musicians who had, at his behest, transferred from the old RNSM into his Divisional band and given up their rank for the privilege. Now only a few years later such transfers were the norm, without giving up rank. After all his own future seemed secure as he claimed that, when he was recruited to serve (only) as the Director of Music of the Portsmouth Band, he was given a guaranteed career to 60 years of age.

His affirmation that it was his careful and skilful management and direction of the band that had achieved all this rung true, but it could possibly have been phrased more diplomatically in view of his forthcoming appointment as the supremo.

However there were other considerations in his mind. Besides providing his Portsmouth Band to enhance his own reputation, he would be severing his very strong links with the City of Portsmouth, where he had conducted the Portsmouth Bach Society and the Portsmouth Symphony Orchestra, a full professional body of instrumentalists engaged by the City Council to provide regular symphony concerts. He claimed that he was the only Director of Music in the Service who took the trouble to pursue such strong associations with civilian musical activities. In turn this widened the scope of his knowledge and thus kept him up to date and in constant touch with all matters musical. Whilst the Bach Society had closed down for the war years, it was Vivian who restarted it in 1946, and on 18th February 1953 he was invited to retain the position of conductor, an offer he gladly accepted. Undoubtedly these outside activities had brought about a close association and regard for the Royal Marines by both the civilian population and the civic authorities in Portsmouth. Inevitably the whole Corps was about to benefit enormously from Vivian's contacts with the outside musical scene when he arrived at Deal.

Then there was the question of his 'Royal' connections. His personal service to four sovereigns was unique in the annals of the Services. He had served in both the Royal Yachts *Victoria & Albert* and in the newly commissioned *Britannia*, as well as accompanying the Royal Tour to South Africa in HMS *Vanguard*. Indeed his promotion to Commander of the Royal Victorian Order in 1954 was unprecedented in military music history. He was very proud of his royal associations, which again augured well for the future of the Royal Marines.

There were also more personal matters. He would be giving up his fine house in Portsmouth, where he had carefully planned the schooling of his three children. Before his arrival at Deal he made it clear that he expected an official residence to be provided, as he maintained he had to live as close to his work as possible to 'facilitate close supervision at all times'. He cited the official quarter provided for his opposite number in the Army, the Director of Music of the Royal Military School of Music, who had such a residence. So started fifteen years occupation of G House in North Barracks, Deal. And of course, he was well aware that he would suffer a considerable curtailment in his financial expectations which he had been privileged to enjoy from private engagements with the Portsmouth Band.

After the expansiveness and freedom of the large house and garden in Southsea, the move to Deal came as a shock to the family. The children found themselves effectively 'in barracks' and the only way out was through the little wicket gate for which there was only one key. Leonie lost the key on one occasion and all hell broke loose as it was, of course, a major lapse of security.

Vivian saw his appointment as the first Principal Director of Music, Royal Marines as a new and challenging concept for the expansion of the Band Service. This title, which he implies he suggested himself, was made after careful comparison of the Army's 'Senior Director of Music, The Brigade of Guards' and the 'Organising Director of Music, Royal Air Force'. Undoubtedly he hit on a title for the Senior Service which gave him added repute.

He also suggested that the appointment should carry the rank and pay of Lieutenant Colonel, Royal Marines. After all he was the acknowledged musical authority within the Royal Navy and Royal Marines. He pointed out that, at the age of 45 and with six and a half years seniority as a Major, over eight years as the Royal Marines senior Director of Music, his rank should fall in line with the other two services. He argued that he had the necessary qualifications and length of service for promotion, and that he felt the whole Band Service would not be slow to realise that, if he remained a Major, their new head presumably was not sufficiently highly regarded to merit special consideration. He sensed this was a most important psychological fact that would not be lost on his musicians. He felt that his new job should have the benefit of a good start. Perhaps he did not take into consideration at that time the differential in pay between similar ranks in the Army and the Royal Marines.

Vivian Dunn's appointment as Principal Director of Music took effect from 1st October 1953, although he had been at Deal since March. He was granted the rank of Local Lieutenant Colonel, which did not, of course, carry any extra pay, on 27th October that year. He and his family moved to Deal. The newly titled Royal Marines School of Music occupied East Barracks.

On his appointment as the Principal Director of Music, Vivian sent the following to all bands and musicians under his jurisdiction:

> On assuming the appointment of Principal Director of Music, Royal Marines, I wish to convey my good wishes and an exhortation to all ranks of the Royal Marines Band Service.
>
> Our traditions are great, therefore:
> Let our bands be splendid and our numbers strong,
> Let our music be harmonious and our tunes melodious,
> Let our rhythm be strict and our intonation true,
> Let our playing be artistic and our balance good,
> Let our practice be constant and our performance ideal,
> Let our drill be smart and our appearance neat,
> Let our ambition be high and our discipline perfect,
> Let our zeal be unbounded and our confidence great,
> Let our service be loyal and our duty devoted,
> Let our future be bright and our spirit undaunted,
> Let our bugles ring out and our drums resound,
> Let us always remember we are Royal Marines.
>
> F Vivian Dunn

The new Principal Director was quick to acknowledge the support he had received, firstly from Major General J E Leech-Porter, but also to his able assistant Major Ian Wray, who had helped to make the transition easy. He also felt that the support from the Commandant General, Sir Leslie Hollis, owed much to the contacts he made during the war working in high circles including the Cabinet Office. He was only too aware of the political scene when the Royal Marines had to make large post-war cuts to their strength.

His arrival at Deal was a great shock to those musicians who had only recently been uplifted by the amalgamation. Those who came from the old RNSM had had a particularly disturbing war and were only just beginning to recover from the effects of losing 225 comrades at sea. They had survived great hardships and suffered a lack of proper musical training for almost a decade. It was most noticeable amongst young Bandmasters and band officers who had not really had the time and opportunity to prepare themselves for leading their bands. They had recently come from the comparatively relaxed atmosphere of Burford to this new

OPPOSITE:
The Royal Marines School of Music, Deal

and dynamic Royal Marines School of Music at Deal. It was an enormous shock to them, particularly when their beloved lyre collar badge, RMB shoulder title and RMBS cap badge were taken away. And on top of all this Vivian arrived from Portsmouth to find himself faced with an enormous task.

All the band officers had passed through the same in-bred system so they found it difficult to accept the radical change readily. In most cases they were unable to see that there was a problem. They believed that the standard to which they had been trained was high enough to meet any foreseeable musical requirements. This apparent lack of musical ambition did nothing to close the cultural gap. The new Principal Director knew that they were wrong and felt their opinions were irrelevant to the long-term future of the Band Service.

Vivian did not understand this attitude and was unwilling to accept it at all for some time. Music was his driving ambition and bringing this ill-assorted group of musicians, whose morale was at rock bottom, up to his own high standards was his singular aim. He did not make friends easily amongst his band officers which is perhaps understandable. However he set about this challenge in his usual manner and soon gained the respect, if not the affection, of the younger musicians, NCOs and Bandmasters who joined the School after 1950. The new breed of Directors of Music gave him their undivided support. A satirical nickname given to him soon after his arrival was 'mustard' but this did not stick and, as we shall see, another more widely used sobriquet took its place.

One of Vivian's first concerns was the promotion system within the Band Service. Previously, aspiring Bandmasters had struggled valiantly, mostly at their own expense, to qualify; but now he put forward a plan for selected Bandmasters to study at the Royal Academy for a year. There they would attend the advanced conductor's course and it is arguably the most significant step he made to ensure the continuing quality of Royal Marines musicianship. It took 18 months to come to fruition.

He also raised the standard of professors at the RMSM for he realised that there was no substitute for producing excellent instrumentalists than having the highest quality teachers. He set up his own small headquarters with a general duties officer as his staff officer and a senior NCO musician as his secretary. A separate Director of Music for the Staff Band was appointed which meant that at long last the Corps had a Principal who could take an overall view of training, presentation and the way ahead. Vivian was just the man for this.

His arrival at Deal coincided with the celebrations to mark the 50th anniversary of the Royal Marines Band Service, which was founded as the Royal Naval School of Music at Eastney in 1903. Between 24-27th September 1953 concerts, both military band and orchestral, Church Parade and a Dinner marked the occasion. It gave Vivian his first opportunity to see his 'new' musicians at work and gauge their standard. It was also the first time he was able to conduct the Boys' orchestra and military band of 50 players whose average age was 16, many younger. He shared the conducting with Captain Tommy Lang and Lieutenant J E Talling. In addition, retired Musical Directors, Major Sam Fairfield, Major Arthur Pragnell and Captain Herbert Kenward, also took the rostrum at the concert on the 25th. All three concerts opened with a new fanfare which Vivian had written specially for the occasion and included themes from the Band Call and the Regimental March. He called the fanfare *The Royal Marines Band Service* and it was played on the Memorial Silver Trumpets.

* * * * *

Although he had left the Portsmouth Group Band he did not relinquish the Directorship of the Royal Yacht Band as was illustrated when the Royal Commonwealth Tour was announced. Much to the dismay of the newly appointed Director of Music at Portsmouth, Captain Ken McLean, Vivian 'took back' his old band to oversee the tour. Although the new Royal Yacht *Britannia* had already been commissioned she did not come into service until 24th January 1954 and the SS *Gothic* was used instead. The following extract from the fairly comprehensive diary kept during the shakedown cruise in October 1953 may have been a foretaste of things to come:

26th October

1130hrs. Band parade for leaving docks
1210hrs. *Gothic* leaves. Band plays marches.
1230hrs. Carry-on
1515hrs. Fire drill. Severe Gale warning
1530hrs. Boat Drill. Bottom's cap blows overboard
1900hrs. Report to D. of Music Weston and Fowler unable to reach band room for instruments. Spencer and Balaam

HM The Queen and HRH The Prince Philip with the Royal Yacht Band aboard SS Gothic, *1953*

	unwell. Gale severe. Dinner Band to carry on with reduced numbers.
1920hrs.	Dinner Band ready at Retinue Mess
1930hrs.	Piano party under Sgt Price, and Dinner Band, enter Anti-Room *(sic)*. Handford falls out, and Palmer turned in. Band plays march. I fall out and muster against the wind on Prom. Deck, and spoil best suit. Sgt Herbert carries on. C/Sgt Leale makes a dash for Retinue Mess door; door locked, musters going up stairs on carpet. Band sadly depleted, so we are told to pack up by D of Music, who also makes a sudden dash past them for the stairs. Sgt Balaam just makes cabin, then musters. Weather very bad. Most of band and Crew feeling unwell.
27th October	
A.M.	Band paraded and rehearsed arrival and departure of Her Majesty. Band inspected in Whites.

As with most Royal cruises, HM The Queen and Prince Philip did not embark in England but joined the SS *Gothic* in Jamaica, the Royal Yacht Band having already embarked on 10th November 1953 and encountered some pretty rough weather for the first week. Vivian noted that the first they

Vivian conducts the Royal Yacht Band on board SS Gothic, *1953. HMAS* Australia *escorting in the background.*

saw of the sun was on the 18th. Two days later the foremast was struck by lightning in yet another Atlantic storm. However, as was his wont, he rehearsed the band in all their various guises, orchestral, dance, church and colours. He reluctantly agreed to allow six band ranks and three drummers to be employed as messengers for the Main Signals Office, though this did have some advantages. The ship arrived, with its band fully prepared musically for any eventuality, on Sunday 22nd November. They then had five days of preparation before the Royal Party was due, and Vivian sent the Drum Major and Bandmaster ashore to the Royal Welch Fusilier's tailor to strengthen the belt hooks on which they carried their swords.

That afternoon, the 29th November, The Queen first saw the *Gothic* alongside Shell Jetty in Jamaica. Being a merchantman, the routine for receiving the Royal Party was rather different from the Royal Yacht. All arrangements had been made for embarkation on the afterdeck while the band would be positioned on the boat-deck above. The Admiral had gone ashore to escort the Queen back and Captain David Aitchison RN was in charge of arrangements aboard. Everything was going according to plan until he was suddenly alerted by the chief yeoman that the barge was approaching the ship, some ten minutes before it was due. Near panic on board as the various reception parties were quickly mustered and the officers and ratings fell in at their respective stations. But no one had thought to warn the band.

A messenger was sent to fetch them as the barge circled the ship. The Queen came up the gangway and was piped aboard. The whole embarkation was being televised with Godfrey Talbot giving the commentary. As The Queen reached the top of the ladder, she paused for a moment as though she was expecting something – the National Anthem? The Admiral and Captain stood waiting expectantly, wondering whether the band had arrived on the boat deck above and after what seemed an interminable pause the roll of the drums preceded the anthem. The messenger had reached the band whilst they were still in their messes several decks below. Rumour had it afterwards that the band had played the National Anthem on the run! However Vivian described it in his diary 'HM was 15 minutes early, causing no little panic, but the band was there on the downbeat.' The aftermath was that The Queen was told the story of the band later, but indicated that she had already given orders that the Anthem need not be played on such occasions in future.

Once again Vivian worked his band extremely hard, particularly when the Royal Party was away from the ship, but at least there was more room for rehearsing than there had been in *Vanguard*. Some of the band resented these long trips away from home but it gave them the opportunity to see parts of the world to which they would probably never visit in any other capacity. Jamaica, Panama, Fiji, Tonga, New Zealand, Australia and Ceylon were all on the itinerary. One day he referred to himself, casually it seems, as 'Master of The Queen's Musick – Afloat'. He enjoyed the joke at W S Gilbert's expense.

One of many incidents on board the *Gothic* is worthy of mention. One Sunday The Queen and Duke attended morning service on deck as the weather was fine. Vivian had a small group of musicians to play the introductions and hymns. First he managed to cut the *Venite* in half coming in with 'Glory be to the Father' quite unexpectedly. This was not a complete disaster as the singing had been rather desultory. Captain Aitchison

Crossing the Line aboard SS Gothic: *HM The Queen captures on camera the antics of Vivian Dunn, left, and HRH Prince Philip, right.*

who was taking the service, had announced that as was always his custom, the last verse of 'Eternal Father' would be sung kneeling. This was a change which had not been communicated to the Director of Music and, to the consternation of all, the band went straight into the final voluntary instead of the hymn. It appears that The Queen nudged Prince Philip and they both rose. Afterwards Vivian appeared at the Captain's cabin to apologise but the former made no admission of his supposed error. Indeed he inferred that the band had played 'Eternal Father' but the congregation had not recognised it! An explanation which the Captain swallowed.

The *Gothic* passed through the Panama Canal on the 29th, the day when the Bishop of Panama took morning service on board and that evening Vivian conducted a small orchestra of 14 at the British Legation when Her Majesty dined there. They crossed the line on 4th December and the musical priorities became the practising of the Tongan, Australian and New Zealand anthems. Apart from playing for Royal occasions on board, with the dance band at dinner most nights, he also ensured that the ship's company had the opportunity to enjoy the band's music by playing for them regularly, usually in the well-deck. In order to raise the standard of his SNCOs, Vivian gave them the opportunity to conduct the dinner and lunch programmes whilst at sea.

It was not all work on the tour, even at sea, and Vivian recalls a deck hockey match during the dog watches between the Royal Household and the ship's officers, for whom he played in goal. On one occasion Prince

Philip bore down on the goalkeeper at full tilt, as the latter advanced, only to receive a swipe on the knuckles. 'Sorry', said the Prince, and they carried on leaving Vivian bleeding profusely. The doctor patched him and for the next evening's encounter, Vivian donned a pair of batting gloves. When HRH caught sight of them he said 'That's a bit pansy, isn't it?' to which his reply was 'Better to be sure than sorry, sir,' bringing the rejoinder 'Well yes, you're probably right'. No further harm was done.

After visiting Tonga, for which Vivian had made some arrangements of Maori music including the Fijian song *Isa Lei*, the ship arrived in Auckland on 23rd December. The following day, he arranged for the band to do a recording for New Zealand radio. After Christmas in Auckland, New Year's Eve was spent at sea, arriving in Wellington at 8am the following morning. As with all Royal visits to overseas cities, the band was involved in many different activities, from general entertainments to street lining, from Ambassadorial receptions to dances. It was in Wellington that Vivian was blamed for bringing unseasonable bad weather! An outdoor concert at the Botanical Gardens had to be cancelled because of the inclement weather as was Beat Retreat at the Basin Reserve, the nearest Vivian ever got to playing on a Test Match cricket ground. Whilst life aboard was nearly all hard work, the band were allowed ten days leave in New Zealand which they enjoyed enormously.

The *Gothic* reached Sydney on 3rd February and when the band visited the Parramatta Returned Servicemen's League Club, Vivian took a mere count of eight to down the ice-cold beer from the ceremonial pint mug! In between official engagements the band were able to see a great deal of the Australian countryside and, during a visit to the outback township of Maitland, Vivian was presented with a cheque after lunching at the local hospital and immediately donated the money to the children's ward. He particularly enjoyed lunching with the Mayor at Bowral, the home town of his great hero Don (later Sir Donald) Bradman. He was able to walk across the hallowed turf on which the great Australian batsman had been brought up.

Vivian subsequently wrote of this part of the tour:

> '*Gothic* has steamed 18,000 miles since leaving England, and to say that the voyage has been a wonderful experience would be almost an inadequate description of such a great undertaking . . . In each country the arrival scenes have been truly splendid. Every place has

SS Gothic *arrives at Hobart, Tasmania*

been different in the individuality of its welcome, but all have been the same in their warmth, sincerity, loyalty and affection for their Queen and her Consort ...

From the Royal Yacht Band point of view it has involved a long sequence of performances of almost every possible kind, from forty-five programmes for luncheon and dinner in the Royal Apartments when at sea, to the Royal garden parties, investitures, and receptions at the various Government Houses. A very full programme of full-scale concerts, studio broadcasts, Beating Retreat, ceremonial band displays has been undertaken. In Sydney alone nine concerts and four broadcasts were given in 16 days, besides journeying many hundreds of miles and participating in a great deal of ceremonial.'

And so the tour continued with visits to Hobart, Melbourne, Adelaide and Fremantle. In Melbourne Vivian met his old friend General Sir Dallas Brooks, a former Commandant General Royal Marines, who was the Governor of Victoria, and then stayed with Colonel and Mrs Spraggett. The Royal Yacht Band joined up with the Band of the Royal Australian Air Force for a concert one day. They recorded programmes in a number of studios and generally made their presence felt everywhere they went. It was after further visits to Ceylon and Aden that the band became anything like operational. Unrest in the Middle East meant that the band was organised into three watches as a precaution as they sailed through the Suez Canal. Although it was not a man-of-war, *Gothic* took every precaution possible to avoid any incident and the band took their active role seriously.

When they reached Malta on 4th May, the whole of the Royal and Naval contingent transferred to the brand new Royal Yacht *Britannia* that same afternoon. They were soon aware of the rather cramped conditions in which they were forced to rehearse, compared with the luxurious spaciousness of the *Gothic*. After calling in at Gibraltar, the Royal Yacht steamed homeward for its first Royal welcome. The whole of the Home Fleet manned ship as the *Britannia* sailed through their ranks. As a special request from the Queen, Prince Charles, then aged 5, was allowed to 'conduct' the band, the young Prince and his sister Princess Anne having joined their parents in Malta. Their arrival in Portsmouth was one of those momentous occasions. Then, on Saturday 15th May, the Royal Yacht *Britannia* sailed up the Thames to Westminster Pier, having embarked Sir Winston Churchill the night before.

Vivian described the scene:

> 'Of all the welcomes, perhaps this last was the greatest, because from the lower reaches of the Thames right up to the Tower of London thousands upon thousands of British people lined the banks for mile after mile to show, as only perhaps they can, their gladness at the return of their beloved Queen to the capital and the appreciation of a task the magnitude of which it is difficult to describe adequately.'

He also noted that the band had a short weekend leave before their duties started again! It was in 1953 that we saw the first Royal Marines Band Service '45' record (EP). Columbia released Vivian's 1940 recording with the Portsmouth Divisional Orchestra of *A Life on the Ocean Wave* and *Heart*

HM Yacht Britannia *moors in the Port of London, 15 May 1954. Painting by Norman Wilkinson. (reproduced by courtesy of Akzo.Nobel UK Ltd)*

of Oak. This became the subject of prolonged correspondence between Boosey & Hawkes and the RM Band Service as we shall see later.

For his outstanding services to the monarchy, Vivian was promoted in the Royal Victorian Order to Commander (CVO) by Her Majesty The Queen. Thus Dunn had served in both Royal Yachts, carried out overseas Royal tours in both the *Vanguard* and the *Gothic*, and attended four sovereigns, an unprecedented achievement by any Director of Music. His Bandmaster on the tour, R H Horsley was awarded the Royal Victoria Medal (Silver). The other honour bestowed by HM The Queen on the Portsmouth Group Band as a result of the *Gothic* tour was that henceforth they will wear the Royal Cyphers of Her Majesty and His Royal Highness the Duke of Edinburgh, surmounted by St Edward's Crown above the cap badge, and on the helmet the Royal Cypher only above the Globe and below the crown, the device in each case being of silver.

* * * * *

Back in Deal, policy matters were soon uppermost in Vivian's mind. He had inherited a system of musical training that bore its roots in the old Royal Naval School of Music. Here Band Boys had been recruited at the age of 14, new entries proving their musical prowess by merely tapping out a rhythm or singing a series of notes. As long as they passed a simple intelligence assessment and interview and were medically fit, they could be accepted for full academic and military training. They were allotted instruments on the basis of physique and mouth and lip formation.

In 1954 there were over 300 boys mostly being trained by uniformed NCO instructors, many of whom had themselves been badly taught in the past and had limited techniques which they were in danger of passing on. This was in stark contrast to the training in the Divisional bands where trained musicians had been recruited directly from civilian life. Vivian Dunn had personally supervised many of these during his years at Portsmouth and ensured that proper musical training had been given to all. This was something rather different, and strong measures were needed to raise the standards.

The first signs of improvement had been in 1950 when four civilian professors were employed as instrumental tutors by the School of Music on its move to Deal. The early ones were mostly string players. Vivian soon saw the benefit of the system and persuaded the Admiralty that, to ensure improvement in the Royal Marines Band Service more musical instruction would be needed. At its peak fourteen such professors were employed, assisted by a number of NCO instructors; an added benefit was that these latter undoubtedly improved their own individual playing and teaching techniques as a result.

Vivian carefully avoided conducting the Boys' Band and orchestra as he believed he should not interfere with their own Director of Music. He was quite clear that his job was to ensure the highest standards in his own Staff Band. But old habits, long engendered in the uniformed instructors and the band officers who had been through the system, were not easily altered. His stand-offish attitude towards his subordinates did little to bridge the gap between two alien cultures. They thought of him as selfish and motivated only for himself.

One example of this came when he found certain weaknesses in his Deal Band and demanded from his successor in Portsmouth that he should draft some of his players from Eastney, including the leader of the orchestra, Corporal Weston, to Deal. Naturally Captain McLean strongly opposed the idea and quite rightly won the day. But it did little to promote happy relations with the newly amalgamated Band Service.

For several years there was a deep suspicion of the new Principal Director of Music. It stemmed from the fact that all his band officers had risen through the ranks and many considered that, as he had not done so, he did not understand the grass root workings. On his side, Vivian found it hard to relate to the old RNSM musicians. Somehow he never seemed to understand the mind and attitude of the old seagoing Band Service ranks who in the course of two and a half year commissions had had little chance to improve their playing and training. This was not what he had been accustomed to with his Divisional Band.

His imposing presence at all times, not just on parade, left many of the old Band Service in awe. Captain Terry Freestone remembers arriving at Deal from two years at sea and seeing the new PDM for the first time, 'scrambled eggs' on his hat, a Sam Browne belt that positively glistened and an individually styled cane in place of the usual brown leather swagger stick. The aloofness and rigidity were palpable. At rehearsal everything was so formal and rigid, with collars having to be done up at all times, and the concentration demanded was unmitigating. He recalls that string players were ordered to remove rings from their left hand as it was 'unprofessional', although this did not necessarily appear to be so when they met up with their professional counterparts in London. Vivian also insisted that all band officers should wear extra long white gloves so that their wrists were not exposed whilst conducting on parade.

Captain Tom Lambert recalls

> 'When I was commissioned he insisted that all band officers should go to Jones, Chalk & Dawson to have their suits "built", and that new caps must come from Herbert Johnson and our boots made by Herbert Lobb. Had we complied with these instructions we would still have been in "hock" and needless to say we ignored them. He didn't like it, but conceded in the end. Later I did in fact have all the right gear, and I must say it made a huge difference to how one felt.'

Terry Freestone recalls an occasion, many years after they had both retired, talking to Vivian when the latter admitted that he regretted that he had not made more effort to get to know, in a friendly and comradely way, the officers of the Band Service while he was serving.

Another problem lay in having so many elderly instruments in issue. Brass instruments had to be replaced by silver-plated wide bore instruments. New clarinets and bassoons were acquired along with a Bechstein Concert Grand for the concert hall. There is no doubt that he used his influence with Lord Mountbatten, who became First Sea Lord in 1955, to precipitate these matters. The transition might not have been quite so easy, or as quick, without such intervention.

One of the factors which influenced the introduction of newer and better instruments was the type of music that the bands were beginning to play. More young Bandmasters became budding arrangers for the concert band, something which Vivian encouraged to the full. This entailed a new concept of exciting symphonic arrangements and these in turn required better instruments, as well as more accomplished playing. By 1960 all the old piston valved French horns had been replaced by rotary valved double horns; and the trombone section took aboard newly fashioned B flat and the more resonant bass, giving them greater flexibility. Cornet players moved to the American inspired long pattern cornet. Vivian established a rapport with instrument makers Boosey & Hawkes which ensured that Royal Marines musicians were equipped with the finest instruments of their trade.

Being a professional violinist Vivian saw to it that new and more expensive string instruments were introduced producing a sweeter and more mellow sound. In his search for a better end result Vivian was more than receptive to those around him. He was told that some instructors were teaching the young boys bad habits. He immediately summoned those responsible for musical training and told them they were to eradicate such bad teaching by giving the instructors extra musical training and lessons in instructional technique. He did this in a remote and imperious way which caused much tooth sucking and resentment. The NCO instructors felt that their professional abilities were being challenged. Whilst his motives were undoubtedly for the benefit of all, his method lacked the sympathetic approach which would undoubtedly have achieved more harmonious results. No-one doubted that he was right but his way of accomplishing it often came into question.

One way of achieving this was his insistence that instructors should play in the regular orchestral concerts. He had established fortnightly winter concerts which were designed to fulfil three purposes. Firstly to raise the standard of orchestral playing; secondly to afford Bandmasters and instrumentalists under training the opportunity to perform and develop the art of conducting in public; and thirdly to foster good relations between the Corps and the townspeople of Deal and Walmer thus establishing the Royal Marines School of Music as a centre of music to which the public may have access. He invited well-known guest conductors and artistes. This was the continuation of what he had started in Portsmouth and which had achieved such wide acclaim from the general public there.

These were held in the concert hall at Deal, mostly in the winter and spring, and on the South Green in the summer, not only to widen and improve the playing and repertoire of the musicians but also to give the outside world an insight into the gradually improving standard. Once again this move was not entirely popular with the band officers and instructors as it interrupted their own tuition and classes. However Vivian was adamant that these concerts would not only show the instructors the high standard he expected of those who were under training, but it enabled the better musicians to play concertos, or movements from them, in front of an audience.

He was always open to advice when it came to the question of brass instruments. One example came to light following a discussion in the *Lord Clyde*, a pub in Walmer run by Billy Monckton, who had been a French horn player in the RN Band Service before World War I. He regularly listened to the BBC programme *Friday Night is Music Night*, in which the BBC Concert Orchestra was often joined by the RMSM Band. He pointed out that the light horn sound, coupled with some bad intonation, compared unfavourably with the BBC professionals. For instance more tone would be apparent if they used wide bore double horns in B flat and F. Intonation could be improved by the correct use of the right hand in the bell. Previously the young musicians had not been taught that the right hand could be used to vary pitch. When one of the General Duties housemasters at Deal, Robin Patteson-Knight, a horn player of some repute, lent his double horn to the first horn in the Staff Band to evaluate, 36 such instruments were ordered within the first year from Boosey & Hawkes.

In 1954 Colonel B J 'Bertie' Lumsden was appointed Commanding Officer of the Depot Royal Marines at Deal. Thus, the two old friends, who had joined the Corps at the same time in the early thirties were thrown together to work as a team. 'Bertie', of course, had introduced Vivian to Mike before the war. It was always going to be a love/hate relationship with two strong personalities vying for supremacy. They were though, such good friends that 'Bertie' was always able to tease Vivian over his pomposity.

Vivian was keen to encourage his very talented soloists of whom there were many in the Staff Band. In working on new arrangements and compositions he directed his thoughts towards these instrumentalists and in December 1954 he took a Roy Turk composition *Where the Blue of the Night* and made a special but particularly demanding arrangement for Band Sergeant 'Taff' Lewis who played it superbly.

At the International Horse Show at the White City in 1955, the RMSM Band from Deal was in attendance. It was the first year that the German National Anthem was allowed to be played at public functions. The German Show Jumping team had considerable success in the early rounds and their anthem was duly played, the band being situated in a bandstand in the arena. In the evenings, at the end of the final event, the band would form up as a marching band and parade in front of the Royal Box. After the final winning team of the day had received their rosettes and trophies the band would play their National Anthem and would then march off to *A Life on the Ocean Wave*. This went according to plan on the first two evenings, but on the Wednesday, with HM The Queen and The Duke of Edinburgh present, the format was changed and it was decided that, whichever national team won the final event, only *God Save The Queen* would be played. It so happened that the German team won the last event and Vivian briefed the band on the sequence of marches – a quick march in to the arena, our National Anthem and our Regimental march – no German anthem, so the band left the parts behind. As the band halted in front of the Royal Box, the Duke of Beaufort came across from the enclosure to tell Vivian that there had been a rethink and the German anthem was now to be played prior to The Queen presenting the Germans with their trophies. Vivian quickly stepped into the band, told them the change and reminded them of the tune, fortunately a well-known hymn. He took his position in front of the band, raised his baton and waited to see what would happen. The Duke of Beaufort ordered, 'Play the German Anthem'.

Vivian directed the drummers to play an introductory roll and looked decidedly pale as he brought in the band. There was a slight hesitancy, then the tune came through, albeit all melody and very little inner parts.

After the march off Vivian gathered the band around him to congratulate them on getting out of a tricky situation. The Drum Major (Charlie Bowden) was told to buy them all a drink – on him, a previously unheard of phenomenon. A reflection on this incident shows the remarkable way in which Vivian was able to avert an embarrassing disaster without any signs of panic and with great sang froid – a gift in itself.

It was at the International Horse Show at the White City in either 1955 or 1956, that another legend was born. During the afternoon performances the band was always conducted by the Bandmaster, while Vivian enjoyed the hospitality of HM The Queen's or the VIP's tent. The occasion was being covered by the BBC and during the afternoon one of their presenters approached the Bandmaster and asked if Lieutenant Colonel F Vivian Dunn would be conducting that evening. On being told 'yes' he asked 'and incidentally, what does the F stand for?' Most of the band overheard this conversation and, to a man, retorted 'Fred'. Charlie Bowden says he immediately went down to the BBC chap and put him right 'His name is Francis' – but 'Fred' stuck, certainly amongst the Band Service ranks for the rest of his life.

The White City provided another amusing sidelight in the late 1950s, this time at the Greyhound Derby, where the band had played many times before. On arrival Vivian discovered that his MOA had not packed his No 1 trousers! This caused great consternation amongst the SNCOs, particularly when Vivian threatened his MOA with 'immediate execution' as he was not going to appear in the wrong rig. The band had come up to London by East Kent coach, whose drivers, in those days, wore company uniform which included navy blue trousers with a narrow red stripe. Fortunately, in the floodlit White City stadium, no-one could tell that the Principal Director of Music was wearing the Drum Major's trousers and the Massed Bands were led by a 'hybrid Drum Major/East Kent coach driver'! History does not relate what the coach driver wore, nor what happened to the unfortunate MOA.

Vivian was keen to spread the virtues of the School's musical training far and wide, and it was in 1954 that two Petty Officers from the Canadian

Navy and one from the Burmese Navy were enrolled for a special course at Deal. This was the start of his remarkable foresight and the firm belief that his methods of military musical instruction were the best in the world.

Although there were some excellent musicians amongst the Boys he became very frustrated by the general lack of improvement in their standards. However, at the end of their training, he ensured that they played in the Staff Band at Deal to gain experience before being drafted to other bands. He still suffered from a lack of confidence in the old type band officers and asked 'outsiders' with musical knowledge, which included some of the housemasters, for their opinions on training methods and how best bad teaching habits might be eradicated. If he felt the advice given was in keeping with his own, he would act fast.

He quietly watched the progress of some of the Boy Musicians who showed outstanding talent. He had so much confidence in their ability, that he invited two of them, J R H Ballard and R J Gee to perform as soloists at one winter concert and both were received with due acclamation. His confirmed interest in choral music was implemented when a School of Music Concert Choir was formed, which added considerably to the scope and interest of the programmes. In the summer, the concerts took place on South Green.

His daughter Leonie became a member of the Royal Marines Concert Choir after she left school. She enjoyed this immensely but initial rehearsals were a nightmare because she didn't read music, and she felt she was always a 'dotted crotchet' behind the rest of the sopranos until she learnt the harmonics by ear. She remembers one concert being a disaster. They were to sing part of the *Polovtskian Dances* from *Prince Igor*, followed by a *Saraband*. The choir and orchestra had their music in the right order, but unfortunately her father had reversed his. He raised his baton to come crashing in with the strident opening of the *Saraband*, while the choir and musicians began sweet and gentle with *Prince Igor*. After two bars Vivian stopped them, turned to the audience and apologised for his mistake, then they all began again with one accord, thus proving that he was human after all! A classic example of Homer nodding.

He also managed to persuade the Royal Marines Office that there should be an increase in the number of Commissioned Bandmasters in the Corps, a step which was warmly received and, in due course, paid dividends for the future. In 1955 approval of his plan came through to send two specially selected Bandmasters to the Royal Academy of Music for a year's conductor's course. He had used his considerable connections with the London musical scene in arranging this, enlisting the co-operation of great musicians and friends such as Maurice Miles and Clarence Raybould. He realised, from his own early days, that these courses would give the candidates a unique opportunity of studying in the right environment, of increasing their musical knowledge and gaining wider experience of their profession. They would also be able to attend opera and chamber music classes to broaden their all round musical ability. Staff Bandmaster Don Guthrie and Bandmaster Doug Haigh were the first to go, followed by Bandmaster Peter Sumner and Band Sergeant Roy Nash the following year. Vivian took great care in the selection of those who should go but it did cause certain rumblings of 'favouritism' amongst those who were not selected. It seemed to them as though the Principal Director of Music was forestalling future promotion boards. Vivian scotched the idea, but there was certainly some ill feeling engendered amongst his SNCOs.

During this period he decided that he should break with the tradition of playing rather stately old-fashioned marches on parade and introduce more popular music with military band arrangements such as *The Saints Go Marching In* and *Thunderbirds.* Of course the Royal Marines Band had been featured in the closing sequences of the film. These were the work of one of his musicians Ray Woodfield who became a prolific arranger later.

On another occasion, the Royal Naval Benevolent Society put on a show at the Royal Festival Hall with the Band of the Royal Marines School of Music. Charlie Chester introduced the programme by looking at the immaculately clad conductor and saying to the audience 'Why does he have to wear spurs to conduct a band? I can't answer that, but it makes him look like Pat Smythe in tights!'

It was in 1960 that Vivian received yet another honour, this time from the Worshipful Company of Musicians, by being installed as a Liveryman. This Company, founded about 1350, and incorporated in the year 1500, has around 250 liveryman at any one time, covering the whole range of the musical spectrum, composers, singers and musicians. He had at last been admitted to the most distinguished company in his chosen profession and, as shall be seen, he eventually became Master of the Company.

In May 1958 a vacancy occurred for the appointment of Drum Major of Portsmouth Group Band. Prior to this, all Drum Majors had come from amongst General Duties SNCOs in the Corps, mostly from the Drill Instructors Branch (formerly MTIs). Acting Sergeant Bugler *Colin* Bowden applied for the post, and although the board was keen to have another GD SNCO, Vivian intervened and Bowden got the job. He had known the bugler since he joined the Band and Drums Company in Eastney as a boy bugler in 1945 and appreciated his potential. This led to a reappraisal of the Bugler Branch and though some GD NCOs subsequently became Drum Majors, the pendulum swung to them all coming from the Bugler Branch, which enhanced the standard and the promotion prospects.

One story is recalled by Drum Major *Charles* Bowden, who had become the Corps senior Drum Major in 1952. Some time during the late fifties, the PDM asked him to go and speak to the RSM, saying that he required the band off parade, where they were attending a squad passing out rehearsal, by 1530hrs as they were required for another rehearsal in the concert hall. Charlie was going across to North Barracks anyway and delivered the message to the RSM who was known to be 'in one of his moods'. The RSM's reaction was 'You mean that *you* want the band to go home at 1530; Colonel Dunn would not send a Colour Sergeant as an orderly. If the Colonel wants me he can speak to me directly.' On his return to PDM's office in South Barracks, Vivian asked Charlie if it was all right. 'Not really, Sir,' and he told him what had transpired. After a while Vivian picked up the telephone and got through to the RSM. His only words were 'I want you in my office ... NOW'. In due course there was a knock on the door, but Vivian continued writing at his desk, with Bowden at the desk opposite. 'That will be the RSM. Shall I go next door, sir?' 'No. You sit there and carry on working.' He carried on writing until here was another knock and finally said 'Come in' without looking up. The RSM entered, saluted, but the Colonel kept on writing. Eventually he said 'Mr -----, the band will be off parade by 1530 hours'. 'Is that all you asked me over for, sir? Couldn't you have used the telephone?', spluttered the astonished RSM. The PDM looked up at him and said solemnly 'I know there are some members of my band who can imitate my voice very well on the telephone. You wanted me to speak directly to you, so I called you over. You surely didn't expect me to come to your office, did you?'

All the while Vivian had been extending and expanding his own compositions and arrangements. In 1955 Warwick Films made *The Cockleshell Heroes*, based on the successful raid by Colonel 'Blondie' Hasler and his team of canoeists up the Gironde river in occupied France to destroy enemy shipping in Bordeaux harbour in December 1942. The young British composer, John Addison, was entrusted to write the film score. However Vivian was asked by Euan Lloyd of Warwick Films to compose the theme music for the film. This was to be in the form of a concert march, which would be incorporated into the background music accompanying many scenes in the film. Lloyd said to him 'I want something that will embody the best of Elgar, Walton and Coates!' A challenge indeed. He immediately realised that strong themes in the modern idiom would be required to make an impact on the film-going public. He wrote:

> 'When commencing work on the project the title of the film kept occurring to me and I conceived the idea of basing the opening of the introduction and the first subject on the rhythm of the words. After some thought, the idea crystallised itself into the subject which I developed from it. The most important requirement of the composition was a smooth flowing yet strong theme of nobilement *(sic)* character in the Trio. This melody began to take shape as the work progressed, and eventually formed the theme which was used in the film. It was a melody which gave plenty of scope for different harmonisation and counter figures.'

Vivian took enormous pride in being asked to undertake this work which, he knew, had to be worthy of the 'Cockleshell Heroes' themselves. He had met many of the marines whilst they were training off the beaches at Eastney during the war. He conceived the outline of the march whilst driving his wife to Ascot and back and the main motif of the march is based on the rhythm of the words 'Cockleshell Heroes'. The final result was a stirring march which has stood the test of time along with marches by other great film composers such as Eric Coates, Malcolm Arnold and William Alwyn. He took the School of Music Band to Shepperton Studios for a day's recording, where they collaborated with the London Philharmonic Orchestra under the direction of Muir Matheson. He wrote afterwards:

> 'For any composer to hear his music splendidly performed is very gratifying, and on this occasion I was no exception, and derived much satisfaction from the ultimate results of one's inspiration being brought so well to fruition.'

The march had its first performance at a School of Music winter concert in October. The world première, in aid of the Royal Marines Association, was on 16th November at the Empire Theatre, Leicester Square. It was attended by HRH The Duke of Edinburgh (Captain General), Earl Mountbatten (The First Sea Lord), Lieutenant General Campbell Hardy (Commandant General) and three United States Marine Corps Generals, besides the two survivors of the raid, Lieutenant Colonel H G Hasler and Marine Bill Sparks along with Douglas Fairbanks, jnr, who was the chairman of the organising committee. Vivian also wrote the *Cockleshell Heroes Fanfare* which was played by a seven piece fanfare team on the main staircase as the principal guests arrived. The evening was supported by a 'pictorial prologue' or pageant depicting heroic episodes from British history with the aid of film sequences, accompanied by the Royal Marines Band. Vivian looked back on it as one of the greatest evenings in his life.

The next innovation that occurred in the Band Service was the changing of the name of Boy Musician to Junior Musician, a title of which he fully approved. This was in line with Admiralty policy for the whole of the Royal Navy. Soon after that HM The Queen Mother paid a visit to Deal, her first there since she was Duchess of York in 1929, to open the new accommodation block in North Barracks; this was followed by an impressive parade on South Green. With his royal connections Vivian was able to advise and assist in the organisation of the event but take a back seat on the day. However he ensured that his daughter Rosemary presented the bouquet to Her Majesty.

One of the major events of 1956 was the centenary of the institution of the Victoria Cross. The Band of the RM School of Music and a Guard of Honour in London led the contingent of veteran holders of the VC in an inspiring ceremony. However before the parade which was due to move off at 11am there was time for the band to fall out for a smoke in the waiting area. After about ten minutes a Guard of Honour of the Brigade of Guards escorting their Colours approached. Drum Major Charlie Bowden gave the order 'out pipes' and called the marines to attention until they passed by. The naval contingent close by was still fallen out and took no notice. Some minutes later an official car drew up and a gentleman in a dark suit and bowler hat spoke to the senior Naval officer present. After the departure of the visitor the Naval officer ordered the guard and band to fall in, at which the Principal Director of Music called him across and demanded to know why he had fallen everyone in with still 20 minutes to go. The Naval officer explained that the 'civilian' was a high ranking Army officer and complained about the behaviour of the men when the Guards had marched past and he had decided to fall everyone in until it was time to move off. Vivian told him in no uncertain words that whilst he might command the Naval guard, the band was not under his command, and promptly fell them out. At precisely 10.58 the Drum Major fell the band in and ordered 'Band Ready'. The Naval guard was still at ease. Vivian marched to his position with the band as the clock struck 11 o'clock. He looked across at the officer commanding the Naval guard and said 'There you are. You've been fallen in for 20 minutes old chap, and now you've bloody well missed the march off!'

At every opportunity, Vivian made sure the Royal Marines bands were in the national spotlight. He had a great gift for public relations and established a particular rapport with the BBC. After all, he had been in at the birth of the BBC Symphony Orchestra. Not only did the band appear regularly on such programmes as *Friday Night is Music Night*, but he ensured they had a share in providing the music for London film premières such as *The Battle of the River Plate*, and *The Yangtse Incident*. He arranged Leighton-Lucas' *Amethyst March* which had been written for the latter film for military band in 1957. There were numerous recording sessions and the like. On one occasion the Royal Marines Dance Band *The Oceanaires* featured in a new film *Indiscreet* in a scene in the Painted Hall at the Royal Naval College at Greenwich. Whenever he could he used his considerable influence and widespread contacts to maintain and exploit the orchestral potential of Royal Marines bands in the firm belief that they were beyond the capability of the Army and RAF. This, of course, was not entirely true, though Vivian could always muster a larger symphony orchestra than the other Services. He also provided a high standard of guest speakers at the annual Band Service reunions.

In 1957, as the result of the excellent playing of Junior L/Cpl John Dixon in a bombardon solo at a BBC concert, he persuaded the renowned brass band conductor Harry Mortimer to come to Deal to listen to a specially selected Junior Band. The juniors rehearsed harder than ever and the result was a fine concert, which was broadcast on 1st April. His encouragement of young trainees undoubtedly paid dividends in future years and laid the foundation of all the Royal Marines bands today. His understanding and love of choral music was also behind the church service at which the Archbishop of Canterbury, Dr Geoffrey Fisher, preached at

St Michael and All Angels, the Depot Royal Marines church when, led by Bandmaster Peter Sumner, 400 boys sang a special setting by Malotte of the Lord's Prayer.

Military Fanfares had taken his imagination and he wrote a number for special occasions, such as *For an Ecclesiastical Jubilee* for the visit by Dr Fisher. This is a very specialised form of composition in which he excelled as can be seen from his not inconsiderable output.*

That summer, the Royal Marines Massed Bands once again provided the main attraction at the Royal Tournament and Vivian had insisted that about 30 young musicians, having just passed out from the Commandant General's Squad, should be included. Just prior to the Tournament, a concert was given at Kneller Hall by the Massed Bands of the Royal Marines and the Central Band of the Royal Air Force, the first time in their history that the two bands had been massed together. Undoubtedly it was made even more memorable by the presence of Wing Commander A E Sims, the Organising Director of Music of the RAF, who had started his career as a Royal Marines musician.

One of Vivian's greatest assets was to spot latent musical talent, and usually his judgement was proved right. However, it did lead to accusations of favouritism. It is of interest to note that Vivian nominated his eventual successor, Paul Neville, to attend the Royal Academy in 1957/58. He had been Vivian's band secretary for about three years, being under close scrutiny by the 'master'. He mixed the duties of band secretary with that of 1st violin in the orchestra. It was during this period that he learnt what the 'Band Business' was all about. Paul Neville wrote:

> 'I learnt to take dictation and present a letter for signature "exactly right". He always strove for perfection in everything and often remarked that music making was the "art of taking pains". During my time as his secretary I noticed the change in him from someone who was very suspicious about everything to do with the Band Service and its members to someone who took great pride in his RMSM orchestra and band. He had an excellent aural perception, a deep knowledge of the score and a fine rehearsal technique which he always said was a result of his years at the Royal Academy playing under the baton of Sir Henry Wood.'

---

* catalogued in Appendix D

The Captain General with the Commandant, Colonel 'Bertie' Lumsden and Vivian during his visit to the RM School of Music at Deal in January 1958

Towards the end of 1956 visits to Deal by both HRH Prince Philip and Earl Mountbatten provided Vivian with the opportunity to show off his bands. He had also negotiated a three-year contract with HMV to record for that company, a signal honour. He knew that not only would these recordings require a great amount of rehearsal and attention, but would also be of incalculable benefit in playing experience and prestige. No doubt there were extra financial rewards too. For the first recording to be made early the following year he set his mind once again to composing a special march. He looked round for a suitable subject. Now that the sea going role of the Royal Marines was being reduced even further by naval cuts in large ships, the Commando role had taken on a new dimension. The marching song of the Commandos was of course *Sarie Marais*, which he had already arranged for military band, so he decided not to use that melody as the basis for a rollicking new *Concert March for Orchestra – Dedicated to the Men of the Green Beret* which he subsequently shortened to *Commando Patrol*. To his dismay it did not have the power and appeal of *Cockleshell Heroes* to become a lasting favourite.

Another word about *Sarie Marais*. Although Vivian had made an arrangement of this before the war and his version was officially adopted as the March of the Royal Marines Commandos on 28th August 1952, it was not recorded until 1964 (*'300 Glorious Years'*). It was not used on a Horse

Guards Beating Retreat until 1958, nor had it been used at any major Corps ceremonial before. Indeed Vivian's score bears the notation 'Original arrangement FVD RMSM 19 May 1958' and it was accredited to Toonsetting.

Although an LP had been released in 1957 entitled *'Royal Tournament 1957'* the one for which Vivian started planning and rehearsing, *'Listen To The Royal Marines Band'* under the EMI label, was released as an HMV recording as *'The Band of the Royal Marines'*. Other than *Commando Patrol* it did not contain another military march, but demonstrated the versatility of the band with such items as *Jesu, Joy of Man's Desiring, Two Little Finches* and *Pomp and Circumstance March No 5* amongst others.*

* * * * *

The friendly rivalry between Vivian and Bertie Lumsden came to a head in 1957, when the Commanding Officer called all his officers together at Deal to explain the new Special Duties List of Officers, which was to supersede the old Quartermaster Branch. In the case of Band Service officers, it was first proposed that they should be identified by the letters SD which would appear in brackets after their rank. Col Lumsden, in his forthright way, said he thought the proposal ludicrous and as an example quoted the weekly band concerts. With a twinkle in his eye, he thought they would last longer as all the concert conductors were introduced by their rank, post and qualification. For example, he said, 'Colonel Dunn will now have to be introduced as Substantive Major Local Lieutenant Colonel Special Duties Bandmaster Dunn, CVO, FRAM, Royal Marines, Principal Director of Music Royal Marines'. The officers found this rather funny, but Vivian was not at all amused. It was the thought of being called *Bandmaster Dunn* that riled most!

Vivian certainly didn't think of himself as a Special Duties Officer. He regarded it as a 'demotion', a reaction probably akin to many General Duties officers put in a similar position. It was a severe blow to his ego and he simply refused to acknowledge the SD tag and proceeded, in characteristic fashion, to rise above it. After all he had not served in the ranks as all other band officers had and felt it an affront to be coupled with them. He had joined the Corps direct from civilian life as had all General Duties

---

* For full contents and release date see Appendix E.

officers, so why should he be 'downgraded' as he thought of it. His pride and pomposity were tested to the full, and only on official service papers were the letters (SD) ever seen against his name.

In a similar vein, some years later, he was briefly refused a British passport, on renewal, by some unthinking civil servant, on the grounds that he had been born in India. His elder daughter, Leonie, remembers vividly the breakfast time when the letter from the Home Office arrived. There was a loud bellow of wrath and he made the classic remark 'That means the children are Indians.' She was quite pleased, because she thought he meant Red Indians! He promptly wrote an indignant letter to the Secretary of State which his younger daughter Rosemary typed for him, and his passport was renewed without further fuss.

During his time at Deal he had formed a strong alliance with the Deal and Walmer Handelian Society, a fine group of singers under the direction of his friend Dr James Hall. His love and affection for the works of Sir Edward Elgar naturally led him to consider *The Dream of Gerontius*, which he had heard the composer conduct some thirty years before in a spellbound evening. In the autumn of 1957 he started to rehearse the choir, gradually adding some excellent singers from the Royal Marines Band Service. For six months he rehearsed them relentlessly, bringing out the full blooded romantic fervour inspired by Roman Catholicism, leading to the death and repentance of Gerontius. It was an electrifying experience for the choir and orchestra to come under Vivian Dunn's baton, a man who so fervently believed that this was one of the finest oratorios ever written. The performance in the Depot church on 28th February was enjoyed by an audience of over 700. Vivian had brought in three soloists of international fame, William Herbert (tenor), Marjorie Thomas (contralto) and Hervey Alan (bass). It was a memorable evening.

He continued to encourage foreign military musicians to come to Deal for some training and in 1958 two colourful Indonesian Petty Officers, Hardjono and Sardjono arrived. He christened them 'Gog' and 'Magog'. One Australian, Sub Lieutenant Don Coxon, recently commissioned, found himself sitting next to Vivian at his very first guest night in the Officers' mess at Deal. The first course was soup and following the master's example, the Australian poured his sherry into the soup. Next day he remarked what a foul taste it was! Another unusual, but welcome, visitor was Drum Major Margaret Davy of the Women's Royal Army Corps who came for a short course in Drum Majoring, under the wing of Drum Major Charles Bowden with whose family she stayed. It is not known whether Vivian ever seriously considered introducing women into the Royal Marines Band Service, but there were Wrens in some of the Royal Naval establishment bands which were trained by Royal Marines Volunteer Band Instructors.

The 1958 Beat Retreat on Horse Guards Parade saw 274 musicians on parade. This was the first time that it was in honour of the birthday of the Captain General and was witnessed by HM the Queen, Prince Philip and other members of the Royal Family. As always months of planning and rehearsal had gone into this great event, the musical programme was carefully thought out and the balance of performers entailed bringing in specialists from other bands throughout the country. Vivian was always quick to praise his own musicians and on this occasion wrote afterwards:

> 'The memory I shall retain of this unique event is of the fine tone of playing of the bands, the excellent drumming and bugling, and the precision of the marching. It was all so very worthwhile, and I know that all who were privileged to take part felt a sense of pride in their achievement.'

Perhaps it was because he had now had five years in Deal developing the Band Service to his ways that he felt the need to spread the gospel further afield. He had always had a great affinity for American music and it was across the Atlantic he looked. He arranged to take 60 musicians to help celebrate the centenary of British Columbia. He had, of course, taken the Portsmouth Division Band there in 1948/49, but other than occasional visits by Royal Marines bands embarked in HM Ships, this was the first excursion by a major band to Canada since he had become the Principal Director of Music. They took part in the Vancouver Centennial Tattoo in the Empire Stadium along with four Canadian bands from the Army, Navy and Air Force and that of the United States Marine Corps from San Francisco. The Tattoo was the first ever to be held in Vancouver and Brigadier Alastair Maclean, the acknowledged international expert in this field, had been engaged to direct it.

Captain Terry Freestone recalls that Vivian found it hard to relax with his band when there was any likelihood of being in view of the public. Indeed it was the practice for the band to travel in No 2 Blue Uniform and they were used to wearing their caps and white blanco-ed buff belts until

A familiar sight as the Royal Marines parade along The Strand, Walmer.
A Church Parade in the 1960s.

after passing Upper Deal church in their coaches. It therefore came as something of a shock to be told that they could discard their caps and belts for the marathon flight to Canada; but they were also politely told that their collars would have to remain done up until they were airborne.

On the first morning of rehearsals in Canada, Vivian, as the Principal Director of Music for the Tattoo found himself confronted by 300 musicians, with variations of musical technique, style and colour of uniforms and methods of drill. They sweated for four days with temperatures in the eighties until he successfully blended them together, producing an integrated band, balanced musically and positioned 'according to the shape and size of their musical instruments and the colour of their hats.' Drum Major Charles Bowden was, of course, in the lead. It was reported that one evening, in between rehearsals, they managed to consume 150 dozen bottles of beer in 55 minutes.

The Tattoo lasted from 23rd June to 2nd July and was seen by 125,000 paying customers. After this exhausting schedule the band was allowed some time off. Vivian was interviewed on the Canadian Broadcasting Corporation's Victoria network where he was able to thank the people of British Columbia for their support. He also announced that they would now be enjoying some free time, which resulted in invitations to play at the Veteran's Hospital and Beacon Hill Park. Vivian decided to go fishing with his staff officer, Captain Alec Horsfall, as he had promised Mike he would bring home a Canadian salmon out of the sea. He fished in the open sea, the narrows, the flat calm and when it was rough, but his catch amounted to no more than two fish. After being accused of baby-snatching he insisted on eating the sardine-like creatures for lunch!

A second LP was planned for 1959 and HMV asked him for an all Alford programme. So Vivian went back to his earlier days for his selection. He had always admired, and enthusiastically played, many of Kenneth Alford's marches. He had studied them in depth in his early days at Eastney and now realised that many of them were no longer available on records. So he set about selecting which of the 17 quick marches could be fitted in. In the end he chose the ten most well known, added the slow march *By Land & Sea* along with two other compositions, the xylophone solo *Two Little Imps* and the waltz *Thoughts*, to add variety. Major Ricketts' two sons attended the recording which took place over two days of exacting playing on 5th & 6th March in HMV's London studios. The record was an instant success when it was released.

The winter concerts continued unabated and his great friend of many years standing Robert Farnon, the Canadian composer, came to conduct one of his own latest compositions. During the season Dr Hubert Clifford conducted another new work *A Cowes Suite* for which Vivian had invited Uffa Fox, the famous yachtsman to whom the work was dedicated, to attend. Indeed Uffa Fox unexpectedly took the platform during the concert and sang a couple of unaccompanied, raucous sea shanties.

The pressure of work during his early years as the Principal Director of Music had an adverse effect on his family life. He drove himself hard to ensure that his concept of a new and improved Band Service would work. He had less time for his family. Leonie and Paddy were away at boarding school, and when they returned for the holidays, they found it was not

Leonie on 'Chips'

easy to mix with the other children. Leonie recalls spending most of her time on her pony and listening to pop music to the intense annoyance of her father. Rosey went to school at Leelands on Drum Hill in Walmer.

Although Mike loved Deal, she became increasingly lonely and found it hard to adapt to life without her children around her. She never complained and busied herself in cultivating a 'mother' image among the young Junior Musicians. In turn they looked upon her as someone in whom they could share their troubles – after all many of them were only 15 years old and away from home for the first time. She called them 'her boys' and took a great interest in their musical careers and was always ready to listen to them and give encouragement. She looked for outside interests and gradually made many friends in Deal, both amongst the people of the town and those at the Depot.

With all his work Vivian found the teenage years of his children difficult and although they took family holidays together, he was less approachable than he had been in their earlier years at Portsmouth. However he did try to involve the family in as many of his engagements as possible. The young 18 year old Leonie remembers accompanying her father to the Royal Festival Hall in 1958 and being introduced to Lord Mountbatten for the first time. She was totally swept off her feet by his charm, good looks, and the interest he seemed to take in talking to her. She was completely tongue-tied and gauche but she cherished that day.

It was during the Spring term of 1959 that Vivian turned his thoughts to composing in a completely different vein. The Depot Royal Marines amateur dramatic society, the Globe Players, had decided to perform a Jeannette Dowling play *The Young Elizabeth* and Vivian's elder daughter Leonie, was cast in the title role. She was pleased to give up her humdrum job in London and come back to live at Deal for the duration and took an 'undemanding secretarial job'. In order to utilise the full range of the establishment's talents Joan Lee, the producer, asked Vivian if he would write incidental music in the Elizabethan style. This was something new, but by using his skills as an arranger and interpreter and inspired by the music of Peter Warlock, a musicologist in the Elizabethan manner, he composed a magnificent score. As someone who was involved in the production the author can vouch that it inspired us all to great efforts. Unfortunately only a very poor recording of it exists; no score has ever come to light. Neville felt it was one of his finest compositions ever, and it undoubtedly played a major part in the Depot winning the Royal Naval Drama Festival that year.

Whilst he was writing the music on his mini piano in the dining room downstairs, Leonie was confined to her bedroom learning her lines. From time to time he would ask his daughter which of two phrases she would prefer at particular moments in the play, such was his attention to detail. Leonie admitted later that, as music was not her strongest suit, she found it difficult to give an intelligent answer. It was some surprise to the director that Leonie arrived at the first rehearsal word-perfect, but she said that as she had spent a lifetime watching her father learn scores by heart so that he could conduct from memory, it was natural that she should do the same. She so loved the music, especially the second movement of the suite he wrote with the *Tower Music*, that she subsequently asked for it to be played at her wedding. The adjudicator of the play mentioned in his remarks how appropriate the music was and that it must be unique to have music composed specially for an amateur production.

Two years later the Globe Players presented *Teahouse of the August Moon* and once again Vivian was asked to provide some incidental music. He wrote three romantic themes *Japanese Motif*, *Willow Pattern* and *From a Japanese Screen*. He conducted the orchestra from the pit during the four performances and his music enhanced the play, turning it almost into a film show. It certainly gave the performers, of whom I was one, an uplift.

Leonie Dunn as 'The Young Elizabeth' at Deal in 1959 for which Vivian wrote special incidental music, later used at her wedding

Vivian, who was always so keen to claim his own royalties and endeavoured to get the question of copyright absolutely right, found himself in a controversy over the music of the Regimental March. In January 1959 Boosey & Hawkes questioned the playing of *A Life on the Ocean Wave* on a new Columbia recording, asking the company for royalties, as Boosey's published the arrangement by Kenneth J Alford 'by authority'. Columbia replied that the version on the recording was a manuscript version by Vivian Dunn and they were paying royalties to the MCPS on his behalf. When he was asked for an explanation Vivian said that they could not use the Alford version as it was written for military band. He went on to say that in September 1940, when at Portsmouth, Columbia had asked him to record an orchestral programme and, as there was no published orchestral version, he had transcribed his own. Before doing so he had spoken to Aubrey Winter of Boosey & Hawkes asking if they had any objection and their reply said that they had none. He added that 'In any case it was thought that the performance would be limited more to Service functions and therefore would be of little value to civilian orchestras. At no time had he decreed that royalties should be paid to the Royal Marines.' It is interesting to note that Vivian's orchestral manuscript had still not been published in 1959.

During 1959 Vivian had fought for the introduction of rod tension drums for the band to replace the old, heavier rope tension ones which had often proved unreliable in the vagaries of English weather. Despite the inevitable reductions in defence spending he managed to persuade the

Admiralty to invest in supplying new drums. During the year many trials were carried out with them with a view to bringing them into service in 1960.

It was around this time that he introduced measures that were to improve the already high standard of drumming and bugling in the Corps. In a 1991 radio interview with Richard Powell on the *Bandstand* programme, he said that he had tried to simplify the effectiveness for the band on parade by introducing specific drum beating routines, either in 2/4 time, *à la brève*, or 6/8 time. He realised that many composers of military marches either did not write a drum introduction or that it was 'not always extremely well done'. As the Corps of Drums, also being buglers, was essentially the most skilful part of the band, anything that could be done to simplify their methods of memorising drum parts, must help. Reducing introductions to about twelve standard ones instead of trying to memorise the one written by the composer, would make sense. He was also concerned about the mouthpieces issued with their bugles. They did not suit each individual and he felt it important that the Royal Marines should have a variety of mouthpieces to satisfy all buglers. It is probable that the initiative came from Bugle Major John Wagstaffe with support from Vivian. A cushioned mouthpiece was introduced similar to that used in a cornet or trumpet enabling a more mellow tone to be produced. It also allowed a bugler to play for longer periods than hitherto.

As has been seen Vivian was always keen for his musicians to take their full part in sport, and in doing so himself, he set an example. He was frequently seen on the tennis courts outside his residence and also in the squash court. He was now approaching 50 years of age, and his days on the cricket field were numbered. The Depot had a particularly strong side, but he played in a number of friendlies on South Green, opening the batting and, with his excellent eye for a ball, treating the bowlers with scant respect. At one stage of the season he topped the batting averages but he was the first to admit that it was difficult to hide him in the field.

Following the success of the Canadian tour the previous year, Vivian had set up enough contacts to be almost certain of another invitation to play at the Canadian National Exhibition in Toronto. The exhibition ran from 26th August to 12th September. From his previous experience there he was intent on ensuring not only a programme that would be appreciated on the other side of the Atlantic, but also included sufficient variety to demonstrate that his Royal Marines Band would prove themselves the finest in the world and the best to represent Great Britain. No doubt it was the presence of the First Sea Lord, Admiral of the Fleet, the Earl Mountbatten of Burma, who opened the exhibition and took the salute at Beat Retreat on the first night, that influenced the choice of band to play there. The relationship between Vivian and Mountbatten during the years the latter was First Sea Lord and then Chief of the Defence Staff was very close and it was speculated that Mountbatten considered that the Royal Marines School of Music Band was his own personal property and it would play for him at the drop of a coin. To a certain extent this was true. He pointed out that the charter of the RMBS was to provide music for the Royal Navy and he was their head. The other side of the coin was that the Royal Marines had the privilege of playing at all the most prestigious events, both in England and very often abroad, besides adding considerably to the high profile of the Corps. Although Vivian usually took all the glory there was no doubt that the very hard schedule resulting in very intensive rehearsals paid dividends. In its turn this improved the standard of playing by the musicians and indirectly made recruitment to join the Royal Marines Band Service even more competitive.

After playing two and half hour concerts every day for a fortnight at the Canadian National Exhibition, finishing up with Beating Retreat each evening, the band went on a ten day tour of some of the principal cities of eastern Canada. Vivian was seldom openly complimentary to his musicians, perhaps because of his latent shyness, but he was extremely generous in his writing. Commenting on this tour in *The Blue Band* he states that the very hard preliminary work put in by all his musicians, more than realised his fullest expectations by the quality and endeavour from every member of the team. Fulsome praise indeed.

Although, as we have read, he claimed that he was guaranteed a career to the age of 60 when he was selected as the Director of Music of the Portsmouth Band in 1931, it is far from clear whether this would apply when he was appointed Principal Director of Music. Certainly no papers have come to light to confirm this and it must be presumed he would retire at the compulsory age of 55 in 1963. However there are indications that even as early as 1959 he was pencilling in a successor, the year after Paul Neville had attended the one year Bandmaster's course at the Academy. Neville was drafted to be the Bandmaster of C-in-C Home Fleet's Band for six months and then promoted to Captain after only two years as a Second

Lieutenant. Although there were several candidates, whom he had already selected to do the year's course at the Royal Academy, he carefully chose newly promoted Captain Paul Neville as Director of Music Training of the Staff Band. As we have seen he had already recognised his ability and now paid tribute to the manner in which 'he has already added new ideas and sound suggestions to benefit training.' Paul Neville then spent a year with the Plymouth Group Band, before taking over at Portsmouth with the Royal Yacht commitment.

Keeping up with all the latest trends and ideas, Vivian arranged to have the band record the orchestral and military band music for a new film about the Royal Navy, *The Navy Lark* starring Ronald Shiner, at Elstree Studios for which he arranged two pieces of music by Max Martin, *The Navy Lark* and *Tradewind Hornpipe*. It was such extra engagements as these that introduced young musicians to a new world, and though there were grumbles from time to time about how hard he worked them, underneath they appreciated what vistas and opportunities he opened for them compared with many other Service military bands.

* * * * *

The 1950s had provided Vivian with a new challenge, which he had successfully taken up. He had blended the old seagoing Royal Naval School of Music musicians with the undoubtedly superior talents of the Divisional bands, into a consolidated, though not always completely united, Royal Marines Band Service. His initiative had increased the repertoire of the bands, he had improved the musical instruments and had insisted on high performance standards. In seven years he had overseen the complete reorganisation of the system of training. He paid particular attention to ensure that all Band Service officers were properly prepared to undertake their task as Directors of Music of the Staff Bands in particular. He had enlisted fine young players from the Royal Academy who joined the Royal Marines for their National Service and he had invited professors from the Academy to visit Deal, examine student Bandmasters and conduct examinations and concerts. He was not slow to use his contacts with the national musical scene and, of course, he occasionally 'tapped' his Royal connections. But above all he had given his musicians a pride in their Service, their playing and their performances. Yes, he had proved to be the right man in the right job at the right time.

CHAPTER 6

Allegro - Consolidation into the Sixties

THE NEW DECADE OPENED on a sad personal note. Vivian's long and close association with the Mountbatten family was suddenly shattered by the news of Edwina's death on 21st February 1960 in North Borneo. Although not within the very closest circle of friends at that time, he was nevertheless close enough to be asked that his band would provide music at the Memorial Service in Westminster Abbey on 7th March. It was a moving experience and Vivian wrote that

> 'It was a great privilege for the band to be able to express, by its playing, the very deep sympathy which all members of the Royal Marines Band Service have for the Mountbatten family. To perform in Westminster Abbey under such circumstances demanded playing of a very special calibre and it was most gratifying that the music played by the band received such fine commendations.'

Earl Mountbatten wrote the day following the Memorial Service:

> 'I am most grateful to you and the Band of the Royal Marines for playing so beautifully during the Memorial Service for my wife yesterday. I have heard excellent reports of your playing from all sides and I am very grateful for all the trouble that you took at such short notice.'

One of the most revolutionary moves in the band's instrumentation which, as we have seen, Vivian had fought for during the fifties, came to fruition in 1960 with the introduction of rod tension drums, side, tenor and bass. These ensured a much slicker, sharper sound and were, of course, much easier to clean and maintain. Somehow it lifted the whole sound of the marching band. The need for a drum skin that did not go soggy and that could stand up to all weather conditions had been proved by the cancellation of a number of Beat Retreats over the years. Legend has it that the new rod tension drums were tested in the showers of East Barracks at Deal. Vivian had supposedly called together a 'committee of taste' which certainly included Directors of Music and Drum Majors, the Premier Drum Company and probably his old friend George Waite from Boosey & Hawkes. In order to prove their resilience to very wet weather a group of buglers, dressed in swimming trunks and plimsolls stood solemnly in the showers drumming – legend doesn't say whether they were wearing Wolseley pattern helmets as well! This, added to the introduction of new instruments, went on steadily during the early sixties.

Perhaps one of Vivian's greatest character faults was his inability to equate with those under him. Maybe it was his shyness, perhaps it was a sense of inadequacy which he sometimes found difficult to face. But, in his dealings with his fellow Directors of Music and Band Service officers, he could seldom bring himself to address them by anything but their surname – occasionally with their rank attached. This undoubtedly niggled many of them. Doug Haigh writes 'I hated him, yet I loved him – but most of all I respected him for all the good that he did for the Band Service. He could charm the hind legs off a donkey and the next minute blast you to kingdom come because of something you had done, which he didn't like.' Doug recalls that, whilst Vivian called his wife Betty, he was always Haigh, even as a captain, and only after he retired did he succumb to the Christian name. This is a recurring theme.

In his letter writing he was most punctilious with his spelling, but seldom used commas. His view was quite clearly that commas can alter the whole meaning of text and without them the recipient is free to interpret them in any way they want without the writer having to commit himself. One of his often heard sayings was 'Music for art's sake, but money for God's sake'. All musicians had a commercial and financial awareness, and he was no exception having played professionally during the early 1930s; an awareness not inherent in the regular Corps. However he was not quite as mercenary as some would believe. He did not always claim his travelling expenses, nor other 'perks', but often paid for these out of his own pocket. Indeed, Vivian did not really care about money, Mike dealt with all his finances, and although his secretary invariably filled in his S542s (travel expense claims) he often forgot to sign and submit them.

His policy for introducing new and exciting music to add spice to the Deal winter concerts was embellished when the distinguished Canadian composer Robert Farnon paid a return visit to conduct the orchestra in his own new rhapsody for violin and orchestra, the soloist being Kenneth Sillitoe from the Royal Academy of Music. In that term, two other distinguished conductors also performed, Maurice Miles and Dr Clarence Raybould, both of whom had special relations with the Corps and who made the Royal Marines Bandmaster students so welcome at the Academy. With these distinguished guests to perform with them, he kept the band, and particularly the orchestra, on their toes the whole time.

Vivian and Bob Farnon had a close understanding of each other's music, one predominantly in the martial vein, the other whose output was in the classical and light music mould. About one of his visits Bob Farnon wrote:

> 'When visiting the School in the 1950s to make music with the RM Concert Orchestra, I was always invited to stay with the Dunn family. One bitterly cold February morning I left for rehearsals (8 hours of them) forgetting to switch off the electric fire in the bedroom. On subsequent visits during winter months I was always offered a hot water bottle! A touch of Vivian's funny side. His humour when giving after dinner speeches consisted in telling jokes against himself: especially amongst musicians.'

At one concert conducted by Dr Raybould, Vivian designed a programme to cater for a large number of soloists, two or three of whom were National Servicemen, with works for two pianos, solo horn, cello and orchestra and a piano concerto. Another National Service soloist that evening, whom Vivian had managed to enlist into the Corps to expand the orchestral range was Musician Norman Webb. When the author, who was the Personnel Selection Officer at the Depot at the time, interviewed this new young entry he asked him what instrument he played. Webb looked me straight in the eye and without even a twinkle, said 'The harp, sir'. At first I didn't believe him, but over the next eighteen months Webb proved his value in accompanying the orchestra in numerous works for harp and orchestra, which they would not have played otherwise. He also showed the versatility of his instrument when he played popular music on the harp at a charity concert. I often wondered what he carried when on the march.

Farewell to Billy Monckton and his wife (behind bar) at the Lord Clyde *pub in 1954. Also in the photograph is George Simpson (left).*

One evening the members of the band invited Vivian to go along to the *Lord Clyde* public house in Walmer to say farewell to the host, Billy Monckton and his wife, who were retiring. He made a presentation to mark the long association and great appreciation of the hundreds of happy hours that had been spent and the thousands of pints that had been drunk at Billy Monckton's by members of the band.

This social excursion with his musicians was comparatively rare for Vivian, whose shyness led to a reluctance to mix too freely with his musicians, except on official engagements, including this Monckton farewell at the *Lord Clyde*!

Vivian's reluctance to accept fully the older RNSM Band officers came to a head in 1960 when he had a confrontation with Captain Tommy Lang, who had been Director of Music of the Plymouth Band since Dick Stoner had retired in 1953. Tommy had had his eyes set on relieving Tommy Francis at Chatham, but the barracks closed down. He was certainly extremely put out at being relieved at Plymouth by Paul Neville, some 23 years his junior and only commissioned three years. In no uncertain terms he made it known to Vivian that he felt he deserved better treatment even though he had reached the retirement age of 55, at least an extension until Neville had more experience. Vivian was adamant and Tommy never forgave him, retiring to the Isle of Man. He never came to

The Canadian composer Robert Farnon was a frequent visitor to the Deal concerts. Here he discusses his À La Claire Fontaine *composition which Vivian later chose as one of his* Desert Island Discs.

a Band Service reunion despite Vivian inviting him personally. The latter was upset by this attitude and very sorry that they were never able to 'bury the hatchet'.

Beating Retreat on Horse Guards Parade on 2nd June 1958 by the Massed Bands to honour the Captain General was another occasion for meticulous and detailed planning. He gathered his team several months beforehand. Whilst he remained in overall control, he left it to his staff to work out the intricate and precise movements which form the essence of the parade. In choosing the music programme he told them to concentrate on showing off the new rod tension drums to their best advantage.

He had more than his usual personal input into the musical programme, composing the Drum Beatings *Ceremonial Ruffle of Drums* and *Emblazoned Drums* as well as the bugle fanfare *Ceremonial Parade*. He also arranged William Walton's *Crown Imperial* for massed military bands and two Handel compositions, the march from *Rinaldo* and the air from *Ptolomy* to create the superb troop *March and Air.* With the inclusion of other arrangements and compositions, *Sarie Marais, Globe & Laurel, Crimond* and *Salute for Heroes*, he had contributed a massive amount of material to this important ceremony.

* * * * *

There were inevitably some amusing incidents and even some frivolous ones. The band was always game for knocking the Principal Director of Music off his pedestal, many of them believing that he did not have a sense of humour.

A legendary incident happened before rehearsals for the 1960 Royal Tournament had started. The Corps' senior Drum Major, Charlie Bowden had had an unfortunate accident at Deal when he broke his arm while stage managing a Depot revue in which this author was a prime mover. It was the day before Beat Retreat rehearsals started. Vivian was not at all pleased at this set-back and considerable alterations had to be made. Drum Major R G Knox from Plymouth took over the senior role and Bugle Corporal (hastily promoted to acting Bugle Sergeant) E Haybittle was quickly 'promoted' to fill a gap in the leading Drum Majors' ranks. This caused a problem as Bowden's fuller figure and Haybittle's height did not match. Vivian told his Supply Officer Music to ring Mr Goss, former Master Tailor at Chatham, and ask him to make a new Drum Major's tunic in two weeks. This was not a request but an order as that was the way Vivian worked. *He* thought of it as a request, but it was always taken by his staff as an order. The tunic was completed on time which must be a record.

It had always been a tradition that, on the final night of the Royal Tournament, the participants engaged in a certain amount of 'skylarking'; women's clothing might be hanging from the field guns crews' rigging; when the RAF Regiment drill squad fired their *feu de joie* a theatrical chicken would come hurtling down from the skies; and so on. But not so the Royal Marines bands – until 1960. Unknown to the Drum Majors and Bandmasters, the 'lads' had decided to play a musical joke. Previously when the participants were dismissed they marched off to the band playing *A Life on the Ocean Wave* once through, then breaking into *Sarie Marais*. The musicians had decided amongst themselves that after the Regimental March they would go into *Colonel Bogey*, played *fortissimo*.

All went well until it came to the march off. The band played the National Anthem and received the applause of the full house. Vivian Dunn brought the band to the ready and gave the down beat for the march off. Colin Bowden, one of the Drum Majors recalls: 'The band stepped off as the drummers played the two rolls and the first thing I heard was a mixture of *A Life on the Ocean Wave* and *Colonel Bogey*. This went on for several bars, but *Colonel Bogey* being a more strident march, it eventually overwhelmed the former and we marched out playing the Ricketts march very, very, loudly!' By the time the bands had halted, one half having exited at each end of the arena, Vivian had run round from the Royal Box and was beside himself with rage. He ordered the Drum Major to send someone to fetch the other half of the band, which was already in its accommodation changing.

They all eventually assembled, over 200 of them, the Principal Director threatening to have the band marched up and down the car park playing *Colonel Bogey* till their lips dropped. But eventually he realised that little could be done about it; the transport was waiting to take them back to all parts of the country. Vivian stood on a soap box and addressed the bands. His mood changed from high rage to philosophical with such remarks as 'After thirty years as Director of Music, I have never heard such a noise ... To think that Field Marshal Montgomery was in the Royal Box ... A great let down for the fine reputation of the Royal Marines ...' and so on. However his impish sense of humour came out when, looking at the assembled throng, he said 'But the worst thing of all was – you played it in the *wrong bloody key*!"

As we have seen before Vivian was not good at sitting down to write a new march unless he had a particular occasion in mind. 1960 provided him with a double opportunity. Firstly he was keen to introduce new marches to the Beat Retreat audience; and secondly the Royal Marines new Commando Ship role coming to fruition with the commissioning of HMS *Bulwark*, providing him with the occasion. Here was a chance to combine the two factors. The result was one of his finest marches *Soldiers of the Sea*. Although it is an original composition with a swinging rhythm, it contains snatches of the theme of the Regimental March. Underneath the melody there can be heard the influence of Kenneth Alford, who had played such a significant part in his early service life. He included the march on his next LP in 1961 along with *Sink The Bismarck* by Clifton Parker which his band had performed at the première of the film.

1960 was also the 21st birthday of the re-formation of the Women's Royal Naval Service at the beginning of World War 2. For their reunion in the Royal Festival Hall he took a band of sixty musicians, compared with the 150 for the Royal Naval Association reunion there earlier in the year. For the WRNS he was invited to compose a new march and he went back into his arranging/composing mode. The result was a gentle quick march based on the traditional 17th century song *There is a Lady Sweet and Kind – I did but see her Passing By*, by Rupert Herrick, which formed the Trio. It was subsequently used on ceremonial occasions as the official WRNS march past. After the first performance before Her Majesty, Queen Elizabeth, the Queen Mother at the reunion, the score was subsequently presented to the Director of the WRNS, Dame Elizabeth Hoyer-Millar at a gathering in the Concert Hall at Deal on 11th October in front of an invited audience, including many former Wrens who lived locally.

Yet a further honour fell his way that year, when he was appointed OBE in the Queen's Birthday Honour's List. On 15th November Vivian, accompanied by Mike, Leonie and Paddy, went to Buckingham Palace to receive the insignia from the Queen. As the children recall Her Majesty seemed to spend an overly long time talking to him and there appeared to be genuine warmth in her smile. He wrote subsequently in a rather pompous manner:

> 'Her Majesty graciously enquired about the work at the Royal Marines School of Music and I hope, therefore, that I may be forgiven for the feeling of great pride in such personal interest.'

During this consolidation period of the early sixties more time was taken up with orchestral rather than military band work. Whilst taking tremendous pride in producing the finest displays on the parade ground, one cannot but feel that Vivian's real love was in the orchestra. Perhaps he thought that there was a limit, which had already been reached in excellence and presentation on parade, and was confident that his staff would continue to maintain the level. He therefore turned his thoughts to new challenges. His programmes became more and more ambitious as he strove to achieve perfection in his young musicians, and despite the hard work and long and sometimes repetitive rehearsals, they admired him. One Director of Music put it this way: 'I am very glad that I knew him because he was an influence on my life that helped to enhance it. He was a builder – never destructive, and although he never forgot, he was very capable of forgiving.'

One of his duties as Principal Director was to carry out inspections of all Royal Marines bands in the country. He usually travelled with the Commandant of Deal, who was a general duty officer, and he made some very firm friendships this way. He always saw these trips as an opportunity to promote his own views, which did not always coincide with the thinking of the General Duties hierarchy of the Corps. One Commandant was very impressed by the detail he went into when inspecting bands and by his probing questions. On one occasion he asked a bandmaster what he would do if he was confronted by a piece of music which required an oboist, when he didn't have such a chap. He made them think about their programmes.

It was always his desire to push his own views and try to persuade the Commandant to present them to the Commandant General's department. Paul Neville writes of these visits:

> 'In order to extend his influence throughout the whole serving Royal Marines Band Service, PDM made regular visits to inspect all bands. I remember his visits to both Stonehouse and Eastney to inspect my bands. On each occasion a very demanding work for both orchestra and military band were selected as test pieces and all NCOs and candidates for promotion were required to conduct something. I know that some band officers and Bandmasters found these occasions terrifying affairs, but if one could produce the right answer, there was nothing to fear. They may not have liked it, but he made everyone sit up, get cracking, and raise the standard of performance.'

As we have seen Paul Neville had already been earmarked as his successor, which indirectly imposed more pressure on him to ensure that everything was not only right, but better than any other band during these annual inspections. Paul recalls an occasion in the early 60s when he and his wife Ann and their two children were invited to lunch with Vivian and Mike who were caravanning in the New Forest. It was all very relaxed and totally at ease, something which was entirely new to the guests. Indeed they were the perfect hosts.

Mike had an enormous amount of entertaining to do whilst at Deal. She nearly always put up distinguished visiting musicians from far and wide in G House for the night when they appeared at the winter concerts. She was a very relaxed hostess, seldom in the limelight, but always in close support. Mike was also very interested in the work of the Junior Musicians and she became a great favourite of them all. She followed the careers and fortunes of 'her boys' as she used to call them. Her own children were of a similar age, Leonie now being 20, so she understood them well and equated with these young musicians.

The 1961 Centenary celebrations at Deal

The centenary of the Depot Royal Marines was celebrated in 1961. In order to present as appropriate a programme as possible for this great occasion, he put on his historical hat and delved into a century of music. The week of celebration started off with a chilly, but nevertheless well attended concert on the ramparts of Deal Castle. Vivian had unearthed the programme of music that had been played at the first church parade after the Depot Band had been formed in 1900 on the same lines as the Divisional bands. (There had earlier been seventeen musicians privately engaged at the Depot.) He rearranged some of the music played on that occasion and then added marches that had been composed by subsequent Directors of Music at Deal, such as Bertie O'Donnell and Frederick J Ricketts (Kenneth Alford).

On Wednesday 31st May, came the unveiling of the Memorial Scroll to all ranks of the Royal Marines Band Service who fell in World War 2. It was a memorable occasion in the Concert Hall, with old and bolds mixing with the present generation of musicians to pay homage to their 225 comrades who were killed during the war. After Colonel R D 'Titch' Houghton, the Commandant, had unveiled the Memorial Plaque with the words 'With great humility I unveil this memorial scroll ...' , Colonel Dunn read the Citation and then called for Leon Young's magnificent *Dedication Fanfare*. It was an unforgettable occasion. It had been decreed since 1953 that 1st June would be the day on which the RM Band Service

In the Abbey Road studios with Brian Culverhouse, the EMI producer responsible for most of Vivian's recordings with the Royal Marines School of Music Band

honours its fallen with a reading of the War Memorial Charter and the playing of Leon Young's fanfare.

Vivian felt enormous pride when his eldest daughter Leonie was married at St Michael & All Angels Church, Deal on 1st July 1961. She remembers the precision of the arrival at the church with her father. Instead of a frantic rush down the aisle to her intended, it was all rehearsed to perfection. Vivian ensured that his daughter waited for exactly the right beat in the music and then stepped off with her left foot and slow marched up the aisle until they arrived at the right spot at exactly the moment the piece finished. She remembers her father squeezing her hand and she was aware of what a big moment it was for him. For music he had written a special arrangement of the *Tower Music* from *The Young Elizabeth* for her.

During the year Vivian worked hard at producing what turned out to be, in many opinions, his finest record. Side 1 was *'Beating Retreat'* and the reverse *'Tattoo'*. It is a very carefully constructed programme of music which contains not only the essential elements of the two ceremonial events but some of the finest military and traditional music with a vibrant Royal Marines emphasis. Almost everything on the LP was written by a British subject. It was released in December 1961 by EMI and subsequently re-released as part of a double LP set by *Music For Pleasure*.

Of the many events of 1962, his ability for one upmanship was seen to good effect during an International Military Band Festival in Ostend. Although there were no prizes to be won and it was entirely non-competitive, he knew that bands from the Belgian, French and German navies would be participating and he was determined to show that the Royal Marines were the best. His pride would have been blunted if this had not been the case. He started off with an advantage as his band was far the most experienced in such displays and he and his musicians of an extremely high quality, but as he described it later,

> '... with malice aforethought it was my avowed intention to ensure that our presentation was complete to the last detail for maximum effect. The weather was wonderful and the crowds enormous, and judging from the tremendous ovation that we received, there is no doubt as to who took the palm. Sparing our blushes, it was a case of planned presentation capturing the imagination of the crowd, as opposed to just marching up and down and doing a bit of static playing. It was most interesting to make comparisons between the bands. There were obviously some splendid players amongst them but when it came to appearance, drill, bearing and finesse there was a great deal left to be desired. I can only repeat how proud I was of our band, for we were representing Great Britain and I firmly believe that our insistence on every aspect of detail is something that is plainly obvious to a critical audience, and that our own chaps realised that it is no mere fetish on our part to see how the other side of the picture can be.'

Ray Woodfield recalls this visit as he was the Bandmaster of the Royal Marines School of Music Band. He writes:

> 'We embarked in a destroyer for passage from Dover to Ostend for the annual military band festival. There were some excellent bands there, and the Royal Marines did their best to go one better. During the festival all the visiting bands were compèred by a Belgian announcer until it came to the turn of the Royal Marines. Vivian strode onto the platform and addressed the audience in fluent German, which received an enormous ovation. Here was the showman *par excellence*.'

This sums up Vivian's philosophy that careful and detailed preparation, intense rehearsals and solid hard work, coupled with a variety of engagements to satisfy all needs, and interesting venues, add up to creating satisfied, competent and dedicated musicians. In their turn they did not always thank him for the treatment they received in rehearsal. Terry Freestone writes: 'He was a great man in the sense that he was right for the time'.

* * * * *

It was in 1962 that Leonie presented Vivian and Mike with their first grandchild, Simon Richard Vivian. Mike was absolutely delighted at the addition to the Dunn family tree, but Vivian was very reluctant to move on to the next stage of life as a grandfather, considering himself far too young at 53 to assume such a role! However, inwardly he was just as proud as Mike and was doubly honoured by the name Vivian being perpetuated.

Vivian would always come into rehearsal and start by saying 'Good Morning, everybody', to which the response was much shuffling of music and mumbling from the band – nobody wanting to respond too positively. This became a little embarrassing all round and one morning, whilst waiting for him to arrive, it was decided that all the band would stand up and in unison call out 'Good Morning, Sir!' – this was even rehearsed. Unfortunately, just before FVD arrived a clarinet player, Musician Shankland, decided to answer the call of nature. While he was out of the hall some members of the band got cold feet and the word went round 'belay the last pipe'. Shankland returned just in time before Vivian walked in and, as usual, said 'Good Morning, everybody', at which Shankland stood up smartly shouting 'Good Morning, Sir!' The two of them looked at each other until Vivian broke the silence with 'Good Morning, Shankland'. After that, Vivian would always walk in briskly and say 'Good morning everybody and we will take the overture from letter A', or some such.

Captain Tommy Lambert offers these thoughts on Vivian:

> 'I know how much I owe him, and that my success – and I believe it to have been that – as Director of Music in Portsmouth and the Royal Yacht, was due in great part to his guidance and patient tuition. One of the things that must have made life difficult for him was that very few people were able to talk to him in the language that he knew best, that is of music. He was a bon-viveur, always happy to share a joke, to share a good meal and quality wine and to speak of the events of the day.'

On many occasions his guest conducting took him away from Deal; a very happy evening was spent with his old Society in Portsmouth, the Portsmouth Choral Union, at their annual concert of Carols and Christmas Music at the Guildhall in December, when the evening was enhanced by the singing of Rae Woodland, the coloratura soprano, and the addition of the girls' choir from Copnor Modern Girls' School.

The remainder of 1962 was almost non-stop work with the Royal Tournament, followed by the Edinburgh Military Tattoo at which he conducted the combined Massed Bands including the Bands of the 1st & 2nd Battalions, The Parachute Regiment and the Band of the Sikh Regiment. For the Tattoo he composed a quick march dedicated to Brigadier Alastair Maclean which he called *Edinburgh Tattoo – Scottish Airs Selection*. This included the fanfare *Edinburgh Tattoo, Green Grow the Rushes-O, Wullie's Gan tae Melville Castle, Annie Laurie* and *Highland Donald.* There was also a slow march arrangement.

He took the family to Edinburgh and they now included Leonie, her husband and their baby Simon. He was so thrilled by his family's presence there that he announced to the audience that the castle that night contained three generations of the Dunn family together. He even mentioned it on the sleeve notes of the LP that was made of that performance. There was no doubt that Vivian had an immense pride in his family values even if, at times, he appeared too busy to pay them more than a nodding acquaintance. This was not so. He adored his family.

With the official retirement age of 55 years looming, although in 1958 he had been promised an extension to '60 on the retired list', Vivian started thinking about buying a house to secure his future. He had a wide circle of friends living in the Kent/Sussex area, particularly amongst General Duties Royal Marines Officers. After so many years in the Corps, he did not want to settle too far away from his main interests, Deal and London where he could keep in touch with both Royal Marines and the music scene. After a particularly happy holiday in the New Forest, he and Mike were driving home and they passed through Haywards Heath where they spied some new houses being built on the outskirts. And so it was that they settled at West Common, half way between Haywards Heath and Lindfield in Sussex, exchanging contracts in October 1963. When his extension of service till the age of 60 was finally confirmed, the lovely house became a quiet refuge from the hustle and bustle of G House in Deal.

Colonel Warner, Rosey Dunn and Vivian at the Warner Theatre London for the film première of PT 109, *16th August 1963*

Early in 1963 he had the opportunity of conducting at the Portsmouth Guildhall a BBC programme for *Friday Night Is Music Night*. It had been ten fruitful and fulfilling years since he left the city but he was well remembered by the packed house. His upbringing as a classical musician made him sensitive to his own skills as a conductor. One Commandant at Deal remembers him saying that when he was going to conduct a concert, he would spend the whole rail journey memorising the music as he felt that any conductor worth his salt should be able to do just that.

There were also two film premières in London that year at which the band was engaged to perform, *Mutiny on the Bounty* and *We Joined The Navy*, each requiring his own special brand of careful thought, preparation and rehearsal. In addition the band performed Beating Retreat in the Pool of London for the C-in-C Home Fleet's visit to the capital and also played at the United States Marine Corps Birthday celebrations.

It was the custom within NATO that each of the nations in turn is responsible for organising ceremonial and social occasions. That year it was the turn of the British and the Royal Marines School of Music was asked to perform as the country's representatives. Vivian selected a full band and drums of 66 performers and took them himself to Fontainebleau in France, where the focal point of the celebrations was to be the Queen's Birthday Parade. He treated each of the ceremonies as a separate event so that each one could be described as tailor-made, and thus made their final presentation unique to the occasion.

About this time he felt that the winter concerts were so popular and in such great demand, that it was time to build a balcony in the Concert Hall to hold an additional 100 seats. Whilst the builders were doing this, alterations were also made to improve the existing seating and the general facilities. The project was expected to be completed by 1st January 1964 and this entailed the concert performances being transferred to the smaller Globe Theatre in North Barracks – smaller that is for the orchestra. This resulted in one incident which hit the national press.

Because the stage in the theatre was smaller, the orchestra was packed in, causing particular discomfort for the strings. Vivian did not think this was a problem. One Friday, the soloist from the Royal Academy was the pretty young lady violinist, Diana Cummings. Despite clear indications during the morning rehearsal that there was not enough room for her, Vivian refused to cut back on the number of fiddles. During the performance of Paganini's *Concerto for Violin and Orchestra, Op.6*, which Vivian appeared to conduct in a more flamboyant style than usual, he managed to scoop the precious violin from the young lady's grip and it went flying. As the *Daily Express* reported it:

> 'The audience packing the Globe Theatre in the Royal Marines Barracks at Deal, Kent, gasped as the violin hit a corporal bandsman before clattering to the floor. The band stopped playing. The audience practically stopped breathing.
>
> Diana blushed. So did Colonel Dunn as he stepped hastily from his podium, retrieved the £1,000 violin and ordered Diana to play on. Diana's mother said last night, "It was probably the best thing he could have done. He got her playing again before the shock hit her."'

After a perfunctory retuning of the violin, the performance was resumed at a suitable score mark and the conductor, soloist and orchestra completed what must have been more a test of nerve than musical sensitivity. It subsequently transpired that there was comparatively little damage to the violin and it was quickly repaired. The trouble was that the violin had been given to Diana by a Trust and she was still paying for it by instalments. It was reported that the following week he gave the band a lecture on the importance of caring for one's instrument at all times!

Vivian was ever conscious of the music copyright laws. In April 1963, Captain Freddie Stovin-Bradford, Chief of Staff to Flag Officer Air (Home)

Vivian introduces a winter concert in the refurbished concert hall

at Lee-on-Solent, sent a copy of the manuscript of a march he had written to Vivian and asked him if he would arrange it for military band. Having heard it played on the piano, the Royal Naval Flag Officer was enthusiastic and wanted to use it as the official march of the Fleet Air Arm – 'all good robust stuff, giving plenty of scope for the trombones, etc!'

Vivian's reply must have dampened the enthusiasm and pride of Stovin-Bradford as he wrote:

> 'Immediately I saw the opening phrase I thought I ought to send you a recording of a march which I wrote in 1949, *Cannatex*, which is the short title of the Canadian National Exhibition in Toronto. The up-beat of the first double bar and the pattern of the descent of the melody in the first two bars of the first subject are very alike. Likewise the subsequent treatment over the dominant harmony.
>
> I thought I ought to tell you about this because, although *Cannatex* is unpublished, it is recorded on HMV and one has to be careful about the infringement of similarity. Will you please think about this matter and let me have your opinion in due course. I like your idea of using the motif of the bugle call *Hands To Flying Stations* in the introduction, and as you say, the treatment has a strong healthy look.'

Stovin-Bradford was not to be subdued; two days later he wrote saying that he had rewritten the passages suggested and thought that these had actually improved the march and given it more of a swing. Chappells subsequently published the march and it is included on several Royal Marines band recordings.

After this exchange it is interesting to speculate on some of his own 'original' compositions, particularly on his quick marches. There is a hint of Alford in many of them, and his orchestral work *The Young Elizabeth* owes a lot to Peter Warlock. But Vivian was always at his best in arrangements – and he attributed this description to many of them assiduously to avoid any hint of plagiarism.

His strict attention to copyright which might affect his not inconsiderable extra income, over and above his Service pay, and his great appetite for anything that might help his bank balance, was not lost on his juniors. Several stories come to light of this side of his character. One former Director of Music recalls the time he was a bandmaster engaged for a two night gig with the Dance Band at the Dome in Brighton, a comfortable money-earner for the musicians taking part. It transpired that 'Fred', who had appeared at this Rotary International Ball in messkit and danced around for just an hour or so each night, had managed to put himself down for a substantial fee, rather more than any of those who had played for six hours each night. When it came to payment the Bandmaster and several of the band refused to sign for the money, claiming it was in contravention of *Queen's Regulations for the Royal Navy* Chapter 39. Vivian called each miscreant for a personal interview and when they refused his demand that they accept the money they were swiftly dismissed by him to await further developments. The disturbing rumour got round that he was threatening them with Court Martial and there was no place like the School of Music for spreading buzzes quickly. The outcome was eventually resolved through the delicate intervention of the RSM and then the Commanding Officer. The latter interviewed the Bandmaster concerned, who endeavoured to put the record straight, and whilst agreeing that some malpractice had taken place, the CO considered the fault was not due to the Principal Director of Music but the advice he had received. The Bandmaster felt it quite a relief to be posted with his own band to HMS *Lion* soon afterwards. He considered he had got his just reward for conscientious duty. Certainly everyone knew where they stood in the future.

On their Silver Wedding anniversary in 1963 Mike and Vivian were collected from G House and escorted through the barracks

On 30th April Vivian and Mike celebrated their Silver Wedding anniversary. It came as a complete surprise to them both when a car drew up outside G House and they were slowly driven off behind the band playing *The Anniversary Waltz*, followed by a number of Vivian's marches. They processed through the barracks, down Cornwall Road and up the road in South Barracks leading to the officers' mess, where they were treated to lunch. When they left the mess the car was 'drawn' by 10 young Royal Marines, echoing back 25 years to the day that Mike arrived similarly towed to St Andrew's Church, Eastney Barracks for her wedding.

* * * * *

In December 1963 Vivian reached the official retirement age of 55. He was still a substantive Major (Local Lieutenant Colonel), equating in pay with Army Directors of Music of the full rank of Lieutenant Colonel. However, exceptionally, he was offered a further extension of five years to take him to the age of 60. A submission was made to the Second Sea Lord that, in view of his outstanding service, he should be confirmed in the rank of Lieutenant Colonel. In order not to upset the other Services, the Commandant at Kneller Hall, Colonel Tuck, was approached through War Office channels seeking his views and how it would be received in army musical circles. The War Office emphasised that the service which Vivian Dunn has given to the Navy was unique in every respect. Tuck pointed out that, in implying that Dunn would be paid at the same rate as a full Colonel in the Army, it must be made quite clear to all concerned that it was a one time measure only in recognition of 'an exceptional service by an exceptional officer'. He said that they also had some exceptional Directors of Music in the Army and there would no doubt be a protest from Lt Colonel Douglas Pope, but he thought that the responsibilities of the Senior Director of Music of the Household Brigade was in no way comparable to that of Vivian Dunn. He added that Directors of Music are extremely lucky in that they make more money from private engagements than anyone else in the Army – none more so than Douglas Pope! Any question of an increase in rank would thoroughly upset the seniority roll and cause endless discontent. The final memorandum from PS12 in the Army is 'Dunn is an exceptional man and we would certainly not object to his promotion'. Thus it was that Vivian Dunn was promoted to the substantive rank of Lieutenant Colonel (SD)(B) on 31st July 1964.

This mention of Kneller Hall and Army Directors of Music, brings into focus Vivian's close relationship with his opposite numbers in the other two Services. Lieutenant Colonel 'Jiggs' Jaeger, Director of Music, Irish Guards, was a very firm friend, as well as a friendly rival. For major ceremonial occasions in London, they always invited each other and their families to their events. Paddy and Rosemary well remember the lunches with copious quantities of champagne in the Chelsea Barracks mess after Trooping the Colour by the Household Brigade. 'Jiggs' was a perfect host, a great friend of the family and an extremely fine musician. Sadly he passed away in 1970, but Vivian always spoke of him as one of the best and he was sorry to lose such a well-respected and close associate. One story that 'Jiggs' related privately but never to Vivian's face: he said to a companion at a Beat Retreat ceremony, 'You see Vivian over there! He is so good at being at ease with senior officers – something I admire so much'. Much can be construed from this shrewd assessment of Vivian's character. It is interesting to note that on his death, 'Jiggs' Jaeger bequeathed his music collection to the Royal Marines Band Service and not to Kneller Hall.

During the fifties and sixties the Royal Air Force had found itself recruiting from the Corps as they could offer longer and more static careers. One who started life with the Royal Marines was Wing Commander A E Sims who became the Organising Director of Music in the RAF as later did Wing Commander Roy Davies. When the latter retired in 1977, his two senior Directors of Music were Squadron Leaders Vic Hutchinson and John Wagner, both of whom had started their musical careers in the Royal Marines Band Service. The Inter-Services co-operation knew no bounds and it says much for Vivian Dunn's reorganisation and training methods that the Army and RAF often followed his lead.

His close relationship with the senior Directors of Music in the Army and Royal Air Force ensured that there was symmetry when on parade together. From his correspondence it would generally appear that he was the one who formulated ideas and then persuaded the others to fall in line. However there was always some give and take but it did ensure smooth working at national ceremonial events. One such was in October 1963 when he persuaded Lieutenant Colonel 'Jiggs' Jaeger to write to the GOC London District saying that for some years at the Cenotaph Remembrance Service the Trumpeters of the Royal Air Force had sounded the *Last Post*, whilst the Buglers of the Royal Marines had sounded *Reveille*. He pointed out that the *Last Post* was composed essentially for the B Flat bugle, and 'being of different pitch it is a technical impossibility to perform this on the E Flat trumpet, unless certain modifications are made, which distort the original melodic shape of the call as shown on the MS attached'. He claimed that this had caused considerable comment in the past with some well directed protests. He did not say from whom. Jaeger further wrote that 'if the RAF Trumpeters were to play *The Rouse*, which is a legitimate Trumpet call, obviously more suited to the instrument in normal use by the Royal Air Force', he considered it would 'show them off more effectively and allay this anachronism once and for all.' Today it is the Royal Marines who play *Last Post* and the RAF who play *Reveille*, but exactly when the change came about has not been established.

Whilst he kept in close touch with the musical world outside the Royal Marines, it sometimes became a source of irritation to the Commanding Officers at Deal when Vivian dealt directly with outside agencies and senior officers over administrative rather than musical matters. The organisation at Deal was that the Commandant of the Royal Marines School of Music was the Commanding Officer of the Depot Royal Marines. Vivian's role was the Principal Director of Music and was directly answerable to the Commandant. His long friendship with Earl Mountbatten, who often rang him up personally, resulted in some friction when he did not always keep his Commanding Officer in the picture. This was particularly so during Tercentenary Year when Mountbatten was Chief of the Defence Staff, and the Commandant sometimes felt himself sidelined over matters for which he was ultimately responsible.

Captain Ted Whealing was a young musician in the Deal Band during this period and recollects:

> 'As a very lowly member of the orchestra in Deal I do recall the abject terror on the faces of hapless trainee Bandmasters and Band SNCOs when FVD entered the Concert Hall. Sometimes he would come in after the rehearsal had started. The trainee conductor, at first blissfully unaware, would be hacking his way through a piece when FVD came in by the back door and sit in the middle of the raised seats at the rear of the hall. The orchestra, of course, would see him but usually gave no indication to the poor conductor! The first he would know of the great man's presence would be the slow double clap of his hands, at which the orchestra would immediately stop playing and a wild look of panic would usually cross the conductor's face. Vivian would then ask something like "what did you think of the playing before the letter D?" The conductor would be in a no-win situation; if he pointed out some mistake he knew he should have spotted it before; if he could not spot anything wrong, he was in for a roasting in front of all hands. Very few could stand up to this treatment.'

* * * * *

The 28th October 1964 marked the 300th anniversary of the formation of the Royal Marines. The following twelve months were obviously to be an occasion for the maximum of ceremonial opportunities and Vivian was forever thinking up new ideas. The year augured well when new and superior string instruments were issued to the band at Admiralty expense. These had been very carefully chosen with the object of enhancing the string tone of the orchestras. As a violinist himself Vivian took the greatest interest in their selection and, as was his wont, ensured that nothing would be second best, even if it was not quite within the budget allowed.

Early in the year the Commandant General Royal Marines, General Sir Malcolm Cartwright-Taylor rang Vivian to say he was having his arm twisted by the Chief of the Defence Staff to adopt *The Preobrajensky March* as the Corps Slow March. He asked if Vivian could produce a tape for Earl Mountbatten to play to the Captain General, Prince Philip. Vivian duly made a new arrangement, updated from the one he had made in 1934, and sent it to CGRM for presentation to Mountbatten to take to the Palace. He added that he thought it would be right and proper for the Corps to have such a fine march officially adopted. Prince Philip's reported reaction was 'Yes, that sounds fine, and I like the Dunn'd up version!' There was no doubt that Mountbatten never let go of an idea and had not really forgiven the Corps for rejecting the march in 1934.

The main events of Tercentenary year were to take place in London during the summer of 1964 with the Royal Marines exercising their traditional right to march through the City with Colours flying, bands playing and bayonets fixed on 22nd July. On the following day Her Majesty The Queen attended a Royal Review at Buckingham Palace, whilst there was a Thanksgiving Service in St Paul's Cathedral on the 24th, where a Royal Marines symphony orchestra of 60 would combine with the Memorial Trumpets, the cathedral choir and organ. These events coincided with the Massed Bands' participation in the Royal Tournament. Vivian oversaw the extraordinarily complicated administration of this week, though he left it to his Directors of Music and staff officers to work out the details.

The first major event was Beating Retreat on Horse Guards Parade on 10th June to honour the birthday of the Captain General, HRH Prince Philip, Duke of Edinburgh, with more than 400 musicians on parade. New and complicated manoeuvres had been dreamt up by the planners and Vivian took exceptional care to ensure the best possible musical programme. He had decided to write a new quick march for the occasion and he came up with *The Admiral's Regiment*, one that has certainly stood the test of time. The score for this march states:

> 'Composed for the Tercentenary of the Royal Marines and first performed by the Massed Bands of the Royal Marines (400 strong) Beating Retreat on Horse Guards Parade, 10th June 1964, in honour of the birthday of HRH Prince Philip, Duke of Edinburgh, Captain General RM. Dated 3rd April 1964.'

For the first time his new arrangement of *The Preobrajensky March* was used as the Troop, the piece that was to become the Royal Marines' official

Beating Retreat 10th June 1964 in the presence of HRH *The Duke of Edinburgh, Captain General Royal Marines*

Slow March. The score of the march was actually presented to the Captain General immediately prior to the ceremony. After the performance, Earl Mountbatten wrote to Vivian on 15th June:

> 'I flew back specially from Paris after the morning's meetings to attend the great ceremony on Horse Guards Parade on Wednesday afternoon. It was well worth the trip for I have never heard a finer performance, or one that thrilled me more. I must have seen Royal Marines bands perform for something like sixty years, first in my father's ships and then in my own, but this was the all-time tops.
>
> I think the "Dunned up" version of *The Preobrajensky March* is really excellent. I was standing next to The Queen and Her Majesty thought it quite outstanding and most moving.
>
> Thank you so much for having taken so much trouble about it. I am delighted that it has now passed into the permanent possession of the Corps, as the official slow march. I handed the music that you had prepared to HRH The Captain General, to pass it on to the Commandant General, just before the ceremony; no doubt you will see a copy of the photograph which was taken on this occasion.'

Earl Mountbatten had inscribed the flyleaf of the score with the words:

> 'My uncle, the Grand Duke Serge Alexandrovitch of Russia, was one of the last Colonels of the Preobrajensky Guards – the Senior Regiment of the Imperial Russian Footguards. King Alfonso XIII of Spain, who married my first cousin, Victoria Eugenie of Battenberg, took an interest, on account of this connection, in this Regiment, and acquired the Music, which he in due course presented to me.
>
> Since 1941 this March has been played by all Royal Marines bands serving under my command. On the occasion of the Tercentenary of the Royal Marines, this Music is presented to them through their Captain General, Prince Philip, Duke of Edinburgh, who also has the above mentioned relationships.
>
> I am proud that it has now been decided to accept *The Preobrajensky March* as the Royal Marines Slow March.'

Vivian was delighted at the response to *The Preobrajensky March* as he was always aware that it was not as easy on the ear as the previous Corps slow march, *The Globe and Laurel.* He once heard one of his musicians whistling it and immediately wrote to Earl Mountbatten assuring him 'that the tune was catching on!' It is interesting to note that a military band version of *The Preobrajensky March* had existed since the last century as it was played by the Guards Band at the Queen's Birthday Parade on Horse Guards on 26th May 1889. Subsequently the first eight bars played in quick time was adopted as the official musical salute for Royal Marines General Officers and it is also frequently used during the Trooping the Colour ceremonies as a slow march in its own right.

This Beating Retreat was followed immediately by rehearsals for the Royal Tournament, in which the Massed Bands were playing an even more prominent part than usual. Vivian was always seeking new ideas for his public displays. In his meticulous preparation, Vivian had set out to devise a new way of showing off the versatility of his band in all its forms. He produced an elaborate plan. The initial entrance and marching display would be by the Massed Bands. On their exit from the arena, leaving the Corps of Drums manoeuvring with ceremonial drum beatings, the band would quickly change to orchestral instruments and take up positions on a mobile concert platform mounted on four lorries. These would be driven into the arena with the orchestra seated, about one third of the way up the arena to give a long view. The piece he had in mind to play was a suitably cut version of the brilliant march movement from Tchaikowsky's *Symphony No.6 'Pathétique'*, which would allow a tremendous wealth of sound and lots of scope for impact. His plan was for this orchestral playing to be superseded by two further lorries bearing his excellent dance band, the *Oceanaires*, driven in from the two angled entrances at the opposite end to the main entrance. He reckoned that, by the use of skilful lighting the symphony orchestra could be withdrawn during the dance band session and quickly reappear as the Massed Bands for a triumphant finale. This was a brilliant new concept, which he kept under close wraps. However it did not come off for various reasons, some of them financial, but it did materialise in a slightly different form four years later, at his final Royal Tournament.

Although he was disappointed that his new concept had not come to fruition, he accepted it in view of the enormous pressures that had been put on the Band Service during Tercentenary Year. However he ensured that the Royal Tournament programme did contain many new and intricate drill movements and unfortunately for the hard working and perspiring musicians the summer proved to be one of the hottest for many years.

The performances at the Royal Tournament were 'interrupted' by yet more Tercentenary events. On 23rd July, Her Majesty The Queen and The

Captain General, dined with the officers of the Royal Marines in the Painted Hall at the Royal Naval College Greenwich. Vivian had carefully thought out the programme of music for the small orchestra that played during the dinner. It was at this dinner, of course, that the Royal Marines were granted the privilege of drinking the Loyal Toast seated, a suggestion prompted during the meal by Earl Mountbatten. Vivian was invited to take port with Her Majesty after the dinner, along with Captain Paul Neville, who had conducted the orchestra. Then came one of Vivian's moments of showmanship brilliance. He had made a special arrangement of Handel's *Music for the Royal Fireworks* for the occasion. As the Royal Party and the officers moved onto the steps of the colonnade facing the Grand Parade, the first rocket sent a cascading scatter of Corps colours and the orchestra played the first notes. The resulting display with its whoosh of rockets, whizzbangs, explosions, its pony tails of sparks and bursts of colour were supplemented by the wonderful music in the warm summer evening. His timing was impeccable; the orchestra reached the final climactic flourish as the last traces of fireworks died away. This was specifically commented upon by HM The Queen in her letter of thanks to the Commandant General.

The following day, Friday 24th July, there was the Corps Thanksgiving Service in St Paul's Cathedral at which Vivian conducted the orchestra of 60 which accompanied the cathedral choir and organ. It was on occasions such as this that Vivian excelled in getting the very best out of his musicians. They lifted themselves and their playing for this great occasion and this was a measure of his flair as a conductor. And there were still two nights of the Royal Tournament to go!

Later that year Vivian took the band back to Greenwich for the Trafalgar Night Dinner – the last to be held during Earl Mountbatten's tenure as Chief of the Defence Staff. For the occasion, Vivian had visited the College earlier to select and train a choir of officers in a specially arranged programme of *Sea Songs and Shanties*. He wrote:

> 'It was quite something to hear that lovely hall resound with the full assembly enthusiastically joining in. After this little party was over, we downed one lot of instruments and picked up others to Beat Retreat in the Grand Square. From all accounts our efforts were appreciated, especially by the foreigners who were seeing and hearing such a presentation for the first time.'

* * * * *

During the year Vivian was in correspondence with Leo Ricketts, the son of Kenneth Alford, over a programme for the BBC to be recorded as a tribute to Major F J Ricketts. We have seen how Vivian had studied his works assiduously at Eastney before the war, and although he had played his marches regularly, he now had the opportunity to acclaim his mentor. He was invited to contribute a large input into the script and the recording went very well.

It was also in 1964 that Vivian was elected President of the Royal Academy of Music Club; he decided to use his year in office to widen members' knowledge of military band music. In November he conducted the Staff Band in a programme at the Academy which he entitled *'The Art of the Military Band'*. He thought very carefully over whether it should be an orchestral concert to show off the prowess of his Royal Marines players, or a military band concert. He came down firmly in favour of the latter as he felt that, however good the orchestra, the Academy audience would hear nothing new, and the Royal Marines could hardly be expected to match the orchestral playing the Academy did every day. The military band was something they did not hear ordinarily and they probably did not appreciate the tremendous scope it had when done very well. He chose some very difficult works requiring expert technique, three of them being original works for the military band, *A Gaelic Fantasy*: *Songs of the Gael* by B Walton O'Donnell, which had been his audition piece when he joined the Royal Marines, *Suite Français* by Darius Milhaud and *Music for a Festival* by Gordon Jacob. The concert was attended by Earl Mountbatten, for whom he played *Malta GC* by Sir Arnold Bax, and many other distinguished guests. Vivian subsequently wrote that it was his object to lead his band to the highest pinnacle of attainment in everything they did. 'I was extremely proud to have been privileged to take the Royal Marines Band Service into our most august musical institution on such an occasion. If I had some small measure of success', he wrote modestly, 'it is because I believe in them and they believe in me.'

When his successful year as President of the RAM Club was announced, Guy Johnson, who had been a new student at the Academy in 1930, wrote in their house magazine:

> 'One of my earliest impressions upon entering the RAM as a student in 1930 is that of a tall and strikingly handsome young man then in the last term of his studentship who, in the role of Chorus-master of the Opera Class, already wielded the power of authority ... We

> are singularly honoured to have as our President this year one who not only is a person of great distinction and charm but is a practical and truly professional musician of the highest musical ideals.'

His perfect dress sense both in uniform and in civilian clothes was envied by all. He ensured his Directors of Music and Bandmasters followed his example, one that continues to the present day. It was therefore quite a surprise one day to see him emerge from the officers' mess at Deal, shortly after the new lovat uniform had been introduced. The band were rehearsing a marching display on South Green, dressed in the new uniform, which Vivian never really took to as he felt it made him look portly. He was also, unusually, wearing a beret instead of his accustomed peaked cap. Drum Major Charlie Bowden was in charge. Captain Ted Whealing remembers the incident:

> 'We saw him come out of the Mess and stand by the tennis courts. We thought he looked different but could not place why. After a few minutes Charlie marched smartly over to the Principal Director, saluted and a short but animated conversation took place during which Charlie reached across and changed the drop of FVD's beret from the left side to the right side!'

Apart from his regular engagements as the President of the RAM Club, to whom he dedicated the fanfare *For a Distinguished Assembly,* he managed to get approval, after a lot of hard bargaining, for a new set of silver fanfare trumpets. In addition, and with the collusion of his old friend Clarence Raybould, he was able to enlarge the music library at Deal particularly with orchestral scores. In due course this would expand the range of works the orchestra were able to play and extend the musical knowledge of the musicians. To complement all this he managed to obtain a grant from the Navy Department for the latest stereo sound recording system for use in rehearsals. For the first time he was able to have an 'instant replay' of music that had just been played for immediate study. This was in keeping with his forward thinking role as the Principal Director of Music, not encumbered by regular daily rehearsals. Another addition to the band at that time was the introduction of navy blue capes for musicians and buglers. He even drew one from the stores for himself, but he does not appear ever to have worn it. Instead he had always had a tailor-made boat cloak with a magnificent crimson lining.

Early in 1965 came the death of Sir Winston Churchill, and the Royal Marines provided four bands for the funeral. The Portsmouth and School of Music bands, totalling 112 musicians, were in the procession, while the Plymouth Band provided the music for the Royal Naval guard of honour at Tower Hill and the C-in-C Home Fleet's Band were stationed near Horse Guards arch.

* * * * *

Advance planning for overseas tours often started nearly two years in advance and even though there were so many major events in the Corps' Tercentenary Year, work had to start on the programme for the following year. It had been in April 1964 that Vivian had written to Brigadier Alastair Maclean, the director of the Edinburgh Tattoo, about the following year's event. It had already been agreed that a Royal Marines band of about eighty would tour Canada and the United States in 1965, immediately following their appearance at Edinburgh. Firstly he suggested that the Pipes and Drums of the Scots Guards and Royal Scots Greys, who were accompanying the Royal Marines to Canada, should also be part of their display at Edinburgh. In addition he considered that the last time the Massed Bands were at Edinburgh in 1962, the total of 200 musicians, including the Bands of the 1st & 2nd Battalions, The Parachute Regiment, was too unwieldy and it had been difficult for the outside flanks to maintain accurate dressing at the narrow end of the arena. Although he had performed these sort of displays for many years in all parts of the world, it showed the minute detail in which he felt it necessary to be personally involved. And these small, and seemingly unimportant points, often made the difference between the very highly polished display that we always saw, and the sort of 'not quite so good' result that sometimes occurred when the organisers were over-ambitious. With his experience he usually got his way, even with the sometimes testy Maclean, with whom he had a great personal friendship. Maclean was a magnificent organiser and director of major events, and Vivian wrote to him about his shows saying that he maintained the 'tradition and majesty of the Service with a touch of Show-biz. This is a highly developed art and very personal to you alone'.

The Edinburgh Tattoo was the only occasion that he and his son Paddy served together, the latter having been seconded as Brigadier Alastair

Maclean's temporary assistant for the Tattoo. He particularly remembers his father wearing his boat cloak for performances as it was a very damp year. He writes:

> 'In fact my father perfected the art of conducting in it with at least half of the crimson showing across his shoulder like Dracula, a most dramatic spectacle especially for television audiences, particularly when he "flourished" it as he raised his baton.'

After the rather damp fortnight in Edinburgh the band were granted 48 hours leave. Although the musicians were glad to have a break, they were more than disgruntled when told they had to take this short leave in Edinburgh, especially as many of the rehearsals for the tour had been during their normal 'time off'.

This was to be the band's first ever official tour of the United States, although bands had visited the New World on one-off engagements before. Vivian's love and respect for the United States Marine Corps bands was well known and now he had the opportunity to savour it to the full. As early as 23rd September history was made when the bands of the two Marine Corps performed together in the USMC Barracks in Washington. Once again Vivian had planned the programme, taking care not to impose too much British military music on his hosts, but ensuring that plenty of our own marches were played. He wrote a large number of compositions and arrangements for this tour, putting in many hours of burning the midnight oil. One of these was a post-horn and coach-horn sextet called *Jorrock's Chase*, for which he got Boosey & Hawkes to make three coach-horns which were pitched in C and convertible to B flat.

The itinerary was as hard and as comprehensive as time and money would allow, with visits to Toronto, Ottawa, Montreal, New York, Philadelphia, Boston, Detroit, Chicago and many others. As with the Edinburgh Tattoo, Brigadier Alastair Maclean was the director and co-ordinator and he and Vivian formed a fine, understanding team. He took his younger daughter, Rosemary, with him as his secretary. They soon found out that the American audiences were very critical and playing in such venues as Madison Square Gardens, Carnegie Hall and Boston Gardens was a treat and a challenge. But Vivian was just as capable of meeting that challenge as he had enormous faith in the musical ability of his band, all 75 of them. This tour probably illustrates the overwhelming respect he had for his band producing the goods. In their turn the musicians respected him for

Vivian lays a wreath on the grave of John Philip Sousa during the tour of USA and Canada in 1965. Drum Major Charles Bowden is extreme right.

pushing them to their limits to achieve such excellent results. It was all about partnership, understanding and working together.

It was also during his tour that he was presented with a framed citation by the Mannes College of Music for 'Master Classes conducted in the Recital hall by Lt Col F Vivian Dunn and the Royal Marines Band, 1965'. Rosey remembers meeting the authoress Monica Dickens who was married to a naval officer, and being invited to their home in Boston. It was while they were there that they met Rose and Joan Kennedy after they had attended one of the concerts. In the official report afterwards, Rosey is described as the ideal secretary and she certainly worked very hard to gain that accolade.

The band had the honour of playing a morning concert at the famous Carnegie Hall in New York. Along with the Pipes and Drums of the Royal Scots Greys and the Scots Guards, and The British Columbia Highland Lassies, Vivian conducted the Royal Marines School of Music in a programme of predominantly British music including his own new composition *Jorrock's Chase*. This was warmly acclaimed by the American audience as was the traditional Sunset finale, although it was only midday! Another popular item during the tour was the Royal Marines Motor Cycle Display Team which played a prominent part.

Whilst the band was in Washington the second time, Vivian led a small contingent of his Drum Major, Charles Bowden and his five Bandmasters to pay their respects at the grave of John Philip Sousa, a man whose works he so much admired. He was always most insistent that as the band worked hard, long hours, they should enjoy as much relaxation as possible and he was as generous with his time off as he was with the work imposed during rehearsals.

Vivian was not always best served by non-musicians, recalls Captain Ted Whealing. It was during this tour that the band was to give a performance at the United States Marines Corps Barracks at Quantico in Virginia. The band was waiting in the wings ready for their first entry playing Kenneth Alford's *H M Jollies*. Unfortunately Brigadier Maclean had decided to do all the announcements and had not hoisted in the fact that 'jollies' in common US Service slang referred to breasts. He then proceeded to Vivian's total embarrassment by adding to the script, and instead of using the 'H M' in the title of the march, announced 'The Royal Marines Band will now enter the arena playing Her Majesty's Jollies!' – and the band marched on for the first ever time to derisive hoots of laughter from some 4,000 US Marines.

One aspect of the Canadian and American tour which left Vivian in a poorer light was over the question of payment for the many Category IV (Private) engagements that took place. When the not inconsiderable proceeds of the tour were being paid out, his assistant Director of Music found his share was no bigger than the highest musician. He marched in to Vivian to complain, receiving the reply that as he had not been officially appointed his 'deputy' he could not receive an appropriate slice, despite having done so much to ensure the smooth running of the whole tour.

* * * * *

For a long time Vivian had pondered about some form of tangible recognition for his musicians, comparing their opportunities with those of the regular marine – not, of course, the financial aspects. Whilst the young regular recruit always had the King's Badge, granted in 1918, to aim at, his young musicians only had music prizes, such as the Cassells Prize. He floated the idea that recognition for the Band Service might come in the form of the Captain General's Cypher to be worn on the tunics of musicians. He realised that any such proposal would have to be most carefully and tactfully made and he enlisted the advice of Major General Sir Robert Neville, who had been Governor of the Bahamas after his retirement from the Corps, and was also closely associated with The Duke of Edinburgh. Although the idea was raised from time to time, nothing came of it until ten years after Vivian's retirement. In 1978, Prince Philip decreed that, to mark his 25th year as the Captain General, there should be instituted the Prince's Badge awarded to the best all round musician or bugler completing training in the year and worn on the upper left sleeve throughout his service. It can be pondered as to whether the initial seed had been planted by Vivian all those years beforehand.

The relationship that had developed between Earl Mountbatten and Vivian Dunn was now very strong indeed and it had become firmer through the Tercentenary Year and *The Preobrajensky March*. Earl Mountbatten was due to retire as Chief of the Defence Staff in the summer of 1965 and he invited Vivian and Mike to a farewell party at Broadlands. In his invitation letter Mountbatten mentioned that the C-in-C Portsmouth had kindly lent him the Portsmouth Command and HMS *St Vincent* Bands to play during the party and Beat Retreat at the end. He continued:

> 'If you are able to come to the party I would be grateful if you could keep an eye on the arrangements as regards music programme, etc., for this my last official occasion with the Royal Marines bands. However it is a long way from Deal and I do not expect you to specially come over from that distance but you might be visiting Portsmouth at that time anyhow.'

In his reply of acceptance Vivian said that he had put it down in his diary as an important event with which 'nothing will be allowed to interfere.' He offered his assistance in any way and hoped that the circumstances would allow that the Royal Yacht Band might be available to supplement the other two bands. However, he pointed out, if the Royal Yacht Band is available that Captain Paul Neville should be in command, instead of the C-in-C's Bandmaster Lieutenant Roy Nash.

His rapport with Earl Mountbatten was very close as the latter had a strong appreciation of music and a keen sense of humour. He loved recounting the story of how, when as Chief of the Defence Staff he was inspecting one of his bands, he asked Vivian for a question he might ask one of the musicians to show off his musical knowledge. Vivian suggested that, faced with a brass player, he might ask 'How is your *embouchure?*' (the art of placing the mouthpiece on the lips). The trombone player to whom the question was directed, far from being taken aback at such a question, answered as quick as a flash, 'Fine, sir! How's yours?' Often when they met later Mountbatten would jokingly ask Vivian 'How's your *embouchure?*'

Vivian was disappointed not to be at Eastney on 27th October 1965, as he was still with the band in America, when Admiral of the Fleet, the Earl Mountbatten of Burma, was installed as the first Life Colonel Commandant of the Royal Marines. However he was extremely pleased that this new post had been specially created for such a champion of the Corps. One cannot help thinking that the liaison and friendship that had been built up between the Royal Marines Band Service and the Earl had quite a significant bearing on the granting of this honour.

Later in his retirement Earl Mountbatten could not let the Royal Marines bands 'get away' with anything, and he used Vivian as his sounding board. At one Romsey Show, held in the grounds of Broadlands, a certain Royal Marines band which had been engaged for the show omitted the playing of *The Preobrajensky March* in their programme. Mountbatten was severely displeased and Vivian had to sort out the ensuing wrangles. There was no doubt whose side he was on!

One of Vivian's principles for Directors of Music was that they should not remain too long with their bands and that they should be moved from time to time to breathe fresh ideas into their work. 1966 was one such year when many of his senior Directors of Music were 'orbiting'. Another innovation he introduced was that musicians on discharge should be entitled to purchase the instruments that they had had on personal loan during their service. He had argued for some time for this change as he felt it would make serving musicians respect and take care of their instruments better, knowing they would be able to keep them on retirement. It would also ensure a continual supply of new and improved instruments coming into the Band Service. It was also in 1966 that SNCOs started to wear scarlet mess dress similar to that worn by the officers. Vivian, with his flair for showmanship, thought this was an excellent step as it allowed his non-commissioned Bandmasters a chance to stand out when they were conducting against the blue of the band.

Another major problem that Vivian had to face in 1966 was that of recruiting. The entry age for Junior Musicians was to be raised from 14 to 15 on 1st April along with other branches of the Services. This was the result of the government's plans to raise the school leaving age. One of the immediate results of this edict was that the Royal Marines had to recruit 100 Junior Musicians in the year instead of the usual 50 and Vivian was afraid that this might lower the standard of those entering. His own policy was that nothing whatsoever would induce him to take in musicians of inferior quality even if this meant a shortfall.

One of his enduring and little praised qualities was his love and encouragement of youth. We have already seen how he and Mike welcomed junior band ranks without being too patronising. It was on one Corps Remembrance Day that the Royal Marines Cadets from Chatham received a letter from the Depot saying they could not be included in the parade at Deal as usual. Their unit Chairman, Colonel Archie Wright, was incensed and soon had the order reversed. They were told that they would be allowed to participate, along with the RMR, RMA and the regular Corps but would not be allowed to march past to the Regimental March. Vivian was sent a copy of this order and found it bewildering. He always had a lot of time for young men who might want to join the Royal Marines in due course. However he decided to comply, but demonstrated his flexibility and cunning by changing to *Sarie Marais* when the cadets marched past. Alan Jordan, who commanded the Chatham Cadets at that time, remembers this warmly and with pride, adding that it was clear from his actions that Vivian had a total commitment for these youngsters who might be the Royal Marines of the future, and more importantly, members of the Corps family.

As often as he could he sallied forth on the golf course, particularly the Royal Cinque Ports. On one occasion he took the son of his great friend Gerry Ross round the course, the young officer Lieutenant Robin Ross being a housemaster in the Junior Wing at Deal. The latter recalls that it was a very demanding course and Vivian, older and wiser, and as always an exemplar of good manners, calmed the nerves of the young man by electing to drive off first at the first tee. Immediately to the right, at ninety degrees, is a small hut where the caddies took shelter and basked in the sun. Vivian took an almighty swing at the ball, completely miscued and it went off the toe of his club scattering the caddies sitting on the bench. The caddies, also being old and wise in these matters were perfectly confident that lightning never struck in the same place twice and resumed their seats. They were wrong; he did it again!

His younger daughter Rosemary was married to John Foster at St Michael and All Angels, the Depot Church, on 1st October 1966. Once again he wrote original music specially for her which was played by a small orchestra at the service.

Towards the end of the year, he had the opportunity of meeting up with his old friend Eric Fenby whom he had 'saved' from military service during the war. Eric now visited Deal as the representative of the Royal Academy of Music on the board of examiners for the Director of Music and Bandmaster examinations. It was during his visit that Fenby presented a copy of his book *Delius as I Knew Him* inscribed 'Vivian Dunn, in token of kind hospitality at the Royal Marines School of Music and best wishes from the author'.

* * * * *

As 1967 approached, Vivian came to realise that this would be his last full year of service. Thoughts naturally turned once again to his successor. As we have seen he had already picked out Captain Paul Neville many years before as his most likely replacement. There was, of course, no Staff College course for Directors of Music. He felt that, with all the opportunities he had had himself of learning music in the fountain of knowledge amongst the greatest musicians and concerts that Great Britain could offer, his successor ought to have a similar, but necessarily shorter, period in London. He enlisted the aid of the Corps Honorary Adviser in Music, Sir Malcolm Sargent, and between them they arranged a one year's musical sabbatical for his successor. Paul Neville recalls his visit to meet Sir Malcolm in Albert Hall Mansions. Along with the PDM, he wore a regulation dark suit, bowler hat and carried a rolled umbrella and, in the taxi en route, Vivian insisted that they stop to buy two pink carnation buttonholes.

The Admiralty eventually approved this arrangement but not before a civil servant in the Ministry of Defence objected to the description 'sabbatical', which was in common use in universities, on the grounds that the Finance Department might regard the detachment as a glorified 'swan' and an unacceptable expense on the Navy Estimates. Vivian adds:

> 'A "study period" was substituted which Sir Malcolm and I privately accepted knowing that, as long as it was approved, it was a case of – "A rose by any other name smells just as sweet!" We often laughed about it and to those whom it affected, and the Commandant General Royal Marines' staff, "sabbatical" is the reference that continues to apply, even if not in official documents.'

In organising the year one of his first considerations was to turn to where his own roots began, the BBC. He arranged that Neville should be allowed unobtrusive attendance at rehearsals of the BBC Symphony and other orchestras, as well as free entry to the Promenade Concerts. He managed to arrange similar facilities with the Royal Opera House, Covent Garden, using his contacts from the past liberally. Here was the 'old boy network' working overtime ensuring his successor would be able to learn about and appreciate the London musical scene. In all this he was helped and, indeed, encouraged by the office of the Commandant General in supplying certain funds for this, besides allowing a year off for the designated next Principal Director of Music.

Paul Neville was promoted to local Major in July 1967 in readiness to take over from Vivian in 18 months time. It had been a difficult choice for Vivian, as a similarly-aged and equally talented musician had also been in the running, Peter Sumner. He too had worked closely with Vivian, firstly as his Supply Officer (Music), subsequently being promoted to Captain in 1961 and becoming Director of Music of the Junior Wing for five years. There was very little to choose between them. Peter Sumner, writing later of those times, confirms a similar encounter to that which Paul Neville had had with the Dunn family on holiday:

> 'I think the fondest memory my wife and I have of him was when I was the Director of Music at Portsmouth and Vivian and Mike invited us and our family to join them when he was caravanning in the New Forest. To see Vivian in shorts and an old pair of plimsolls, playing with my children and thoroughly enjoying himself was a revelation. This was a side of him that had hitherto been quite unknown to me, and it was wonderful.

I shall never forget his warm understanding of my problems when I decided to retire prematurely. He knew and sympathised with my frustration at the fact that I could never attain the pinnacle of Principal Director. He realised that my job with the C-in-C Fleet's Band was keeping me away from home and my teenage children needed me there. He wrote me an excellent reference for the teaching post for which I had applied and wished me well.'

1967 was another Beating Retreat year on Horse Guards Parade, the last of Vivian's 'reign'. With just over 300 musicians on parade and perfect weather it was once again a resounding success. He would have liked to compose a new march for this farewell occasion, but neither the inspiration came nor was the time available. As we have seen, he found it very hard work to compose music that was satisfactory to his own high standards, and he was certainly not going to produce anything that was only 'fairly good'. On the other hand he did compose a bugle fanfare *Freedom of the City* and a fanfare for bugles, trumpets and band entitled *For a Royal Birthday.*

One new feature of this Beat Retreat was noted favourably when his old friend Major General Sir Robert Neville wrote to him 'Ever since I heard the Russian bands burst into song, I have always wished that we might introduce it into the programme.' Vivian had decided that Elgar's *I Vow To Thee My Country* should be sung by the band and he trained them for it. The band were not quite so sure and their singing was so ragged that he threatened to stop their weekend leave. This produced a remarkable effect and it forged ahead as planned during rehearsals at Deal. However many of his band officers expressed their doubts about the singing being heard in the vast expanse of Horse Guards Parade, and he was eventually persuaded to drop the idea. It would seem that General Neville must have been present at a rehearsal where they did burst into song, and not at the London ceremony on 8th June.

Of this Beating Retreat Vivian later paid tribute to all those whose work had made it a success. He wrote:

'I am happy to say that the weather was perfect and the ceremony acclaimed as the best we have ever done. This was due to the efforts of the planning committee formed by Directors of Music Royal Marines and the immense amount of hard work contributed by all

> ranks taking part. During the years that I have been responsible for the Massed Bands activities of the Band Service I have never known such dedicated work put into the preparation by the members of the various bands. Never on any occasion was there a lack of effort and resoluteness from one single man and I wish to pay my tribute to all for the loyalty and response that I was privileged to receive.'

His love of the Unites States of America had been rekindled during the summer when he was invited by Dr Russell L Wiley, the Director of Bands at Kansas University to be the guest conductor and lecturer for three weeks at Beaumont and Kansas. The reason for the invitation was that it was the custom for the music and art departments of American universities to hold Summer Camps after the end of term. These were attended by young musical students. Lamar State College in Beaumont had 650 young musicians on their course for a week, while at Kansas there were 870 taking part in a six week long course in all forms of musical appreciation and instruction. Vivian found himself conducting a symphony orchestra of 110 one day and a concert orchestra of 90 the next. He found it a rewarding experience and he appreciated that the Americans were quick to recognise ability and develop it to its natural conclusion.

Afterwards he endeavoured to compare these young American students with his own Royal Marines Junior Musicians. He said that in comparison with young players in this country (excluding the Royal Schools and our RM Band Service) he felt generally the standard in the USA was higher at the comparable age levels because they began younger and worked harder during their formative years. However in the age group 18 to 20 our own Royal Marines instrumentalists compared very favourably with a definite advantage in tone and resonance; likewise in the bass and euphonium sections. He considered that our rich quality had the edge over their baritones and sousaphones, some of the latter being made of lightweight plastic which could not compare with its brass counterpart.

On this tour he met Paul Gray for the first time when he collected Vivian from Kansas City Airport and they became great friends over the following years. Paul was the conductor of the 312th Army Reserve Band and had invited Vivian to be guest conductor. Indeed Vivian stayed with the Grays on many future occasions and he later became godfather to their daughter Tacy. It was somewhere he could relax away from the public eye.

Paul recalls the occasion that Vivian gave them a bottle of Drambuie as a housewarming gift. They decided to broach it straight away and Paul filled up eight ounce glasses with it, and then proceeded to drink his down right away. Vivian sat and sipped his. Paul understood why when he realised he couldn't stand up. They called their drinking sessions 'score reading' and they spent many happy evenings together.

Some years later, on another visit to the Grays, Vivian wanted to get his hair cut and Paul took him along to his own barber where they were told there would be a short wait. It was very hot and Vivian was dying for a drink. On being told there was a pop-machine in the back, he spent some time hovering over the machine which seemed to be a maze just to find where to put a quarter in. He eventually returned with a drink and sat down to wait. When the barber saw him he exclaimed 'That Goddam Limey's drinking my last beer!' It seems he had hidden a beer under all the soft drinks for the end of his day and somehow Vivian had copped it.

Paul Gray wrote that Vivian had a tremendous musical influence on him; he had guided and shaped his character, more than any other person that he had known. This is repeated very often in similar tributes from those in the United States. No wonder he was such an ambassador for Great Britain.

After this brief tour, he was invited to be the guest conductor with the United States Navy Band, the USMC Band, the United States Army Band and the USAF Band at the Watergate and Capitol in Washington, DC. This would have been a unique occasion as no foreigner had ever been invited to conduct all the principal military bands in succession. Unfortunately his visit was sadly cut short by the death of his brother Geoffrey and he flew home for the funeral.

This was yet another sad occasion as the two brothers had been very close even though Vivian was somewhat older. Although geography prevented them from seeing more of each other they had been bound in brotherhood by their common love and dedication to music. Vivian and 'Chiffer' had managed to meet only occasionally in London and had been closer than many realised.

* * * * *

In November he received a letter from Earl Mountbatten, now retired as Chief of the Defence Staff, which included:

> 'I am sure you will be delighted to hear that Peter Morley, the producer of the television series of my life and times, has firmly decided to use *The Preobrajensky March* as played by your band at Deal as the theme music for the series. I hope this will popularise the Royal Marines bands as well as the music and the tune.'

The subject of the 12 part television series had arisen more than a year earlier when Earl Mountbatten had visited Deal as the first Life Colonel Commandant of the Royal Marines. He had arranged with Peter Morley to send a film crew to cover his visit and was anxious to get some good footage to use as an introduction. Writing privately to Vivian, Mountbatten said that he was responsible for suggesting the idea of using 'a good shot of as big and smart a Royal Marines band doing a slow march and playing *The Preobrajensky March*'. He added 'I am so keen that the Royal Marines Band should get the greatest possible publicity on TV, and therefore I hope you will be able to arrange an adequate number of musicians to put up a fine show.'

Thus 34 years after he first offered the score to the Royal Marines, Mountbatten, through Vivian, had found a way of bringing this music to a wider audience. Indeed his tremendous support and friendship with Vivian did much to enhance the reputation of the Band Service and to ensure that it was always in the public eye.

Yet another sad occasion later that year was the death of the Corps' Honorary Adviser in Music, Sir Malcolm Sargent. He attended the funeral at Stamford Parish Church and later the memorial service in Westminster Abbey. The appointment of Sir Malcolm had been made partially at Vivian's behest and it had heralded the introduction of the sabbatical year and an even closer liaison with the Royal Academy and the London musical scene.

Vivian now entered his final year in the Corps and he was determined to make the most of it. His diary was overfull as he prepared himself for a musical life outside the Corps which he had served so well for 36 years. Another visit to the United States was planned as well as his dining out of the Corps at Eastney.

An interesting visit by the Minister of Defence, Gerry Reynolds, took place in January in which Vivian was able to show off his 'empire'. Shortly afterwards his old friend Leon Goossens, one of the country's greatest oboists, played in a winter concert with the band, and Vivian used his interest and contacts to host a visit from the BBC Music Quiz show *Strike a Note* in which three Royal Marines musicians pitched their knowledge against three professionals, Harry Rabinowitz, Ernest Tomlinson and George Chisholm, with Steve Race as adjudicator.

Vivian's annual inspection of Royal Marines bands did not often include the farthest flung. However he took this last opportunity to visit HMS *Terror*'s and 3rd Commando Brigade bands in Singapore, where he was able to see at first hand their working environment and he was also presented with a mounted Commando dagger. During his farewell visit to Lympstone he opened and named the new Ricketts Hall, a fitting tribute to one of his greatest mentors.

One of the last marches he wrote whilst serving was the *Holbrook March* for the Royal Hospital School in Suffolk. This came as a request from the former, long-serving Secretary to the Admiralty, Sir John Lang, in April 1967. Because of other engagements Vivian was not able to complete the march until early 1968, which coincided with a visit by HM The Queen Mother. Following a meeting between Sir John, Vivian and the Headmaster, several ideas were discussed including the possibility of basing the march on a Suffolk folk song. Several tunes were suggested but in the end he decided to write an entirely original composition and he said 'he hoped to make it a worthy swan-song, as it were.' He then discovered to his dismay that the school band's instrumentation was 1st, 2nd & 3rd B flat cornets, 1st & 2nd E flat tenor horns, 1st & 2nd baritones, 1st & 2nd B flat trombones, B flat euphonium and E flat bombardons, plus bugles. This was a challenge for anyone. Vivian then suggested writing words, but the Headmaster tactfully declined the offer, being very aware of what small boys could do to the words of any song. Unfortunately Vivian was in the United States for the first performance, but he made sure he found an opportunity to take the band, which was already well rehearsed, through his march.

Another visit to Boosey & Hawkes factory was made, not only for discussions on the latest trend in instrument design, but also to cement the strong relations he had built up with this great firm, with whom his son

Paddy had worked for a period. He also arranged for yet another visit for Junior Musicians to visit Boosey & Hawkes later in the year.

Conducting at the Royal Tournament 1968

After his failure to get his ambitious plans into fruition for the 1964 Royal Tournament, Vivian was even more determined to succeed in his last appearance at Earls Court. He started planning a year ahead and by November 1967 was able to put his ideas on paper. Briefly they were to commence with an opening by eighty bugles and drums in a three minute display, followed by a Symphony Orchestra of ninety musicians playing the last movement of *The New World Symphony* by Dvorak, the march movement from Tchaikowsky's *6th Symphony* and his *Tarantella* from *Capriccio Italien*, being rounded off with Elgar's *Pomp and Circumstance March No 1*, the whole lasting five minutes. The *Oceanaires* Dance Band of sixteen players would then take over for four minutes and the display would culminate with the Massed Bands of 200 for the last eight minutes. He considered the music to be played very carefully as he felt they must avoid trying to educate the public or be accused of being too clever. Ultimately the Massed Bands marched into the arena to his *Tribute to Alford*, an arrangement of five of the composer's best known marches. The only worry was whether the Dance Band would appear too small in such a vast arena. For the 80 buglers on parade, he wrote yet another bugle march *Bugles and Drums*.

The day after the last night of the Royal Tournament, Vivian left for America yet again at the invitation of Kansas University where he spent two weeks as their guest conductor. He was amused by a story told by the

Dean of Kansas who had enquired of some of his students what they thought of Colonel Dunn. The answer came back 'Gee – he's fine, and he talks just like the Beatles!' This was immediately followed by the invitation which he had received the previous year but had not been able to fulfil, that of conducting the four major military bands in the USA in Washington, DC. He was the first foreigner to be so honoured.

His son Paddy (Patrick) was married to Ann Crook at the Depot Royal Marines Deal church on 30th March 1968. His practice of writing or arranging wedding music for the family continued. He scored an arrangement which he called *Wedding Music for Patrick and Ann,* based on Paddy's old school song *Carmen Carthusianum* and *Annie Laurie* for full orchestra. Although never recorded at that time, Captain David Cole has recently done so, and it is a stunning piece of music.

A tribute to John Philip Sousa came when, for the final time whilst serving, he made a studio recorded LP *'The Royal Marines Play Sousa'* under the EMI label. Brian Culverhouse who had been his recording producer for the past 15 years, reveals:

> 'It so happened that I was selected from the HMV Company's recording producers to ensure that the company had a new catalogue of well-known marches and I felt that, despite my own service in the Grenadier Guards, the ideal choice for the project would be the Royal Marines bands.
>
> I was invited by Colonel Dunn to visit the School of Music at Deal to listen to the band and discuss the programme in detail. It was indeed an eye-opener for me to observe the comprehensive training that every musician receives there and the meticulous manner in which Col Dunn was preparing the band for the recording. The programme was agreed upon and the recording sessions took place at the end of which I was a complete convert to the world of the military band and have been an ardent advocate ever since.'

During their fifteen years working together they made thirteen LPs covering every facet of the band's repertoire and it was hailed as an annual event to which they both looked forward. After some three weeks of rehearsals at Deal, Vivian would take his band up to the largest of the HMV studios at Abbey Road, St John's Wood and they usually took about 9 hours to do the actual recording. On one occasion the Beatles preceded the Royal Marines recording and Vivian sat through part of their session.

He was absolutely horrified at the number of 'takes' and technical 'enhancements' required to achieve a finished piece.

Brian Culverhouse pays tribute to Vivian's meticulous attention to detail during rehearsals as being the key to the success. The two men built up an understanding and rapport which they both valued greatly. As a special tribute, their last Royal Marines recording together was made in Guildford Cathedral in the weeks before Vivian retired. It was appropriately titled *'Music of Pomp and Circumstance'*. It contained many of Vivian's favourite pieces and he described it as:

> 'This recording presents a new sound not previously heard to any great extent anywhere in the world – the combination of band and organ in a specially designed programme. The tonal qualities of each lend themselves excellently to such a partnership, as the brilliance and sonority of the band blend perfectly with the grandeur of the organ. The lovely acoustic properties of the beautiful cathedral enhance the sound to a remarkable degree, making the performance an exhilarating, sumptuous and rewarding experience. The programme is devoted entirely to English music and the works are ideally suited to the imaginative treatment that was conceived.'

In his sleeve notes to the recording he was able to pay generous tribute to his two great friends, praising the talented young organist, Barry Rose, and EMI's Brian Culverhouse for his shrewd judgement, inspiration and enlightened ideas which had achieved so much during their 15 years collaboration together. Their co-operation did not end there as, after Vivian had retired, Brian Culverhouse became his producer when he made recordings with the Light Music Society, Bournemouth Symphony and other orchestras in the 1970s.

Earl Mountbatten was the Guest of Honour at the 1968 Band Service Reunion at Eastney. This, as always, was an all ranks dinner on 21st September 1968, and the last to be attended by Vivian as the Principal Director. The Drill Shed had been fitted out with an awning and striped red and yellow bunting covering the strutted roof, multicoloured chandeliers, masses of flowers and almost fully carpeted. It had been transformed beyond all recognition. 243 members past and present of the Royal Marines Band Service gathered for this memorable evening, along with many distinguished guests from the regular Corps, Directors of

The Band Service reunion dinner 21st September 1968. Earl Mountbatten was the chief guest and Charles Bowden the Master of Ceremonies.

Music from the Army and RAF, representatives of the Royal Academy of Music, Boosey & Hawkes and others. Drum Major Charlie Bowden was the Master of Ceremonies for the evening.

After the Loyal Toasts, Lieutenant Tom Merrett proposed the toast 'Absent Friends'. Then the principal speaker of the evening, Earl Mountbatten, gathered the assembled company around him and paid tribute both to the Band Service and to the retiring Colonel Dunn, finishing with the appropriate pun 'Well done, Dunn, or if preferred – Dunn, well done.' Vivian replied, recounting his own 37 years service in the Royal Marines, and thanking the Corps for giving him the privilege of serving four sovereigns in the Royal Yacht and tendering his gratitude to all those musicians who had given of their best to make the Royal Marines Band Service the finest in the world. He ended by wishing Paul Neville every success, saying that he was confident that he would receive the same support and loyalty that he himself had been so fortunate to enjoy.

* * * * *

In his final message to his beloved Band Service in their magazine *The Blue Band* Vivian wrote:

'It has been my privilege to serve the finest Corps and certainly the finest Band Service in the world and looking back over the long span of 37 years of my service, a host of memories recur which remind me it has all been thrilling and very worthwhile. I believe that I belong to a happy band of brothers which has made me say that I would gladly do it all over again. I have always been fortunate to have very splendid people around me and to work with. Therefore I wish to pay the greatest tribute and give my sincere thanks to the Officers, Senior NCOs, Junior NCOs, Musicians, Junior Musicians, Professors, Instructors and last, but by no means least, my long suffering Secretaries who have supported me in all my endeavours. Likewise to the succession of Commandants of the RMSM, and the officers and all ranks of our great Corps with whom I have been proud to serve.

My work has always been a challenge to me as my aim has been to make the Royal Marines Band Service second to none. Others must judge whether this ideal has been achieved but I know that all, without exception, have worked very hard and with the greatest goodwill to attain this. I know, also, that I have always been utterly uncompromising in my demands to live up to the very highest standards. I have never offered any apology for this because to my mind nothing can ever be accomplished if it does not bear the stamp of endeavour, perseverance, loyalty and dedication to match professional skill. My good fortune has been to receive all these marvellous qualities in abundance from the most senior to the junior ranks. My gratitude therefore knows no bounds as in addition to all this there has been a bestowal of friendship and cheerful understanding which transforms hard work into an ultimate pleasure.

Any tribute that I pay would be incomplete without praise for the noble Corps of Drums of the Royal Marines. In company with the members of the Band Service I count them among my best friends and it must never be forgotten that their sheer determination and skill, when set even the severest task, has brought a distinction to our bands that stamp them as unique.

The culmination of my work, I have realised, has come in three main events. Beating Retreat on Horse Guards Parade during the Tercentenary Celebrations in 1964, when the largest Massed Bands in our history was produced, and again in 1967 with slightly smaller numbers. But thirdly and particularly the Royal Tournament, 1968. This involved the widest range of our playing roles and undoubtedly it was a great tribute to be able to present a new look *Finale* in the shape of a quadruple display by the Corps of Drums, Symphony Orchestra, *Oceanaires* Dance Orchestra and Massed Bands. All in twenty minutes aided and abetted by the willing backroom boys led by Captain Robin Patteson-Knight RM and Sergeant Lewis Toyne. At each of these performances the will to achieve has been tremendous and the remarkable thing is that I have never once seen a sour expression or a single reluctant dragon in spite of the magnitude of the undertaking.

Saying goodbye is never easy and I was deeply touched by the kindness and sincerity of my leave taking when visiting the bands in Singapore earlier this year. I fear that my words of thanks are very inadequate but I wish all serving members to know how much I appreciate their wholehearted and wonderful co-operation and the ex-members to realise what makes things possible in these days.'

In saying their own farewell to Colonel Dunn, *The Blue Band* thanked Mike for being the 'finest liaison officer that ever was', a liaison officer between the top brass and the spit and polish. Mike always had an ear for even the most humble of junior musician. In her 30 years of marriage, the last 15 years at Deal, she had witnessed that miracle peculiar to military schools of music and the Royal Marines in particular, the transition of the raw recruit into a more than competent musician. She was on Christian name terms with many of them and they regarded her with genuine affection. She was always on hand behind the scenes at pantomimes and plays enthusiastically helping with make-up, prompting or handing out mugs of coffee. At a farewell concert given by the Junior Musicians, Mike was presented with a gold bracelet from the Junior Musicians and teaching staff at the School. The inscription read affectionately:

'To Mrs M J [sic] Dunn
From My Boys and The Staff of Junior Wing'.

The Blue Band's editorial offered their sentiments and feelings in one word 'Ichabod', which the *Oxford English Dictionary* explains as 'glory to the departed'.

During his 37 years in the Royal Marines, the last 15 at Deal as the first ever Principal Director of Music Royal Marines, Vivian was acknowledged to be in a different class to anyone else in the Royal Marines Band Service or any military band in the country for that matter. He was always at his best rehearsing and conducting. He was probably at his worst when dealing with subordinates, especially over non-musical matters. He never really worked out the rank structure other than that the rest of the Band Service was junior to him. He was often rude in public to Commissioned Band Officers and showed few of them any lasting friendship. However, surprisingly few ever showed any long-term resentment.

Many felt that, after more than ten years at the helm he ought to have accepted some of the shortcomings of the old Band Service, and that there should be a lighter touch at the tiller. He seemed incapable of accepting this and there is clear evidence that the only person in whom he could truly confide was Drum Major Charlie Bowden, which created a degree of antipathy from many band ranks.

What most people overlook is that, unlike all other Royal Marines and Band Service officers, he had received no formal military training, except the few weeks of parade ground work and some military lectures which he had volunteered to attend when he first joined. All he had to fall back on was his extensive musical training, and it is not surprising that his ideas of leadership were somewhat old fashioned. His man management skills, in common with a lot of musicians, were not in tune with those of his military counterparts. His success derived almost entirely from his musical prowess and certainly not from his abilities as an administrator.

It was also true from the tributes of so many band officers, that they owed their whole career to the support, encouragement and guidance that Vivian imbued. This, coupled with a sense of pride, professionalism and musical achievement was what most will remember. However hard they were pushed, or even bullied, Vivian's all-powerful influence made the musicians and the Band Service what it is today.

At his farewell Guest Night in the officers' mess at Deal, with many of his family around him, he was 'serenaded' after dinner by his Directors of Music and band officers. Between them they did not make the most balanced combination, and many of them were a little rusty in their instrumental ability. Vivian was invited to conduct them in a newly scored piece and, despite his efforts at controlling them with the baton, the erstwhile 'musicians' took it upon themselves to play *stringendo!* The result

Vivian conducts the Directors of Music and others at his dining out from Deal, September 1968. Left to right: Tom Merrett (hidden), Jim Mason, David Hathaway-Jones, Roy Nash, Paul Neville, Leo Arnold, Bert Farlow, George Manuel (standing), Wally Shillito, Ray Woodfield (hidden), Tom Lambert, Malcolm Cavan, Peter Sumner, Dick Place, Chris Taylor (hidden) and Doug Haigh.

Vivian presents the Horse Guards painting to the Officers' Mess

was not quite up to the standard of musicianship he had striven for during his service, but it was a nostalgic evening. He presented the officers' mess with a specially commissioned painting of the 1964 Beating Retreat on Horse Guards Parade. This now hangs in the office of the Principal Director of Music at Headquarters Band Service Royal Marines in HMS *Nelson*, Portsmouth.

Before he finally retired he wrote a comprehensive appreciation of the duties and responsibilities of the Principal Director of Music in the light of his fifteen years in the appointment. It is a well thought out and considered document, but in it one can see touches of the 'do as I say' attitude, rather than the 'do as I do' philosophy. He wrote at length on administration, promoting some excellent ideals, but in his own years in the job, he had been found lacking on several counts. However his emphasis on paying the utmost attention to detail in all matters was certainly one which he totally upheld himself. His description of using the winter concerts at Deal as 'match practice' gives a glimmer of his own love and dedication to sport.

His conclusion that the principles upon which any PDM should work were to be an optimist and never a pessimist; to be positive and never negative; and to be completely dedicated to your work. These ideals have been practised by all the subsequent Principal Directors. Words of wisdom indeed.

In saying his farewells and visiting all the departments, he arrived at the office of the Supply Officer (Music). Here he reluctantly handed in his ceremonial band cape, not really worn as he had always preferred his 'Dracula' boat cloak. This was subsequently reissued to the newly promoted Lieutenant Graham Hoskins. On suggesting that he might be measured for a new one, the young Director of Music was promptly told that he was being ungrateful. Was he not aware of the intrinsic value of this cape, hardly worn; and that if he was ever to set out to walk to France whilst wearing it, he would safely make it to the other side! 'Our Father, which art in Deal'!

Vivian and Mike left G House in Deal with mixed feelings. Retirement is never easy to contemplate, but after so many years of living in an official residence, Mike was particularly looking forward to moving into her own house, the one they had bought in Haywards Heath in 1963. It had been let for some time, but now it was to be their family home. It had already been decided that a studio should be built onto the house, and into this moved the mini piano, the stereo, a desk, typewriter and a mountain of Royal Marines band memorabilia. Drum Major Charlie Bowden and his wife Betty spent a considerable amount of their spare time travelling up from Deal to get everything shipshape. Betty made a wonderful collage of RM and US bands' badges and insignia which when hung covered the whole back wall.

Before he left Deal as Principal Director of Music he paid tribute to his secretaries, who undoubtedly took the brunt of the administrative work load and his occasional outbursts. He recounts that one who has already been named in this story was once asked 'What does FRAM stand for?' He was given the reply 'Fred's Right 'And Man!'

CHAPTER 7

Cadenza - Fulfilment and Challenge

One week after his official retirement date, his 60th birthday, Vivian was honoured in the New Year's Honours 1969 with a Knighthood in the Royal Victorian Order – the first military musician ever to achieve this. To Vivian it came as the fulfilment of more than 37 years of service in the Royal Marines. Perhaps Earl Mountbatten's congratulatory letter reveals more than he actually says:

> My Dear Vivian,
> No Knighthood in the Royal Victorian Order has given me so much pleasure as the KCVO The Queen had conferred on you in the New Year's Honours. Please accept my heartfelt congratulations.
>
> You were the first and only Officer of the Royal Marine Band Service ever to have been made a substantive Lieutenant Colonel and now you are certainly the first Officer in any of the Band Services of the three Services to receive a Knighthood on the termination of your career.
>
> I am sure you realise that all the rules and regulations lay down that nobody below the rank of Major General, and preferably Lieutenant General, can receive a Knighthood. It is therefore a true measure of the exceptional services you have rendered to military music in the widest possible sense that this recognition has come to you.
>
> Added to this there is the fact that the Royal Victorian Order is in the personal gift of The Queen to recognise services to Her Majesty. The services you have personally given both as Director of Music in the *Gothic* and on board *Britannia* and later as Principal Director of Music in arranging the bands and programmes for all Her

> Majesty's trips form the solid basis for this award but I am sure this will give the greatest possible pleasure throughout the country.
>
> When I introduced you to the Editor of the *Daily Mirror* I took the liberty of telling him in strict confidence that there were strong hopes that your exceptional services would be recognised in this remarkable way and I hope he will not have forgotten this.
>
> Finally, let me thank you for your charming letter of 19th December. My son-in-law, Lord Brabourne, told me that of the many letters of thanks which I had received he considered yours was by far the most intelligent and perceptive. I agree with him.
>
> With all best wishes to you for the New Year and for your new career in civil life.
>
> Yours very sincerely
>
> Mountbatten of Burma

In his telegraphic reply, Vivian merely said 'Very proud of KCVO. There is no doubt whom I must thank. Best Wishes for spectacular success of your Television series.'

But there was much more behind this, as Mountbatten had almost 'spilled the beans' when they met at the première of the new television serial *The Life and Times of Earl Mountbatten* on 18th December. Vivian later said he had misconstrued the Earl's congratulatory remark on this occasion, thinking it referred to a possible appointment as Honorary Colonel Commandant of the Royal Marines Band Service. In reading through Vivian's citation for his KCVO, the hand of Mountbatten is quite clearly seen in the wording and praise.

The summary and recommendation for his knighthood included:

> 'There is no doubt that in the past fifteen years Lieutenant Colonel Dunn has transformed the Royal Marines Band Service. The fine reputation once enjoyed is now immeasurably more so. The inspiration and influence he has untiringly given the Band Service has yielded great dividends and the Band Service is one of which the Royal Marines are jealously proud.
>
> It is now some 14 years since Lieutenant Colonel Dunn was rewarded by her Majesty for his personal services and yet he has continued to direct his energies to that end. As the Principal Director of Music, Royal Marines, Lieutenant Colonel Dunn has exceeded all

> that could be expected of him. He is well known, both nationally and internationally, and his reputation as a Director of Music is unique in the three Services.
>
> It is recommended that the outstanding service which Lieutenant Colonel Dunn has continued to give to the Royal Marines, coupled with devoted personal service to Her Majesty The Queen and other members of the Royal family are such that Her Majesty the Queen may wish to consider further rewarding his efforts before final retirement in December 1968. Such a reward to the most outstanding military Director of Music of his day would delight the Military Music world of all three Services.'

On the day of his investiture at Buckingham Palace, Vivian shared the glory with another eminent musician, Dr Arthur Bliss, Master of the Queen's Music, who was being similarly knighted with the KCVO. Two famous musicians similarly honoured on the same day was indeed a rarity. Mike, Paddy and Rosey accompanied him to the Palace, as Leonie and her family were living in Zambia at the time.

One of his Directors of Music, Captain Tom Lambert wrote about Vivian that he had the extraordinary capacity for turning a very ordinary player into a really good player. It was a mixture of encouragement, bullying and hypnotic magnetism. Many a musician in the Staff Band at Deal who performed in the winter concerts was transformed by a session of what Lambert nicknamed 'the mangleyisation box'. This was a small room at the back of he concert hall into which Vivian summoned musicians of whatever rank, with the crook of his finger, if he thought they were not giving of their best. He 'mangle-ised' them with a verbal lashing that made the culprit ashamed at their lack of capacity, or their inattention. Lambert recalls that few musicians survived more than three or four of these tongue-lashings without a very considerable improvement in their performance.

Just a month after his official retirement, on 29th January 1969, Vivian was accorded a reception at the EMI headquarters in London, supposedly, he thought, to mark his retirement. He was surprised but pleased to hear that Earl Mountbatten was to be there and indeed they arrived in the same car. He was even more surprised to be ushered in first and be received by a fanfare from the Royal Marines School of Music Fanfare Trumpets.

Earl Mountbatten presents an EMI Gold Disc to Sir Vivian on 29th January 1969

Rather like television's *This Is Your Life* he found himself surrounded by a large gathering of famous people, representatives of the musical profession, many personal friends and his family who had all been let into the secret. Amongst the guests from the musical world were Sir Adrian Boult and Mr Harry Mortimer, while Admiral Sir David Luce and Lieutenant General Peter Hellings, the Commandant General Royal Marines were among the senior Service chiefs.

After a welcome and introduction from Sir Joseph Lockwood, the chairman of EMI, Earl Mountbatten, wearing his Corps tie, presented Vivian with a Golden Disc with the words 'Don't drop it, old boy ... it's solid gold!' Vivian was completely taken aback, being entirely unaware of this great occasion and the honour being bestowed upon him. The disc was to mark the sale of over one million records by bands of the Royal Marines.

Believing it to be a simple farewell party, he had prepared what he described as a totally inadequate response, but he was very quick to emphasise that it was not through his efforts alone that EMI had so honoured him but that it was equally as much for the Royal Marines Band

Service. He said that it should be kept by the Band Service, and it is now on display in the band room of the Royal Marines Museum. He wrote about this momentous day:

> 'I wish to do honour to the splendid band and the many fine instrumentalists whose musicianly skill and dedication to the demanding tasks over the years it was my privilege to be associated with. Each and everyone one of them will, no doubt, remember that I never believed in leaving anything to chance and that I made great demands on them at rehearsal. Perhaps from their point of view to an exhausting degree. I knew from long experience that every player must not only be able to play his part perfectly but belong and contribute to an ensemble of sound whose quality of tone and balance had the stamp and distinction of the Royal Marines. I am grateful for the unstinting support that I have always received because I am sure everyone realised, in spite of the hard work, that recording is the highest form of our art and the most rewarding.
>
> It takes really fine players, who play with a wonderful sense of goodwill, to make records and they must have great belief in their work. In addition there must be an infinite capacity for the big match temperament to reach the highlights just when required, aided by an element of luck and the ability to "catch it while it is flying!" Atmosphere and the right feeling are essential and often humorous happenings or a few cryptic remarks make all the difference in relieving the technical tension, smoothing difficulties and paving the way for a performance that has the stamp of class. In this specialised field, to play well is minimal, to play superbly, with its tremendous physical and artistic demands, comes from being what we are – Royal Marines musicians who are proud of their accomplishments. Only better than the best is good enough.'

Soon after his retirement the Commandant General wrote to Vivian in March 1969 and invited him to become the Honorary Colonel Commandant of the Royal Marines Band Service and Honorary Adviser in Music to the Royal Marines. He accepted this with some aplomb, being particularly thrilled at the thought of following Sir Malcolm Sargent in the latter role, there having been no such appointment since his death in 1967. Although Vivian had a letter of congratulation from Earl Mountbatten, his appointment was never confirmed.

Far from retiring at Haywards Heath Vivian quickly got down to work. The writing of *The Mountbatten March* was prompted by a short note in March from the former Chief of the Defence Staff saying that he had received a letter from Musician B Hobbs, serving at Deal, asking his approval to name a march after him to be called *Mountbatten*. He wrote to Vivian:

> 'My reason for writing to you is that you may remember having told me in confidence at the dinner at Eastney that it was your aim after your retirement, and you had time to write a march, to call it *Mountbatten*. If this is still your aim clearly you have priority in every sense of the word and could I then have your permission to tell Hobbs my reason for refusing the request.
>
> On the other hand you may not have felt any inspiration and may not be wishing to go through with your original suggestion which was only a tentative one, in which case I propose to accept Hobbs' request.'

The thought of someone else writing a march dedicated to his great mentor, spurred Vivian into action. Of course he was still contemplating writing such a march, but he claimed he had not yet found the right musical inspiration. Indeed it was almost exactly a year later before he sent a photocopy of the pianoforte score to Broadlands and expressed concern about the exact wording of the title. He said that, after consulting a number of people the preferred title was *The Mountbatten March*, with *Earl Mountbatten* second choice and just plain *Mountbatten* third. He emphasised that the preferred title had the correct dignity, does not follow any other pattern, like the marches *Viscount Nelson* or *Trafalgar* and most important for posterity, was sufficiently brief to come easily to mind. There was no doubt that at that time he had not found the right tune, as he had already written two marches which he described as 'quite good in themselves, but were not sufficiently individual to you'. He intended to write a march that would stand the test of time, and from past experience of his marches this might seem a fifty-fifty chance.

His strength had always been in arrangements, using identifiable tunes and then giving them a strong march theme, coupled with an interesting trio. Thus it was that he decided that he would try to incorporate the four major aspects of Mountbatten's career – Admiral of the Fleet, Life Colonel Commandant of the Royal Marines, Colonel and Gold Stick of the Life Guards. He felt he should not lean too heavily on any particular one, but wrote an introduction of eight bars with snatches of *Rule Britannia*,

A Life on the Ocean Wave and the *Slow March* of the Life Guards. The trio was predominantly *The Preobrajensky March*, while the other pieces were woven into the later sections. In justifying this hotch-potch of tunes without much originality, he said that his principal themes were entirely original and that he had cunningly and tastefully treated the 'reference tunes' without over-stressing them. His aim was to create a march for marching and ceremonial purposes with a strong impact in the classical style. He felt that the key to the march must be an impression of greatness; in other words 'a mighty march' – his words. He also appreciated that it had to have a catchy quality to give it durability. He also told Mountbatten that it would never be produced until he had the Earl's complete approval.*

By March 1970, Vivian had completed the new march and then had a private recording made by the Band of the Royal Marines School of Music in May, sending a copy to Earl Mountbatten saying that 'it was recorded at 7½" and it had been played twice through to save him rewinding the tape.' Unfortunately Mountbatten's tape recorder only had speeds of 3¾" and 1⅞ths. By an oversight he played it through at 3¾" and wrote 'I was very sad to find it turned out to be a rather doleful slow march'. He soon borrowed a recorder with the right speed and wrote to Vivian saying how very pleased and proud he was, even though 'the reference to *The Preobrajensky March* is more difficult to distinguish'.

Unfortunately it was too late to include *The Mountbatten March* in that year's Beating Retreat, but it was played by the Massed Bands privately when Earl Mountbatten visited Deal on 5th June to witness the final rehearsal of the programme for Beat Retreat. It had its first public showing the following year at the 1971 Royal Tournament and the first recording was made at the Festival Concert of Brass Band Championships at the Royal Albert Hall Concert on 22nd April 1972 in the presence of Earl Mountbatten, when Vivian was invited to be one of the conductors. Prior to this he had written to Mr F C Buttress of WD & HO Wills, who sponsored the championships, saying the fanfare *Flourish of Trumpets* had been specially commissioned by them for the record and to herald the arrival of Earl Mountbatten at the concert. At the last minute its title was changed to the more appropriate *Supreme Command* and was conducted by Harry Mortimer.

---

* This march is discussed by Major Gordon Turner in Appendix B,

Four winning teams from the best of British brass band music combined to give this memorable concert, along with the Luton Girls Choir. Vivian shared the conducting with the great brass band conductor, Harry Mortimer. It was two further years before there was a Royal Marines recording of it when Captain Jim Mason with the Band of the C-in-C Naval Home Command included it on his Polydor label record *'Famous British Marches'*.

During Vivian's retirement years he undertook a considerable amount of work with Harry Mortimer in his promotion of brass bands, and acted as an adjudicator on many occasions at the annual Brass Band Championships at the Royal Albert Hall.

* * * * *

We have already seen that Vivian had very little time for such matters as tax returns, leaving his financial affairs entirely in the hands of an old school friend and later his accountant Alan Cowdy. Through the years they exchanged some highly amusing correspondence. Only weeks after Vivian left the Royal Marines Alan wrote to him as follows:

> Dear Vivian,
> HM Inspector of Taxes Dover to HM Inspector of Taxes Cardiff:
> "Any signs of Dunn's current return form yet?"
> HM Inspector of Taxes Cardiff to HM Inspector of Taxes Dover:
> "You must be joking. Did you ever get it less than ten months overdue?"
> HM Inspector of Taxes Dover to Secretary:
> "This man ought to get knotted"
> Literal minded Secretary to Board of Inland Revenue:
> "HM Inspector of Taxes recommends Dunn for getting knotted"
> Board of Inland Revenue:
> "Corrected message to Chancellor – Dunn recommended for getting knitted"
> Chancellor to H Wilson . . . .
> If only Wilson had said "Oh Lord" at that point, you might have got a life peerage!

Whatever the cause, my warmest congratulations. I won't even charge you for writing this letter.

Yours sincerely

Alan

PS: But all future fees at time and a half, of course!

And later that month on the 20th January 1969, Alan Cowdy wrote:

Many thanks for your letter – now back to work.

(1) A photocopy of the Revenue's advance reply to your request for a moratorium is enclosed:

Whether Portsmouth or Oxford or Thame
Every damn year it's the same
You're put down for appeal
In Dover or Deal
And poor old A.C. gets the blame

(2) You are not entitled to your Post War credits. The fact that your actual certificates are undoubtedly lost doesn't matter – fill up the enclosed form and let me have it back

(3) As you will now be engaged on your memoirs, I thought you would like your oldest tax assessment – for 1930/31. It seems to relate to a period before you joined the Services. In spite of the low tax rates, the tax in relation to income seems pretty steep. I don't think it's worth appealing now.

etc, etc.

Paddy says his father was the most appalling example of how not to conduct one's personal administration, to the extent that he loathed paperwork and simply could not be persuaded to even look at his bank statements or deal with the elementary essentials of bills payment and cheques paying in. (Even in 1998 Paddy was still finding unpresented royalty cheques dating back to the 1950s.)

* * * * *

As can be seen Vivian had no intention of withdrawing from the music scene in his retirement and soon offers to be guest conductor at concerts throughout the country began to pour in. It was his classical orchestral conducting that was in demand as much as his military band expertise.

Coupled to this was his love and deep knowledge of choral singing. One such concert in aid of the Malcolm Sargent Cancer Fund took place at the City Hall, Newcastle-upon-Tyne on 22nd November 1969, when he found himself on the platform alongside his old friend Harry Mortimer, with the stage filled with the Low Fell Ladies Choir, the Hexham Male Voice Choir, the Prudoe Gillemen, and three colliery bands from Easington, Craghead and Harton and Westoe. In the programme was Vivian's *Salutation: Tribute to Sir Malcolm Sargent* which he had written for fanfare trumpets and full orchestra in February 1969 and was played at the inaugural Royal Albert Hall concert. Vivian was always willing to conduct charity concerts in aid of the Malcolm Sargent Cancer Fund For Children, and he devoted a lot of time and energy to promoting this cause.

Earlier that year on 6th September he had been an adjudicator at the British Open Brass Band Contest at the King's Hall, Manchester, along with Gilbert Vintner and John Carr. This was his first adjudication in these championships and it turned out to be quite a marathon all day affair which required careful listening and total concentration while the 21 competing bands went through their paces.

* * * * *

After his retirement Vivian was asked on a number of occasions how the title of 'Her Majesty's Royal Marines' came about. Although he racked his brains he was never quite sure. However he did write:

> 'The title "The Band of HM Royal Marines" raises an interesting question as it is, strictly speaking, incorrect and should be "The Band of the Royal Marines".
>
> I never wished to raise the question as to the authenticity of the prefix HM, nor have I ever done so; since its application to the Royal Marines dates from the late 1920s or early 1930s. It adds distinction to our title and we are the only service to which it applies by custom.
>
> There is a connection through the nickname given to the Corps by the Royal Navy – perpetuated by the march of the same name by Kenneth J Alford – *H M Jollies*, and I believe it is through this association it was never queried by the Royal Marines when advertising the appearance of the bands. The Corps never uses such a prefix.
>
> Its origin can be attributed to a Mr A.E.V. Dennis, who was entertainments manager at Eastbourne at that time and added the

> prefix (for dignified reasons) publicising all Service bands playing at that resort. It is a fact, however, that an order was promulgated by the Army Council prohibiting such use for Army bands and has remained so to this day.'

Whilst this explanation may not be the ultimate answer, it is yet one more example of how traditions come about, and is now, over 70 years later, lost in the antiquities of time.

On 6th November 1971 Vivian was honoured in a rather different way by being invited to be Roy Plomley's guest on *Desert Island Discs*. His eight pieces of music he described as a choice of nostalgia. He wanted to hear extracts from pieces of music that meant a lot to him at particular times in his life. There was no great surprise that his first choice should be the wonderful chorus *Praise to the Holiest in the Height* from Sir Edward Elgar's *The Dream of Gerontius*', conducted by Sir Malcolm Sargent, all aspects of which had such a profound and long lasting influence on his life.

His second choice went back to his Queen's Hall days when he recalled Wednesday nights, which was always Bach night. He said that Sir Henry Wood used to produce a number of arrangements of his own, and the show piece which always brought the house down was the *Prelude* from Bach's *E Major Partita* for solo violin. Vivian had, it may be remembered, chosen this sonata when he auditioned for the BBC Symphony Orchestra over forty years earlier. His third choice also came from his student days but in a rather different vein. In the late twenties the young musicians were intrigued by the world of jazz and he bought a record which he played over and over again until it wore out. He then wrote the music down and played it himself. He described it as a marvellous piece of wonderful, stylish fiddle playing by Joe Venuti entitled *Wild Cat.*

It was inevitable, of course, that Vivian chose *The Preobrajensky March* of which he had not only made the definitive arrangement but also it had the Mountbatten and Royal Marines associations. His fifth was also predictable, but in introducing *A Life on the Ocean Wave*, he remarked that it was one of those tunes which has a marvellous lift to it, it seems to take the weight off your shoulders and is so easy to whistle and sing. But he added that as he had the privilege of serving in the Royal Marines for so long it meant a great deal to him personally.

His sixth choice recalled one of his many lasting friendships. It was Robert Farnon's *À La Claire Fontaine* played by the orchestra of the Light Music Society conducted by himself. He described it as a wonderful example of the composer's work which had something ethereally beautiful about it, satisfying his musical appetite. In turn the composer publicly acclaimed Vivian's recording of this famous piece as by far the finest he had heard. For his penultimate choice he said that he had one great favourite amongst the classical repertoire, *Jupiter – the Bringer of Jollity* from the *Planets Suite* by Gustav Holst. He chose it because it brought back memories of his time in the BBC Symphony Orchestra under Dr Adrian Boult, and it was a piece that has tremendous excitement, ebullience and marvellous writing. Both these pieces were subsequently played at Vivian's Memorial Service.

For his final choice, he returned to Royal music and picked the splendour and majesty of sound in William Walton's *Crown Imperial* march. It had to be played by his own band of the Royal Marines with himself conducting. When asked to pick just one among the eight, he had no hesitation in choosing *The Dream of Gerontius*, a recurring favourite throughout his life. There was certainly no room for Ravel's *Bolero*! As a luxury item he asked for a piano stool, complete with an upright piano, but inside the stool there would have to be plenty of manuscript paper, a number of pencils and a good supply of rubber. And a pen, too!

There is an irony in his love/hate relationship with Ravel's *Bolero*, a piece which he had specially arranged for military band for the first post-war Eastney Tattoo. Mike loved it, but Vivian found it began to pall. It is related by one of his successors as Principal Director that there was an occasion when Vivian was conducting the overlong piece and the pianist lost his way because of the large number of repeats. When Vivian brought it to its exciting climax, the pianist just kept on going! He resolved never to play it again. Mike's fondness for *Bolero* went back to her love of dancing and when Torvill and Dean used it for their world winning ice-skating performance, she just loved it. Indeed she had the last word, because she ensured that it was played at her funeral.

A few years later he was interviewed on Toronto radio for a programme *Men of Brass* by Henry Shannon. In this were played Kenneth Alford's *Army and Marine*, his own *The Mountbatten March* and *Sarie Marais*. It was during this interview that he admitted to the story of a terribly cold winter's day at Eastney when he discovered, just as the band had fallen in on the parade, that all the brass instruments had frozen. He sought permission for the band to fall out and take the instruments indoors to thaw them out. No sooner were they back on parade than they completely refroze. He described the noise that came out as the funniest he had ever heard; no bass, no trombones, no cornets – a proper pip-squeak sound.

In touring the country for engagements, he often came across former Royal Marines musicians who had now become players in eminent orchestras. On Saturday 15th January 1972, he conducted a *Gilbert & Sullivan Night* with the City of Birmingham Symphony Orchestra and Birmingham School of Music Choir as one in their season of Gala Pop concerts. He found at least three former Royal Marines in the orchestra including Eddie Bosher. This concert was recorded and issued on the EMI label in April.

Soon after this, Vivian contracted peritonitis and spent seven weeks in hospital, the last three weeks in the Royal Naval Hospital, Haslar. He had not often been seriously ill in his life, having maintained a fitness through constant exercise. When he was discharged he found he had managed to reduce to his wartime weight, which had been rather exceeded in his retirement. He felt this was also very good for his professional image! Even Lord Mountbatten commented on his new slim line when they next met, saying he wish he could do the same!

His contribution to the United States musical scene had been recognised, in 1969, by the unprecedented honour of being elected as an Honorary Member of the American Bandmasters Association, the first foreigner ever to be admitted. It was this distinction which led him to attend many conventions in the United States over the years that followed. He was able to study the principal American Service bands in detail and was frequently invited to conduct at universities. Having studied European and Commonwealth military bands during his Service career, he was probably the most informed and knowledgeable musician in this field. He was not slow to pass on his wide experience to the young and thence came a succession of invitations to appear in the United States. Later Vivian became a member of the executive committee of the John Philip Sousa Memorial Foundation and an international jury panellist. He had also been awarded the Sudler medal, one of the highest military music honours in the United States, of which he was very proud.

He was not afraid occasionally to have a little 'dig' at his American friends. When addressing a conference on *'The Marching Band'*, he paid tribute to the spectacular displays that provided entertainment at football matches. By European standards, he said, they were numerically huge, based on 'extravaganza extreme' with universities vying with each other to produce ebullient marching patterns, often at a very fast tempo, complete with Drum Majorettes, cheer leaders and colour bearers. However, when it came to drill symmetry he pointed out that the Americans were greatly assisted by the 5 metre patterns marked on the grid iron, an advantage which British bands do not have (nor would they wish it otherwise) because they are trained to overcome the more difficult operation with ease!

During his visit as guest conductor to the Troy State University Symphonic Band in 1973 Vivian was honoured by the Academy of Wind and Percussion Arts. He was awarded their 9-inch silver statuette, a silver medallion and an engraved certificate, which were described as the 'Oscar' of the band world. The AWAPA award was presented at a performance by the band for 'his truly significant and outstanding contribution to the furthering of the excellence of bands and band music'.

After his return from this three month visit to the United States, he was invited to be the guest conductor at a Sunday concert of Bournemouth Symphony Orchestra, mostly of music by British composers. His friendship with Earl Mountbatten had certainly blossomed fully by this time and he invited him, his daughter Pamela and her husband David Hicks to the concert. Earlier that week he had made a recording with the orchestra entitled *'English Music Through the Ages'*. While Vivian was in Coronado, California, he had stayed at a house near San Diego which had a fine English library. In it he had found a book *The Mountbattens* by Alden Hatch, which Lord Mountbatten did not have in his own library, and Vivian arranged a swap with them for the book *Louise Mountbatten, Queen of Sweden* which the Earl duly autographed.

The following month his American connections were recognised when he was guest conductor at the Civic Centre in Southampton for a *'Salute to Sousa'* evening with the Royal Marines Band from Portsmouth, the Band of the Irish Guards and the Southern Band of the RAF. Once again Lord Mountbatten was able to attend.

In 1973 Vivian joined the Royal Marines Historical Society and not only contributed a number of articles through the years, but also was a source of knowledge for musical researchers, whom he helped liberally. In 1978 he addressed the Society after their Annual General Meeting on the history of the Royal Marines Band Service. It was the 75th anniversary of the Band Service and it was appropriate that the talk took place at Eastney where the Royal Naval School of Music had been formed in 1903. He dwelt at length on the tragic decision made in 1921 to dispense with the civilian professors as a financial economy which resulted in a poor standard of teaching and influence. He said that no one seemed to realise then that what began was tantamount to in-breeding, as there was much enthusiasm for shore based 'square numbers', which did not necessarily produce the best Band NCOs as instructors. Many fine Directors of Music struggled against this burden, and in the 1930s the RNSM bands could be recognised by the sheep-like vibrato of the cornets, poor thin tone, bad intonation and indifferent performances.

He continued by explaining that it was the lot in those days for promotion candidates to have to pay heavily for lessons and travel to London, swot late into the night and be on parade as usual next morning. His solution, when amalgamation came about in 1953, was to see that such facilities were provided, whereby promotion was encouraged and gained because of the Service and not in spite of it!

His 1974 North American trip, again lasting a couple of months with the American Universities and later in Canada, culminated in an engagement in Hawaii. Whilst he was in San Diego, he was invited aboard HMS *Jupiter* by HRH The Prince of Wales. On his return Lord Mountbatten asked Vivian if he would send a complete set of band parts of *The Mountbatten March* to the Regimental Band of Princess Patricia's Canadian Light Infantry to play at their Diamond Jubilee Trooping of the Colour, as his daughter Patricia, Lady Brabourne, would be present as their new Colonel-in-Chief. Lieutenant Colonel Paul Neville, then Principal Director of Music, duly arranged this.

His programme of invitations to be guest conductor took up most of his time, as he always assiduously researched each piece of music to be included, even though he might have played it many hundreds of times before. Never did he approach a concert without full preparation. His trip to Canada to play at the Festivals of Toronto and London, Ontario in January 1975 was no exception. He returned just in time for the annual Royal Marines Band Concert at the Royal Albert Hall. During that year he conducted the Royal Philharmonic Orchestra and made recordings with the Bournemouth Sinfonietta and the Scottish National Orchestra, the latter being an entirely Russian programme with music by Tchaikovsky, Borodin and Glinka.

His continued interest in the works of Sir Edward Elgar, under whom he had played *Gerontius* when he was still a student, ensured his presence at an address to the Elgar Society (London) in January 1976 given by his old friend Yehudi Menuhin, who autographed Vivian's programme 'To recall fifty years'.

* * * * *

On the 1st January 1977 the International Military Musical Society was formed. There had earlier been a Military Band Historical Research Society, but it had foundered after a few years with unpaid printers' bills. Like many similar well-meaning clubs it had been essentially run as a one-man band and although it served a very useful purpose in bringing like interests together, it had never progressed beyond the first phase. The Military Historical Society had a Band Section and it was from this that the IMMS was formed. George Brinkley and Harry Plunkett were behind this new venture and a meeting took place on 25th September 1976 at which fourteen members met to elect officers and form a committee. They had already agreed to ask someone distinguished in military music to be their President and Vivian was invited along to meet the new representative members of the society before making his decision.

Thus it was that Vivian became its first President. Although, according to the rules of the Society, the presidency should have been renewable every three years, he never offered himself for re-election neither did anyone on the council want him to stand down and thus he remained their president until his death in 1995. Indeed at the IMMS Annual General Meeting on 12th March 1983, his wholehearted support of the activities of the Society were recognised when he was elected President for life, and they were very honoured to have him as their head. In his acceptance speech, Vivian quipped that this could be a longer sentence than that given to a murderer!

Vivian worked ceaselessly for the Society, diligently ensuring that its aims were maintained; namely those of promoting military music and accord throughout the world. He always tried to put a positive slant on the Society's endeavours and his long presidency probably helped to overcome any difficulties which arose. The first chairman, George Brinkley, commenting about the years that led up to the formation of the IMMS, wrote that there were times when, with all the trials and tribulations, he considered giving up but it all turned round when Vivian agreed to become the President. The latter made a point of never interfering with the Chairman of the Society or the UK (Committee) but was always ready to help and advise those who sought it from him. Undoubtedly had it not been for the President's international renown, the IMMS would not have achieved the status it enjoys today.

He made it his duty to attend as many of the Society's meetings at Kneller Hall or the National Army Museum, and apart from addressing the Society on several occasions, he was instrumental in inviting some very distinguished speakers from the musical scene. However they did not always get off lightly as he would test them with very searching but interesting questions after their talks. One presentation he particularly enjoyed was given by Paul Taylor, a retired architect with a deep interest in bandstands. The speaker produced a great number of slides showing the endless variations in designs. Vivian was in his element as he recognised and reminisced about many he had played on during the 1930s.

On 15th February 1977 he was winging his way across the Atlantic once more, this time to be the guest conductor again at the Troy State University in Alabama for three weeks, where the students had wonderful opportunities for making advanced music with a symphony orchestra and large bands. Vivian, although in his late sixties, found these trips inspirational and an edifying experience. He had always enjoyed working with young musicians and these American students had a freshness and keenness about them which he found musically stimulating. They in turn learnt a tremendous amount about the art of conductorship and playing, which their generally younger tutors were unable to impart. None of them had such a wide musical spectrum as Vivian.

Vivian conducting a high school band on one of his visits to the United States

Later in July he was invited for another visit. He was amused by a note in the programme of a concert he was conducting at the University of Kansas Midwestern Music and Art Camp. In an evening which included a concert choir, a symphony orchestra, a concert band and a symphonic band, he found himself described as 'Sir Dunn conducting'!

In 1977 the Sussex Division of the Royal Naval Reserve were honoured with the Freedom of Hove. Vivian was asked to write a march for the occasion which he finished on 12th April. It was based upon two Sussex folk tunes, *Blow The Wind I Oh* and *Three Maidens* and was dedicated to the Captain, Officers and Ships Company of HMS *Sussex*. Titled *The Royal Naval Reserve March*, he hoped it might be used at the Military Music Pageant at Wembley Stadium on 30th June when HM The Queen reviewed the Reserve Forces. However to use a title containing the word 'Royal' required Royal assent. Whether it ever received such is not known, but the march was not played on that occasion.

Another march written around this time was *The Royal Regiment*, which had been commissioned by the Canadians for HRH The Prince of Wales on the occasion of his visit to the Royal Regiment of Canada as their Colonel in Chief. The dedication on the score reads 'Dedicated to Lt Col Brian S McCool, Hon Lt Col, and the Officers and Men of the Royal Regiment of Canada in admiration and affection after a long association from 1941'. The theme of the march is based on their regimental call and contains the tune *God Bless The Prince of Wales*.

It was in 1977 that Vivian approached Lord Mountbatten with a view to helping with the United World Colleges, which the latter had founded many years before. Nothing seems to have become of this, though he would undoubtedly have tried to organise a concert in aid of them if asked.

* * * * *

The assassination of Earl Mountbatten in August 1979 had a profound effect on Vivian. Suddenly and unexpectedly he and lost a great friend and mentor. This spurred him on to finish a work which would epitomise the great figure in music, something which the Earl loved so dearly. He was already well advanced with his plans for *The Mountbatten Suite*, of which the concert march *Man of Action* was to be the third movement. He noted on the score 'Orchestra and Concert Band. The Mountbatten Suite 3rd Movement. Man of Action. FVD 15 Nov 1979'. A clever insertion in the march is the popular song *Has Anyone Here Seen Kelly?*, a reference to Mountbatten's captaincy of HMS *Kelly* in the early years of the war.

The Suite was to be in four movements:

'Prelude – *Man of Destiny*'
'Pastoral – *Broadlands, the Serenity of an English Country House*'
'Concert March – *Man of Action*'
'Epilogue – *Classiebawn Castle, For Whom the Bell Tolls For Thee*'.

By April 1980 Vivian had completed the orchestral work *Broadlands*. On the score he noted '2nd Mvt – Romance Pastoral – Broadlands – The Serenity of a Country House – FVD Haywards Heath April 1980'. Arthritis in his hands was setting in and it was probably this that prevented him from writing the final movement *Classiebawn Castle*, as long periods playing the piano became increasingly painful. At a concert on the Corps Birthday in 1982 at Deal, Vivian conducted *Broadlands*.

Earl Mountbatten's funeral in Westminster Abbey and his Memorial Service in St Paul's Cathedral both saw Vivian pulling out all the stops in memory of his great friend and champion. Perhaps one of the most memorable musical moments in the whole service was when the full Royal Marines School of Music fanfare team accompanied by Westminster's great organ, under Lieutenant Colonel Jim Mason, played Vivian's *Supreme Command* as the cortège entered the Abbey. The BBC's recording remains, to this day, one of the most poignant and dramatic of his career.

In 1980, Vivian had the opportunity to pay tribute publicly to his great mentor. The annual Royal Marines concert at the Royal Albert Hall was performed on two successive nights for the first time and renamed the Mountbatten Festival of Music. The Principal Director of Music, Lieutenant Colonel Jim Mason, invited Vivian to conduct the musical tribute to Earl Mountbatten. This was the first and only time he conducted at one of these concerts. In the presence of HRH The Princess Margaret and Countess Mountbatten he opened with the fanfare *Supreme Command* and followed it with *The Mountbatten March*. After the regimental slow march *Preobrajensky* came the concert march and 3rd movement of his new Mountbatten Suite *Man of Action*. His presence on the platform inspired the musicians to a supreme effort – and their response was near perfection. After the concert he told his daughter Leonie 'that their performance was an example of snap, crackle – and a lot of Pop!'

As the President of the International Military Music Society, he paid a visit to Denmark in August 1981 at the invitation of Mogens Gatzwiller, who directed the Slagelse Military Tattoo, a combination of international military and civilian contingents. On the final night he was privileged to sit in the Royal Box alongside Her Majesty Queen Margarethe of Denmark, the British Ambassador and other distinguished guests. He was particularly pleased that the Band of the 2nd Battalion, the Green Jackets, were amongst the British bands taking part as they were the successors of his father's old regiment, the 2nd Bn KRRC. His old friend Major Gordon Turner was the musical director of this fine tattoo.

In 1981 he paid his almost annual visit to the United States when he attended the conventions of both the American Bandmasters Association in Kansas City and the National College Band Directors Association in Atlanta, Georgia. He subsequently conducted several university bands besides hearing presentations of many established American composers,

The only occasion Vivian conducted at the newly named Mountbatten Festival of Music at the Royal Albert Hall was in 1980 when he was able to pay a personal tribute to his friend and mentor with several pieces dedicated to Earl Mountbatten

such as Alfred Reed, Martin Mallman, James Barnes and Claude T Smith. In return he arranged many concerts in the City of London for visiting American youth symphonic and concert bands. Their venues included St Paul's Cathedral and the Barbican Centre, and he did a great deal to cement the relations between the youth of the two countries. After Vivian's death, Dr Al Wright, President of the John Philip Sousa Foundation, wrote:

> 'Sir Vivian guest conducted my 'United States Collegiate Wind Band' each summer when this *ad hoc* group of High School student band musicians concluded their three weeks concert tour of Europe and England with a Gala Concert in St Paul's Cathedral. This conducting appearance was always followed by our entertaining him and a guest or two for a wonderful evening of dinner and dancing at London's magnificent Savoy restaurant – an event he jocularly referred to as a 'Beano'. This went on every July for some twenty years and he attended (but did not conduct) his final concert with us in the summer of 1994.
>
> During his visits to America, Sir Vivian was much admired and extremely well respected for his musicianship and sensitive conducting throughout the USA. His British reserve, his 'spit and polish' demeanor and his warm regard for all things of excellence in music

> of all kinds made him especially welcome. Whenever and wherever he appeared as a visiting professor or a guest conductor, his musicianship won him the admiration of his colleagues and his wisdom won him the admiration of his students.
>
> Sir Vivian will be long remembered and admired in the United States for his elegance, his musicianship, his demand for excellence, and for his wit and charm. He was everything an American thought that a British "Officer and Gentleman" should be.'

His continued interest in young musicians led him to accept an engagement conducting the National Youth Brass Band of Great Britain at Norwich at Easter 1982. His joy in rehearsing these young enthusiasts was coupled to the excellence of their performance. During what turned out to be a very long hard day he rehearsed what was quite a good band into a concert ensemble of some brilliance. He took the opportunity of introducing them to two of his compositions, the Fanfare *Supreme Command* and *The Cockleshell Heroes March*, and the programme also included many of his own favourites, including Gordon Langford's *Fantasia on British Sea Songs*. The entire band was exhausted by the end of the evening but elated with what they had achieved. Whether any of these young musicians eventually joined the Royal Marines is not recorded.

His love of the works of Sir Edward Elgar has already been mentioned, so it was a particular honour for him to be invited to address the Elgar Society for a second time, dwelling on the effect the great composer had had on his own musical education and subsequent thinking. He said that he had endeavoured to 'spread the gospel' on Elgar throughout his career among the military band fraternity, not only his renowned marches, but also his many fine orchestral works.

Vivian was invited to speak at many conventions and seminars both at home and abroad. He was always in constant demand as he was an undoubted master in his own subject. He was particularly thrilled to be invited to address the Institute of Instrument Technology in May 1982, as he felt that the foundations of musicianship must inevitably lie in the instrument itself. He had long admired the dedication and expertise of those who made musical instruments. 'Indeed' he said, 'where would the music profession be without them?' Without the skill of the instrument makers and the research that produces the technology of implementing

ABOVE:
Vivian's interest and involvement with youth orchestras was one of his main preoccupations during the 1970s and 1980s. Pictured here adjudicating.

RIGHT:
His annual visits to the United States invariably involved at least one recording session

magnificent craftsmanship in all branches of manufacture, no band or orchestra could do justice to the works of the composers and the artistic creativeness of the players.

In June 1983, about 30 members of the Netherlands Branch of the IMMS visited the Royal Marines Barracks at Eastney, where Vivian was able to show off the surroundings in which he had first joined the Corps and spent 21 years there. Lieutenant Colonel Graham Hoskins, the Principal Director of Music enlightened the Dutchmen on the current Royal Marines band scene and this was followed by the Band of the Commander-in-Chief Portsmouth, less the Royal Yacht element who were away on duty, performing ten of his marches, the composer explaining the significance of each. As a member of the welcoming party, the author can vouch for the fact that the visitors were highly impressed on that beautiful June morning. This was a typical example of Vivian cementing international military music relations in the most personal way.

His interest in light music culminated in 1984 with his appointment as President of the Vintage Light Music Society, which had been formed for the enthusiast of Light Music on 78 rpm records. Although a classical musician and subsequently a military musician, Vivian had always had an ear for light music and felt the British variety was the best in the world. From his early days as a student he had kept up with the latest developments in music and his choice of programmes for military band concerts always contained a fair selection of light music. In his presidential address he said:

> 'The present generation of music administrators tend to regard any suggestion of the quality in the programmes of fifty years ago as "saccharine", "old hat", "outdated and outmoded", with an attitude of "never again" and "over my dead body". We are here for progress! But like vintage wine, old masters, craftsmanship and beauty, there are jewels in light music that have stood the test of time and would be a revelation to those hearing them for the first time.'

Along with the hard working Honorary Secretary of the Vintage Light Music Society, Stuart Upton, he urged the BBC to promote more *bona fide* light music in their programmes instead of 'saturating the listeners with pop, rock and reggae, perennially delivered *fortissimo* as an assault on the ears almost from morn to night'. He felt that, of all the agencies that could influence the public's choice of music, the BBC's position made it the most likely to succeed.

His annual trip to the United States in 1983 found him teaching Advanced Conducting and lecturing on World Band History to Troy State University in Alabama. He attracted large classes and found that his students 'applied themselves diligently'. They already had a good grasp in their subjects and asked searching and intelligent questions. Their musical facilities were first class. He proclaimed that the art of teaching is centred on communication and that his rapport and patience with the young musicians was exceptional. In their turn the Americans revered this fine military figure, whose musical knowledge seemed to know no bounds, and when asked how they got on with Sir Vivian, the answer came back 'He's sure got us fired up!'

Stephen Pearce, of Foley, Alabama, was a student at Troy University at that time and recalls fond memories of his encounters with Vivian. He had been asked to pick the visitor up from the airport and take him to his lodgings in Dill Hall 104 which was in the University near the music department. He writes:

> 'Sir Vivian taught classes in conducting, history of the march and twentieth century masterworks. I signed up for everything. Those two summer sessions are some of my fondest memories of my musical education. He gave this gift to all of his students. He made us think and play to levels that we never believed were possible. He

would say "Don't be a time beater."

One of my favorite stories that he shared with us at Troy was concerning his visit to John Philip Sousa's grave. He had noted that there was no mention on the memorial that Sousa was the former conductor of the United States Marine Corps Band. Sir Vivian mentioned the omission to the right parties and the oversight was corrected.

It was Sir Vivian's teaching that made such an impact on my life and my approach to the students I now teach. He called me "Rocket Man" as things come easily to me and he would occasionally have to fire a rocket up my rear to get me going!'

* * * * *

In 1984 he persuaded the Master and Court of the Worshipful Company of Musicians to promote a competition for British composers with a prize of £1,000 for a 'Suite in Three Movements'. He felt it was high time that there should be, after 75 years, a competition which might promote a number of talented young musicians to come forward. The last such competition had been held in 1909 when Percy Fletcher won with *Woodland Pictures*, which was still in the international repertoire. Gustav Holst's well known *Suite No 1 in E Flat* was unplaced!

The problem was that running such a competition involved a lot of time-consuming work, made even harder when they were faced with about 100 entries. There were few people in the Company who were willing to take on such a commitment and it was left to Richard Crewdson, Clerk of the Worshipful Company, and Vivian to run it. At the final judging stage, when the high standard of submissions had been short-listed to three, with the help of Lieutenant Colonel Graham Hoskins, the Royal Marines Band went to London to play these specially written suites of music for adjudication. The judges, with Vivian in the chair, were Harry Mortimer, Vilem Tausky and Victor Fleming. They 'came in on time and to budget' with the winner being Bram Wiggins with his Canadian Suite *Big Sky Country*. This was played the following year at the Mountbatten Festival of Music when the composer was able to hear the Massed Bands of the Royal Marines give it the full treatment. Once again Vivian had been instrumental in cementing the strong ties between the Royal Marines and the Worshipful Company of Musicians – a recurring theme.

A change in his usual conducting schedule came in early 1985 when he was invited to Norway. Although in his late seventies, he still displayed the enthusiasm for new pastures which would have been eschewed by many younger men. In Oslo he conducted the Norwegian Army Staff Band whom he described as 'excellent responsive players'. He had ten hours of rehearsal with them, stretching most of them further than they had ever been before, and they produced a very fine broadcast for Norwegian Radio. It was in this broadcast that the new composition *Big Sky Country* had its world radio première. He described the performance as magnificent. During his stay he was welcomed by Major General and Mrs John Hardy and the British Embassy staff and met up with his son Paddy who was serving in Norway at the time with 3 Commando Brigade. Vivian was not quite so impressed by the February weather when he wrote 'But by God, the snow! Ten feet high on the roadsides and damned cold. All right when you got inside and the Norwegians are very courteous and generous.'

More often than not Vivian was equally generous with his praise which he found encouraged others in their performances, although there was sometimes a sting in the tail. After a page and half of rapturous remarks and some well-founded comment, including constructive criticism, he would add, in what seemed like an afterthought, 'Oh by the way, don't always rely on your proof reader to get the difficult musical names spelt right in the programme!' Several Directors of Music received such letters, being admonished subtly by this musical elder statesman.

The following year found him in Rotterdam for the first time since 1945, when he had toured with his Portsmouth Divisional Band at the end of the war. This was at the invitation of the strong Netherlands Branch of the IMMS and particularly his old friend and Vice-President of the Society, Colonel J P Laro. The tenth anniversary Netherlands Military Tattoo was held at the historic castle of Breda, but this was the first time Vivian had attended. He described it almost beyond praise and went on to say that he was well aware of the world class standards of the Dutch Service bands. Not only were the traditional elements of a military tattoo present but he was particularly attracted to the sixty young ladies from the Jorien Peeman Ballet School who delighted the audience with their display of dancing to a Latin rhythm.

Vivian was often asked, both at home and abroad, for radio interviews. After all, music is a sound, not a visual experience and radio was the best medium. In December 1986 he contributed to three programmes with Angela Rippon, herself the daughter of a regular Royal Marine. She explained how, as a child, the parade ground at Stonehouse Barracks was her extended playground, and how she was enthralled by the sight of musicians in white helmets marching in immaculate formation and to the sound of their own band and corps of drums, which had left an indelible impression on her. On being asked whether the Band Service had changed over the fifty years since then, Vivian enthused about the current standard of musicianship. He said:

> 'The purpose of the military band has basically remained unaltered. It is for the marching of troops, allied to which there is a far greater area of morale, playing to the public and performing music that will bring great satisfaction and reward to those who listen to it.
>
> If a regiment is on the line of march it is headed by its band and it is important that the quality and excellence of the marches that they play makes for better stepping for the troops who follow. It quickens the pulses and it makes chests stick out; and it develops a sense of pride. There is something about the British race and all that they inherit which can be found in some of the music performed by military bands.
>
> However today, young people who are to be found within the ranks of the military bands are well versed in modern instruments and modern techniques of recording, the result of years of study and enthusiastic application; and they are therefore prepared for even the most extraordinarily difficult contemporary music.'

In another interview two years later, hosted by the renowned broadcaster Richard Baker, Vivian *'Compared Notes'* with the current Organising Director of Music of the Royal Air Force, Wing Commander Eric Banks. Obviously the question of combining the three Services musical training arose, but it was swiftly pointed out that both Canada and Australia had been down the same road, but had now reverted back to their individual Service again. They both agreed that the standard of young musicians joining now was so much higher than three decades ago. The increased flexibility of the young Service musician was apparent in their answers. Vivian remarked:

> 'Nowadays young musicians entering, both men and girls as well, have an expectation of an extremely good professional career. The

> basis of it, of course, lies in teaching ... and flexibility. One of the important aspects is when you consider morale in ships and I quote the Royal Marines Band that went to the Falklands. They had an excellent dance band, guitars and all that sort of thing, that was so marvellous for our troops. It doesn't exactly fit into the curriculum, but bands are expected to be up to date and to be able to perform music of every kind.'

One unusual, and perhaps unbelievable, article was published in the *Knoxville News-Sentinel* in March 1987 when he was the guest conductor of the University of Tennessee Concert Band. He had been friendly with the band's Director, Dr W J Julian and his wife Faye, for a number of years, a friendship built up by frequent visits. In the newspaper article we are astonished to read '... Sir Vivian is so down to earth that he had Gail Hunter, Julian's secretary, play Queen Elizabeth as they re-enacted the ceremony in which he was knighted.' One is left to draw one's own conclusions on this purported happening!

He was absolutely delighted at the birth of his first great-grandson in 1987, Jason Simon Vivian, and was over the moon about it, announcing to anyone he met that he was now a Great Grandfather. In his retirement he had grown more and more fond of his enlarged family as more grandchildren appeared and his love of youth shone through what others might regard as his austere exterior.

During his visit to the United States in 1987 he was invested with the Star of the Order of Merit of the John Philip Sousa Foundation, at the convention of the American Bandmasters Association, the only Englishman ever to be so honoured. This was part of his annual visit and teaching commitments with the Universities of Tennessee, Michigan, Kansas and Troy. He always gave the impression he felt that American Universities had the upper hand over their British counterparts in the realms of music teaching, particularly with a military emphasis, which was why he accepted their invitations so readily. He was quick to point out that the United States Collegiate wind bands and their associated wind ensembles were peculiarly American in their concept and that we did not have anything in England on that scale at the college and university level. It was not the same as our own fine brass bands which, whilst encouraging young musicians to join them, did not have the firm foundation that the Americans of like age possessed.

Vivian was able to reminisce about his long association with the Malcolm Sargent Cancer Fund for Children, of which he was a Vice President. This had been set up at the instigation of the Promenaders in 1968 at a schools' finals concert organised by the Yamaha Music School at Bletchley. By 1987 there were 70 Yamaha Schools in the United Kingdom with over 6,000 young students, the finalists winning through various local and regional competitions. That year he was able publicly to pay tribute to Sylvia Darley, the general administrator, on the award of the OBE for her work with the Fund which, since the inception of the annual Massed Bands concerts at the Royal Albert Hall in 1973, had been one of the two beneficiaries.

He regularly attended the Service of the Royal Victorian Order which was held in St George's Chapel, Windsor, with a reception afterwards in the Castle. The Royal Family all attended when possible and he was very honoured to be in such royal company. He was particularly impressed by the wonderful singing of the chapel choir, harking back to the days in Winchester where his interest in choral music first came alive.

1988 was memorable as Vivian and Mike celebrated their Golden Wedding anniversary. A huge party was held at an hotel in Cuckfield in which as many of the family as possible gathered. In addition his best man Kit Boothby with his wife, along with Toni Hancock (née Adams), who had been one of Mike's bridesmaids, were there to join in the reunion. This was the last time they all met as sadly both died within two years. The occasion was crowned by the receipt of personal telegrams from Her Majesty The Queen and Queen Elizabeth The Queen Mother. This was exceptional as the rule now is that standard Palace telegrams are sent for Diamond anniversaries only.

One occasion which he could not miss was the IMMS visit to Knightsbridge Barracks on 23rd September, as the guest of the band of the Blues and Royals, under Major Roger Tomlinson. It was a particularly nostalgic moment when he was invited to conduct the band in Elgar's *Cockaigne Overture* and his own *Cockleshell Heroes* march. He recalled that it was over 60 years since he had last conducted the Band of the Horse Guards when his father was their Director of Music and had allowed him to rehearse the then Royal Horse Guards (The Blues) Band as part of his studies. He was then a mere teenage student at the Royal Academy. The choice of Elgar's music was particularly apt, as was that of Lieutenant

LEFT: *Vivian was clothed as the Master of the Musicians' Company on 9th November 1988. With him at his installation are the great violinist Yehudi Menuhin and the famous conductor, Sir Charles Groves.*

RIGHT: *The Musicians' Company. Left to right: Lt Col Graham Hoskins (PDM), Lt Gen Sir Martin Garrod (CGRM), F V D, Paddy, Col J J Thomson (Commandant RMSM)*

Colonel George Evans, Vice President of the IMMS, who followed him by conducting his old band in *'Theme and Variations'* by Walton O'Donnell, the man under whom Vivian had studied composition all those years ago. It was a very emotional experience.

Perhaps his crowning achievement came on 9th November 1988 when he was made (clothed as) the Master of the Worshipful Company of Musicians. He had been a Liveryman since 1960 and regularly attended their functions and dinners. During his year, which had many memorable moments, HRH The Duke of Edinburgh was admitted as an Honorary Freeman of the Worshipful Company. Lieutenant Colonel Graham Hoskins, who had been invited to attend as Vivian's personal guest, recalls the moment when Prince Philip stood in front of the Master to swear allegiance; 'It was an unbelievable scenario to see the HRH standing to attention in front of Vivian like an errant schoolboy!' For this particular ceremony he wrote a *A Selection of English Songs* and inscribed the score with 'Arranged for the Installation of HRH The Duke of Edinburgh KG as an Honorary Freeman of the Worshipful Company of Musicians. Performed by a Baroque Quintet from the RMSM, Stationers Hall, 30 March 1989. F Vivian Dunn. Master.' The arrangement consists of *A Fine Old English Gentleman, Early One Morning, The Lincolnshire Poacher, Drink To Me Only, Drinking* (which FVD noted as requiring 'a good bucolic

During Vivian's year as Master of the Worshipful Company of Musicians, HRH *The Prince Philip was admitted as an Honorary Freeman*

tone!'), *John Peel, Here's a Health Unto Her Majesty* and *Rule Britannia*. The quintet was made up of flute, oboe, B♭ clarinet, bassoon and serpent – the instrument which helped provide the bucolic tone – and was conducted by Captain David Cole, also a Liveryman of the Musicians' Company.

In this momentous year, he invited Sidonie Goossens, the renowned harpist, as his private guest to the annual dinner, a gesture which she said was the highlight of her career and harked back to their days together in the BBC Symphony Orchestra in the thirties. His other principal guests were Lord Menuhin, Sir Charles Groves and Dr Al Wright.

1989 was the year Mike sustained a nasty fall and broke her femur. She had been increasingly unwell and Vivian was torn between being with his wife and continuing his outside engagements. Many of these were pushed aside as he spent more time at Haywards Heath. They were both now well into their late seventies and the strain of such a hectic life was beginning to show. But Vivian would not admit it easily.

He was deeply distressed and angered when he heard of the IRA bombing of the Royal Marines School of Music at Deal on 22nd September 1989 when eleven young musicians were murdered. He immediately hastened to Deal to offer his support and condolences. Mike and all the family felt this tragedy very deeply as Deal had been their home for so many years and the children were particularly attached to it having spent their formative years there. Amongst a number of concerts around the country which helped raise money for the Relief Fund, was the City of Birmingham Symphony Orchestra, which still boasted two former Royal Marines in their numbers. Eddie Bosher and Jeremy Ballard organised a concert on 18th October at which Vivian was invited to conduct Sir Edward Elgar's *Sea Pictures – Five Songs for Contralto and Orchestra* with the renowned soloist, Penelope Walker. As the concert had been put on at such short notice the audience was smaller than had been hoped, but the following night, at another CBSO concert, their conductor, Simon Rattle, made an announcement about the bombing and arranged for 'buckets' to be passed round. The result of the two nights was more than £5,000 for the Relief Fund.

For some years Vivian had been the President of the Brighton and Hove Branch of the Royal Marines Association. During 1990 he took a particular interest in raising money for the Queen Alexandra Hospital, Gifford House, Worthing. He arranged a concert by the band of the Corps of Royal Engineers. The Secretary and Matron of Gifford House had asked him to write a song to mark the occasion, for which he wrote both the words and music, though one of the patients did submit a set of lyrics. For the Open Day he was asked to be the Guest of Honour of the London Taxi Drivers Benevolent Association for War Disabled, which raised funds for Gifford House and took patients out for trips. They kindly picked him up and returned him to Haywards Heath.

He joined another august body in 1989 when he became a Fellow of the Royal Society of Arts on 9th October, the President of the RSA being HRH Prince Philip, The Duke of Edinburgh. Three years later, one final honour came his way when, on 9th November 1992, an Honorary Doctorate was bestowed on him by the Guildhall School of Music and Drama, with whom he had had such a close association over many years. He looked a fine figure, not perhaps as upright as before, but immaculately dressed complete with mortar board and gown, when he was presented with the diploma by the Lord Mayor of London, Sir Brian Jenkins.

He was often asked, in his retirement, why he did not follow his father and grandfather into the Army. His reply was always short and to the point – 'Somebody had to take the right turning sometime!'

CHAPTER 8

Rallentando - A Positive Retirement

As we have seen, during his retirement from the Royal Marines, Vivian had never felt the need to stop working. He was particularly keen that others should learn from him as he had learnt half a century before. He had always been quick to recognise that he would not have risen to the top of his profession without the enormous help and encouragement from his mentors. His were mostly from the orchestral world, and now, here he was, the acknowledged master of the military music world.

In an address to the students of the Royal Military School of Music at Kneller Hall, he propounded some of his theories, hoping that at least some of his ideas would rub off on those who would inevitably command the major army bands of future years. He was not insular in his thoughts as he believed that he was in a position to pass on his considerable experience to Bandmasters of all three services in equal proportion, and indeed he delivered similar talks in the United States.

He pointed out the value of academic study in the musical genre; how hard work, diligence and dedication towards successful qualifications were the way ahead to emulate their distinguished forebears, the Godfreys, Winterbottoms, O'Donnells, Ricketts, Millers, Dunns, Williams and Mackenzie Rogan, to name but a few.

The art and principles of military musicianship he presented in the form of a 'Theme with Nine Variations'. Firstly he felt that pride in one's profession was most paramount in one's attitude to what and who you are and what you stand for. Whatever Regiment or Corps a musician owes allegiance to at the time must be the prime object of your endeavours at any given moment. He put integrity second in his variations, a determination to engender trust in everything one does and says, high levels of professional and personal behaviour so that those under you look up to you. They may moan and groan at an insistence on hard work to raise their standards, which may make you unpopular. Whatever else you do gain the confidence of your commanding officer and those with whom you work. Enjoy the fellowship of mess members and take a full part in regimental functions, both social and sport. He also suggested it was a good idea to gain the respect and friendship of those who looked after the funds.

Education came third in his priorities. Make sure you not only gain knowledge in your musical profession, but seek to write good English and learn to speak and converse well. This is most important when talking to senior officers and he felt that a bad accent was tantamount to bad intonation in music. There is no snobbery in this, but carelessness will spoil the image. However he was quick to point out that any exaggerated posh or phoney accent would count against you. 'There is nothing worse than being an amateur gentleman' was one of his catch phrases. He pointed out that Bandmasters and, more particularly, Directors of Music, became public speakers when performing with their band. Announcing needs study, thought and practice in a natural voice. The cultivation of a foreign language provides unrivalled opportunities in these modern times. Under education came teaching, which is the art of communication. The attainment not only of musical qualifications and diplomas is essential, but study for Bachelor of Arts degrees is an excellent way of refreshing brain cells and enhancing reputations. There are many Directors of Music in all three services who have graduated in this way.

By way of surprise, he put musicianship as low as fourth in his variations. Whilst being the hallmark of one's professional endeavours, it encompasses the ability to interpret and perform the widest range of the musical repertoire. Music must be an all consuming interest wherein considerable time must be spent on arranging and composing, even if the latter gift is not given to everyone. Many who have risen and studied thus far will have natural ability in their favour, but he believed that mental effort was needed to attain the heights from quite modest beginnings.

Vivian conducting with the score in his head, not his head in the score

Probably the dearest to most aspiring Bandmasters' hearts is conducting. In principle, he said, it means a clear beat without eccentricities. If coupled with a good ear and a keen sense of pitch, not necessarily 'perfect pitch' which is comparatively rare, it avoids bad intonation and musical errors. However each individual should be encouraged to develop his own sense of style coupled with the ability to read and interpret a score. He emphasised the paying of attention to accuracy and detail at rehearsal as well as performances through meticulous preparation. He encouraged the study of eminent conductors but warned against imitation by creating one's own individual style. It is musicianship which counts, not baton waving. Whilst warning that the conductor may be just as guilty as a musician in playing wrong notes, he said 'Conduct with the score in your head – not your head in the score!'

A band is only as good as its conductor is an old saying, but it is true. Never adopt an attitude of 'I know it all, don't argue with me'. He always felt that many of his players, particularly professionals, could teach even a good conductor a thing or two. It was good to criticise oneself.

Variation No 6, he entitled Personality and Appearance. He felt it was essential to develop an alert, cheerful and optimistic approach, combining it with a sense of humour, encouraging others to do the same without losing control of situations. He stressed the importance of smartness and bearing not only when in uniform but also in civilian clothes. A little extra spent on good clothes not only gives personal satisfaction but also creates the best possible impression. The aim is to be recognised for who and what you are and stand for; in other words dignify the position.

Leadership and administration are needed to command with confidence. In a military environment this should need no explanation, but as with all things, set a good example and think out problems before issuing orders. Meticulous planning might get a band to the right place at the right time but it would never make them play better. Conversely if the administration fails, morale suffers. The creation of a good team spirit amongst a band is essential. His penultimate variation was business acumen, knowing the commercial and morale value of a band. Make sure you sell it well, and ensure that every man knows exactly what is due to him in an engagement. Good publicity is all important but never overplay the band.

His final variation and probably the most serious aspect of bandmastership is the avoidance of pitfalls. Although it is sometimes said that the musicians' creed is 'Art for art's sake; but money for God's sake', this attitude must be avoided. It all comes down to honesty in the end.

In repeating these points before a number of different audiences, Vivian tried to paint the picture of the perfect Bandmaster. In doing so, he did not admit some of his own shortcomings. A close scrutiny of his theme and variations will reveal a few cracks in his armour. Those who served with him will know these only too well, but certainly on the musical content of his ideals he could hardly be faulted

Paul Neville recalls that he always felt that Vivian was a remarkable rehearser both with orchestra and band. Indeed he went so far as to say that he felt that Vivian left his best performances in the rehearsal room. Although the latter propounded the virtues of the art of conducting, he was not himself always the most relaxed of conductors. His anxiety for achieving the ultimate performance, plus nerves, sometimes resulted in gestures and tempi at odds with the work done in the rehearsal room. This

His final appearance on the rostrum was on the occasion of an International Military Music Society visit to the Central Band of the Royal Air Force at Uxbridge on 17th June 1994

had the effect of unsettling the orchestra and it is arguable that had he developed a more relaxed relationship with his players then he might have been able to achieve even more in his performances. The musicians were sometimes frightened of playing a wrong note. This was probably only occasionally the case, and apparent only to the pure musician. The audiences certainly appreciated his performances on the rostrum.

* * * * *

When the International Military Musical Society arranged a visit to the Central Band of the Royal Air Force at Uxbridge on 17th June 1994, Wing Commander Barrie Hingley, the organising Director of Music, invited Vivian to conduct the band playing *Cockleshell Heroes*. This is believed to be the last time he ever conducted a band. At the time he was using an upturned golf club as a walking stick, and upon seeing this a string bass stool was brought over for him to sit on. He firmly dismissed this, but courteously stood as he explained to the audience and the band how he came to write the march. At the completion of the piece both the band and the IMMS audience gave him a rapturous ovation.

His grandson Simon Langston remembers this day well as he had been the willing chauffeur and drove Vivian to the meeting, something that he had done many times since 1993. He writes:

> 'I purposely kept a low profile as I didn't have much to contribute in terms of conversation amongst enthusiastic followers of band and classical music. Instead I merely observed the immense respect my Grandfather commanded from the many awe-struck fans who would almost bow and scrape before him; and equally his own charm and humility in dealing with such situations.
>
> By the time of the performance, Grandfather was very unsteady on his feet and was helped to the podium. He joked that he wished he had brought his "zimmer". However, you could literally see the physical surge of energy and total composure that took control as soon as the baton was in his hand. I saw for myself the utter respect the band members had for him and the stage presence which emanated from the podium.
>
> The whole experience was very moving. I was watching a man who had experienced so much during his lifetime, whose best years were a long time gone and yet who still had control of all around him.
>
> Grandfather was very kind, considerate and thoughtful and our many journeys were often very quiet, both of us believing only in saying what was necessary. Often an outburst of "pom-te-poms" and a wave of the hands would break the silence as he reached the crescendo of the music in his mind. This attribute served to reinforce my opinion that Grandfather was totally engrossed with music. To me it is no wonder he was such a giant in his field; if you can concentrate and focus enough on any subject, you can achieve wonders – and he did. I am very proud to have been associated with a legend.'

Later that year on 22nd November he was again invited by the IMMS when they visited the Band of HM Royal Marines in Portsmouth. However he was rather unwell, and although Captain David Cole sent a car to Haywards Heath to collect him, the family telephoned to say that he was not well enough to travel. Soon after this, at the last committee meeting of the IMMS he confided to the UK Chairman and Vice Chairman that, on his doctor's advice, he should start to reduce his commitments and give up the Presidency. He was quite adamant that he wanted to oversee a smooth handover, and was very much against remaining in office when he was no longer able to make a worthwhile contribution. However the committee did not accept this and Vivian remained as President until his death the following year.

Sport had always played a great part in his life and he spent many happy hours watching cricket particularly at Hove, having been a member of Sussex County Cricket Club over twenty years. He later achieved his long held ambition to become a member of the MCC. The author remembers him telephoning in 1985 and asking how he could be elected at his advanced age, knowing that the normal waiting list was about twenty years. He said that he had achieved most of his lifetime aspirations but this one had so far eluded him. One of his proposers was the famous cricket commentator and after-dinner speaker Brian Johnstone, who had also proposed him for membership of the Garrick Club; another was Ian Wallace, the well known baritone, and the third was General Sir Ian Gourlay, a former Commandant General Royal Marines and captain of Royal Navy cricket. He said that his membership of this illustrious club gave him more pleasure than many of the professional accolades which had been bestowed on him. His passion for cricket never diminished and to the very end of his life, when he was too frail to attend even local matches, he would sit in front of his television set, turn up the sound *fortissimo*, ignore the world around him and watch every single match. Although Mike showed considerable tolerance for his behaviour, it nearly drove the rest of the family mad!

In his retirement Vivian played a reasonable amount of golf, and one of his regular partners in singles and four ball matches was Alan Toze. He writes:

> 'His impressive stature and bearing rather overawed me at first, but he immediately put me at my ease by offering his hand with, "Hello, Alan, my name's Vivian. What's your handicap?" This made it evident that he did not wish to be "Sir-ed" and he happily joined in the leg-pulling, backchat and exaggerated histrionics which are normal in friendly games.
>
> Being a heavy man, he found the hills on the course a bit taxing, and he once slipped and sat down heavily on a down slope, slithering some yards in the mud. He roared with laughter at first, but lapsed into military language when he saw the state of his trousers. Again, in a close singles match, my approach shot to the crucial hole had a lucky bounce, giving me the match. "Oh well",

> he chuckled, "Can't fart against thunder, eh?" This coming from such an eminent musician was most endearing.'

There was one aspect in which Vivian luxuriated and that was his compositions of fanfares. Altogether he wrote more than 30 of them. Bob Farnon comments:

> 'A Fanfare is not the easiest of pieces to compose without it sounding contrived and ordinary. It takes a master of brass instruments to produce a flourish of trumpets such as I heard from above me during Vivian's Memorial Service at St Martin-in-the-Fields. The brilliance of the music shook me to the core, and the composer of this work was Sir F Vivian Dunn, whose creativity throughout his lifetime covered canvases large and small, encompassing music in a light vein to the splendid sounds of the symphony orchestra.
>
> His years of experience as an orchestral player, followed by his appointment as Principal Director of Music at the RM School of Music, resulted in the finest brass band and orchestral performances by British servicemen, many of whom became professional musicians in the concert world, TV and radio, and recording studios throughout the country. I don't believe he was ever aware of this accomplishment.
>
> Sir Vivian understood the importance of the conductor's empathy towards the musicians. "I have played under the baton of the best and worst. I should know." His words.
>
> It was a special privilege to have known such a great man who became, not only a personal friend, but a great hero.'

The Wardroom officers of the '*Vanguard 1947*' tour held a reunion every five years which Vivian enjoyed attending. At the last *Vanguard* reunion that he attended HM The Queen Mother requested that Vivian should meet and escort her. During the evening they had to negotiate a flight of steps, which proved to be a nerve-wracking experience for the onlookers as neither of them were particularly steady on their pins. He also met up with his old chum, Frank Gillard CBE, who was the BBC commentator for the *Vanguard* tour. Of the reunion held at the Caledonian Club in 1993, Gillard wrote :

> 'The Royal Ladies (two Queens and a Princess) usually honour this reunion with their presence. On the last occasion, in 1993, Vivian brought along a tape playback outfit, and at one point in the proceedings he and Princess Margaret got together quietly in a corner

> of the large reception room to listen to something. It happened by pure chance that I was nearby at that moment. The music on the tape was – would you believe it – *'N'Kose Sikele'* [sic], the very performance I had recorded during our tour all those years previously. Princess Margaret had obviously asked to hear it once more, and she was still enchanted with the song. She got Vivian to play it again and again, and spotting me, drew me into the conversation. We are having one of those reunions again this year, but alas without Vivian. However I have a cassette, so I shall continue to enjoy Vivian's music, and his memory.'

* * * * *

A disappointment in his life must have been that none of his children took up music as a profession. There was no lack of pushing by him in the early stages of their development. Although he later accepted that their individual lives were for them to live, after so many continuous generations of music makers, it was sad to see the line come to an end. It is often said that musical talent sometimes skips a generation to emerge later, but there does not even appear to be any outstanding musical talent in his grandchildren, nor even his great grandchildren. One unusual family coincidence happened in 1997. One of his grandchildren Jamie Dunn, a newly qualified sound engineer for the BBC, found that his very first outside broadcast assignment was the decommissioning ceremony of the Royal Yacht *Britannia*; thus, in a way, completing something of a circle, recalling that Vivian had been the Director of Music on board for her maiden voyage.

It was a great shock to the family when cancer was diagnosed. He was too distraught to speak of it, even to his own family. However he showed them a letter from his consultant and left them to draw their own conclusions. He remained cheerful and optimistic to the end. When asked how he felt, his remark would be something like 'a bit slower over the ground than I used to be'. He found it increasingly difficult to walk but refused to use a walking stick; instead he upended a couple of his golf clubs and used these to hobble around. This sort of eccentricity appealed to his consultant, who spared him a great deal of time. Vivian never complained and held the firm belief that somehow he would recover. His determination remained strong.

There is always a bitter sadness about meeting a distinguished person in their declining years. For 80 years Vivian had maintained his sartorial standards, passed on this important facet of life to those under him and supported as far as he was physically able, all the musical events that had been his life. Thus the author last met him at the Royal Albert Hall at a Mountbatten Concert, the annual Royal Marines band and orchestral concert. That evening he was a frail figure, along with Mike, sitting in a box and enjoying the scenario in which he had first performed more than 65 years before. We chatted, mainly about England's cricket prospects and recalled our happy times together on the field and when we had lived next door to each other at Deal. His body may have been weak, but his mind was as active and acute as ever. Indeed the warmth of the two elderly figures towards each other was no more apparent than in some bantering between them. On one occasion Vivian got very agitated because he couldn't find his hat, until Mike pointed out it was on his head! She also, in her quiet and amusing way, suggested to Vivian one day when he was going to a funeral, that it might be a good idea if he stayed at the crematorium to save time. This was the wonderfully unseen relationship they had with each other.

Later that year he attended his final Worshipful Company of Musicians Installation Dinner at the Stationer's Hall. He sat at the top table but somehow there was an emptiness about him and for the first time in living memory he was not as spruce and well turned out as usual. His jacket was open and he had an old belt holding up his evening dress trousers. Suddenly he really was an old man on the sideline of life. Graham Hoskins said it was one of the greatest sadnesses of his life to see him like this. He described how, at the end of dinner, Vivian struggled from his seat and left the dining room with the other members of the top table; but instead of going with them for further coffee and liqueurs, he asked for a chair to be placed at the top of the small set of stairs between the dining room and anteroom, where he sat. Everyone had to pass him as they left the room and he was able to say an emotional, personal farewell to all who had been present at the dinner. He knew he would not see them again, and he didn't. It was sad to see a hunched figure that had adhered to a lifetime of enviable standards of dress, suddenly being reduced to the very ordinary. Near the end, the bubble had finally been pricked and a genuine, but unremarkable person was seen to exist beneath the carefully sculptured veneer shown to the world over his lifetime. It took supreme effort and total dedication to 'tread the boards' so effectively right up to the end.

For the last time he visited Deal for the Band Service Reunion on 25th September 1994, only six months before his death, when he was able to say farewell to many friends. With him are Lt Col Richard Waterer, the Principal Director of Music, and his wife Sue.

One can only admire the spirit which drove him to believe in himself and make this final gesture to the exclusion of all else.

He attended his last Band Service reunion dinner on the 24/25th September 1994, by now looking very frail. His lung cancer had taken a firm hold and he was desperately ill. However he was quite clear in his mind that he was attending this dinner, as he had the one at the Musicians Company, with the express purpose of saying a final goodbye to all his friends. His spirit and resolve were as strong as ever but the physical effort it cost him was enormous. The family had once again tried to dissuade him from going but he simply would not listen to them. He intended to carry out what he perceived as his 'duty' to the end.

He found time to chat with as many old friends as possible that evening. On the following morning, after the church service, the orchestra played *Cockleshell Heroes* as he and the congregation left the church. He managed to walk to the drill field where he took the salute at the end of the band display before Lieutenant Colonel Richard Waterer and his wife Sue ushered him into their car to take him home. That was the last time most of the old and bold band ranks saw Vivian. Peter Sumner wrote afterwards:

> 'I shall remember him for many things – the man who took the Band Service by the scruff of the neck and shook it into real professionalism; who set me on the path to promotion and gave me a deep and abiding love of conducting; who always set the finest example of

> devotion to duty and loyalty to one's own principles; who was always immaculately turned out – but above all as a very caring and understanding man, who whilst not accepting fools gladly, readily appreciated personal problems and was prepared to make allowances wherever possible. There were times when he could seem unsympathetic but this was because he never spared himself, and sometimes expected everyone else to do the same.'

With only a few months to live he attended the Brighton Royal Marines Association guest night, and as their President he gave a welcoming address to their guest of honour, Major General Robin Ross, whose career he had championed every step of the way. Although the family tried to dissuade him from attending, he said that nothing would deter him. He would carry out his duty no matter what, as a mark of respect to the son of his old friend, Gerry Ross.

His sense of humour remained intact. When asked by Rosey 'How are you feeling today? General malaise?', he came back quickly with 'Never heard of him!' All three children remained in close contact during the final months as far as their work would allow. He was visited regularly by Care Nurses, and as time went on both day and night nurses popped in most days. He was always so grateful for even the simplest tasks the nurses and the family performed for him.

Mike always preferred to believe that he was suffering from any other illness than cancer. They both refused to accept the finality of his condition. Mike was very poorly herself, receiving regular treatment for leg ulcers. When Vivian was finally moved to hospital for his last two weeks, the nurses adored him; his humour, positiveness and optimism were abundantly apparent.

On Sunday 2nd April the two daughters, Leonie and Rosey were with him. He was heavily drugged with morphine, but when he opened his eyes, he immediately recognised them and said, as he always did 'How nice to see you. Tell me, how is Mummy? Is she all right?' His last thoughts were with his wife of 57 years. He died later that night.

He passed away peacefully on 3rd April 1995, aged 86 years, having achieved most of his lifetime ambitions. He always acknowledged that he had been born under a lucky star, but it had been his driving ambition, devotion to music, loyalty to the Royal Marines Band Service and sheer hard work that had led him to the honour of becoming the first military musician ever to be knighted. His funeral at All Saints Church, Lindfield, Haywards Heath on 10th April saw a full church for which the current Principal Director of Music, Lieutenant Colonel Richard Waterer, had very kindly offered the band and two buglers from the Royal Marines School of Music. They were supported by Dr Barry Rose at the organ, an old friend whose playing in Guildford Cathedral had so richly enhanced Vivian's final recording with the Royal Marines in 1968. Amongst the large congregation were all five former Principal Directors of Music. A large contingent from the Brighton and Hove Branch of the Royal Marines Association turned out and lined the route as the coffin was borne away.

The programme included music by Elgar, Walford Davies and Eric Coates. The Reverend Dr John Watson, a former Royal Marines musician and a long term friend took the service and gave a moving and inspiring address of the man whom the Band Service had affectionately known as 'Fred'. He included the apocryphal story of the boy musician who, when faced with the end of term exam question 'Who is the patron saint of music?', unreservedly wrote 'Saint Vivian'. As the service came to an end, the rousing strains of *The Globe & Laurel* filled the church as the body of Sir Vivian was carried on its final journey, led by Standard Bearers of the Royal Marines Association. The congregation then filed slowly out to the sounds of *Cockleshell Heroes* with its insistent rhythm, its triumphal coda and its bright optimism breaking through. He was buried in Walstead Cemetery in Lindfield to the strains of Last Post being sounded by the two Royal Marines buglers.

The detailed *Daily Telegraph* obituary concluded with the words, *'When he raised his baton, it was like a call to arms'.*

This was followed by a memorial service at St Martin-in-the-Fields in London on Friday 7th July 1995, at which the Commandant General, Lieutenant General Sir Robin Ross gave a moving address. The 'house' was packed, the music wondrous and one could almost picture Vivian on the podium, his handsome, upright figure, dressed immaculately with just the right amount of shirt cuff showing, conducting his orchestra, who that day played their hearts out under the direction of Lieutenant Colonel Richard Waterer, in his memory.

Her Majesty The Queen, His Royal Highness The Duke of Edinburgh and Her Majesty Queen Elizabeth The Queen Mother were all represented at the service. In his address, General Ross remarked that he had found himself in the presence of HM The Queen a few days after Vivian had died. She expressed her sympathy and told him that Vivian had been one of her heroes, 'And,' she added, 'he had such marvellous legs!'

With the orchestra and the Band of the Royal Marines School of Music were the Organist and Choir of Sutton Valence School, Maidstone, which John Watson had kindly arranged. The selection of orchestral music while the congregation were arriving included music by J S Bach, Robert Farnon, William Walton, Ronald Binge, and Sir Edward Elgar. For the service the musicians switched to concert band to play Holst's *Jupiter* (from the *Planets Suite*), two of his favourite fanfares were played and the Master of the Worshipful Company of Musicians, A M W Davies, read from *Music and the Mind.*

In concluding his address General Ross summed up his own thoughts, and those of the large congregation, when he said:

> 'Above all, perhaps, Vivian Dunn understood quite clearly the value of military music. That which forms, if I may say it, part of the fabric of our nation and which sadly, at this time of constant pressure on defence cuts, seems to be forgotten. He was a man among men the like of whom we rarely see. In thanking God for the life of Vivian Dunn, no words in my view more appropriately can express my feelings for him than those describing the martyrdom of Mr Steadfast in John Bunyan's *Pilgrim's Progress*: "So he passed over and all the trumpets sounded for him on the other side." '

Whilst the large congregation were leaving his own *The Globe & Laurel* was followed by his arrangement of *The Preobrajensky March* and finally by the enduring march *Cockleshell Heroes*. Vivian would have been very proud.

Subsequently a Charity Concert was held in tribute to Sir Vivian Dunn, and attended by HRH The Prince Edward, the US Ambassador and the Commandant of the United States Marine Corps. It was held in the Guildhall, the City of London, on 22nd October 1996. The proceeds were divided between the Royal Marines Museum and St John Ambulance. The Guildhall was packed and the distinguished audience was treated to a fine

The Memorial Service to Sir Vivian Dunn at St Martin-in-the-Fields, 7 July 1995

concert demonstrating all the facets of the Royal Marines bands' range. Starting with an orchestral concert, which was followed by a sumptuous buffet supper, there came a military band concert before the evening was completed with an outdoor Beat Retreat. Vivian would have been overwhelmed, not only by the professional quality of the musicians, but also by the large number of his friends who attended the memorable evening.

Mike never really got over Vivian's death. She had not been in good health for many years. Their marriage had been a wonderful partnership. Outwardly Vivian had been 'on the move' ever since they were married, whilst Mike, remaining mostly in the background, had been a tremendous source of support, not only for her husband but for the whole family. When he died she simply lost her reason and will to live and her health declined very rapidly. Despite her immobility and frailty she was adamant she wanted to stay in the house they had shared and loved for so many years. She said she wanted to feel Vivian's presence near her. Some member of the family managed to visit her every weekend, for the three years she lived on after Vivian. It was a strain on them, but at the beginning of 1998 they had no option but to move her into a nursing home where she could receive 24-hour nursing care. She did her best to put on a brave face but the family were aware how unhappy and lonely she was. On the morning of the 26th June she slipped peacefully away to join her beloved Vivian.

Lady Dunn had also set out her funeral arrangements and had asked that the Reverend John Watson should conduct the service. During those past four difficult years he had been a source of comfort and solace to Mike. He wrote to her frequently and she expressed much pleasure that one of 'her boys' had thought so much of her. One of the most poignant moments during the service was the inclusion of *Ave Maria* which had been played at their wedding almost 60 years ago to the day. Jon Yates (also one of Mike's 'Boys' but now professor of trumpet at the RMSM) and Band Colour Sergeant Jason Burcham came over from Portsmouth specially to play this. The funeral was held in All Saints Church, Lindfield and her ashes were laid to rest alongside Vivian's grave at Walstead at her request 'with a smile and a prayer for them both'.

* * * * *

Probably one of Vivian's greatest achievements was his encouragement and development of musical talent within the Royal Marines Band Service. He had been quick to recognise outstanding musicians and could foresee what the future might hold for them if they were to work hard at it and, as he would put it, follow his example. We have already seen how Paul Neville had been picked out as a likely successor many years before his own retirement. His introduction of the year's conducting course at the Royal Academy had much to do with this selection. He always felt that the art of conducting was the most important asset of any Director of Music. This coupled with a wide range of musical knowledge, extending far beyond the military field into the classical repertoire was necessary to develop young talent and ensure the long term future of the Royal Marines Band Service.

He never suffered fools gladly and those who were not prepared to work and study hard, to widen their knowledge and pass their learning on to their charges, were quietly passed by. Unfortunately this sometimes led to accusations of favouritism, and though there may have been a few cases, it is not generally justified. There were very few band officers who did not suffer his wrath at some stage, but most acknowledged his intransigence and were able to say that they owed almost their entire careers to him. The compliments paid by so many that have been included in this book show much more than their personal appreciations of what he did for the Royal Marines Band Service. Vivian encouraged those under him to compose and arrange, while he was not afraid to introduce new and modern works into the repertoire. Had it not been for his example and understanding, the Royal Marines would not have had so many outstanding musicians. Paul Neville's marches *Silver Bugles* and *Sword of Honour*, John Ware's *San Carlos*, Peter Sumner's *Zeebrugge* and Richard Waterer's *Royal Salute* are excellent examples of the continuing quality of Royal Marines composers; and the many sumptuous and exciting arrangements made by countless others such as Ray Woodfield and David Cole who followed him owed much to the superlative teaching methods set up by Vivian and given to musicians of all ages which helped them develop their own individual styles. There are others too numerous to mention. No doubt Michael McDermott, the present day master of arrangements and compositions at the Royal Marines School of Music, can be grateful for being brought up in a Corps where all facets of music are taught and those best suited to individual talents are enlarged.

Gone are the days of what used to be called 'reluctant dragons', and Vivian's exhortation for educational and musical qualification ultimately produced Directors of Music with Bachelor of Arts degrees in addition to their musical diplomas. His influence can still be felt more than 30 years after he retired.

When the redevelopment of Eastney Barracks, Southsea into private flats and homes was completed in 1995, the new road which stands on the old parade ground outside the church was named 'Dunn Close' in his honour. It was here that the weekly church parades used to form up after the service; it was here that he and Mike had been married. The last time they stood there was at a farewell concert on the closure of the barracks in 1991. He will never be forgotten.

And thus another chapter in the Dunn family has drawn to a close. The illustrious career of Lieutenant Colonel Sir Vivian Dunn KCVO, OBE, FRAM, FRSA, HonGSM, RM is over. His life span, covering as it did all ten decades of the twentieth century, saw him learning, making and teaching music in all its many forms. What he did for the Royal Marines Band Service cannot be underestimated, but one only has to compare the breadth and depth of his compositions and arrangements with those of many other leading composers of this century to see how unique were his achievements. In addition to this he headed a professional organisation over

1,000 strong at its peak with national, international and Royal commitments. Only then can we appreciate the full measure of his contribution to the musical scene of this century. He once wrote:

> 'The writing and composing of a humble march is a very difficult thing. To achieve originality, structure, design, good tunes, good instrumentation, harmony, all that sort of thing. If you can write a good march you're a good musician.
>
> I have everything to be grateful for in my life. My family, the Band Service, invitations to conduct and teach at many universities in the United States, the prestige of the Worshipful Company of Musicians, Presidencies of a number of Music and Service Societies have allowed me to fulfil the commitment.
>
> You are placed in this world to do good, and if it lies within your power, it is your bounden duty so to do. Therefore it may not be entirely inappropriate to quote the words of the song "I Did It My Way!" '

APPENDIX A

The Orchestral Music of F Vivian Dunn

An Appreciation by Alastair Mitchell LGSM

For someone who composed in a mainly homophonic style (i.e. the combination of instruments or voices sounding melodically alike) it is prudent to consider Sir Vivian Dunn's orchestral music in context with the state in which British music was during the period 1930-31, the years when Sir Vivian was a member of the BBC Symphony Orchestra.

This was the time when British music sounded quintessentially 'British', mainly through the work of Ralph Vaughan Williams, who was synonymous with all that is best in English symphonic music, and Sir Edward Elgar, who reinforced native faith in English musical heritage. That quintessence was a stimulant for all composers of that time, and it is readily seen in Sir Vivian's *Romance Pastorale: Broadlands*, subtitled *The serenity of an English country house*, the second movement of *The Mountbatten Suite*. The first performance was given on 28th October 1982 at the Royal Marines School of Music, Deal, the orchestra conducted by the composer.

The scoring for strings and harp arpeggios of *Broadlands* reflects upon a bygone era; here, we are in the world of the tone poem when orchestral colour and the work of Debussy and Ravel in the early part of this century were to leave their 'hallmarks' of style. Much of this is to be seen in Vaughan Williams' *The Lark Ascending* or Elgar's *Introduction and Allegro* for strings.

Strings open the work softly, and as an evocation of the countryside (the trees and the river Test flows through the grounds of Broadlands) the oboe makes its first entry in the seventh bar, like a shaft of sunlight illuminating a dark corner in the river. This tone colour painting is almost reminiscent of the opening of the *Andante* of Schubert's *Great C Major Symphony*, though an imperceptible reduction of tempo to introduce a solo flute, accompanied delicately by a bass clarinet, solo horn, harp and strings with the marking 'sostenuto'. Here one is tempted to equate this with the dawn chorus. In the character of the instrument, a solo bass punctuates the score rhythmically with pizzicato crotchets. A pastoral duet is now heard on oboe and flute, this being the main theme on which the whole of the work is based:

Example 1

This is accompanied by soft syncopation, which intensifies and appropriately broadens. Second violins double-stopping, and divided violas and 'cellos producing an unmistakable, quintessential 'English sound' (the device Elgar and Vaughan Williams used) and in which the second violins and violas are an octave apart. After further intensification, the majesty of this music is implemented by four horns and trombones making their first entry in a section marked *piu mosso*. Seventeen bars later Sir Vivian reminds us of who the occupant was of *Broadlands* by letting the bassoon, third horn, first and second trombones and the first cellos play the introductory fragment from *Preobrajensky* accompanied by tremolo strings and stylistically written in 12/8, giving the piece a Wagnerian touch. The timpani signal the approach of the closing section with four distinct crotchets, another Elgarian even Waltonian characteristic, and two bars in the relative minor key of D in order to provide a bridge back to how the piece began. It closes with the same serenity evocative of a splendid summer's day idyll on the river, and allowing a solo violin to display the compass of the instrument and, in the last bar, a harp glissando, one of those romantic devices that Sir Vivian chose to include in his music *Portrait of a Lovely Lady* (12 February 1961) which includes an enticing theme for horns:

Example 2

No other instrument could sound this passage in such a seductive manner. Unfortunately no first performance details of this are known.

The concert march *Cockleshell Heroes* is usually performed nowadays in a version for military band arranged in 1956 by W J Duthoit, then professor of instrumentation at Kneller Hall. However it started life as an orchestral march and was first performed as such by the orchestra of the Royal Marines School of Music, conducted by the composer in a programme leading up to the world première of the film *Cockleshell Heroes* on 16 November 1955 at the Empire Theatre, Leicester Square, London.

The opening bar (set here in short score) provides the nautical motif on which the whole piece is based:

Example 3

After the first rousing twelve bars of alternating tuttis and bridge passages heard in an antiphonal style, cellos, basses and bassoons provide that essential SBS element of 'something sinister lurks below sea level'. But since this pattern:

Example 4

is broadened to:

Example 5

on strings and woodwind as the main cantabile theme of the slow section, it is easy to see that 'something sinister', i.e. the heroes, is on the side of the right.

Example 4 recurs once more as a lead in to a restatement of the cantabile tune used as a finale to the march. One can sense a certain surge of the movement of sea water, and there is a temptation to compare this music to the heavy surge of water depicted in Mendelssohn's *Hebrides Overture*. After the introductory scene setting which takes some 27 bars in 2/4 time, the essence and spirit of the music establishes itself as a very fine concert march.

Although 225 bars long *Cockleshell Heroes* may appear to be of unequal proportions (it is certainly not divisible by four or eight), but taken as a whole the sound and structure is nevertheless complete, simply because of the breezy, nautical style, making this one of the best known of all Sir Vivian's marches.

Cockleshell Heroes matches Sir Vivian's dictum that a good march relies on '... originality allied with sound musicianship and the ability on the part of the composer to invent excellent tunes, harmoniz(ing) them soundly and invest(ing) his invention with ingenious counterpoint.'[1]

Man of Action is the third movement of the *Mountbatten Suite*, written and first heard at the Royal Albert Hall on 6th February 1980 in a tribute to the late Admiral of the Fleet. Four Royal Marines Bands were conducted by Lieutenant Colonel J R Mason MVO, and, as the title implies, this is an active and exciting piece which only relaxes for the middle, slow section with its Elgarian, some may say, heroic associations. Sound in rhythm, stylistic attraction and similarly structured to *Cockleshell Heroes*, *Man of Action* is based on a breezy, main tune introduced in the twenty-second bar, and sails through the whole work, evoking the delight of steering through a Force 6 wind. As in *Cockleshell Heroes*, there is an Elgarian influence in the middle section marked *molto expresso*. Every good march requires a contrasting slow section, and in it Sir Vivian makes appropriate use of *Kelly from the Isle of Man*, a very popular tune dating back to the early 1930s. *Man of Action* is a good example of being a nautical *perpetuum mobile*, though in the closing bars there is the suggestion that one has turned into the safety of harbour, having been negotiating an exhilarating and satisfactory course, the final goal being represented by an orchestral gong. The same sort of feeling, this writer admits, evoked by the end of the third movement in Vaughan Williams' *Sea Symphony*.

* * * * *

The use of incidental music dates back to at least the Shakespearean times, especially for entrances and exits, alarums and excursions, and such music cannot be interpreted as characteristic of a composer's style. He can only enhance upon a certain dramatic moment, for instance by composing a short fanfare for the entrance of royalty or some other dignitary. The incidental music, referred to as *Japanese Motif*, written for the play *Teahouse of the August Moon*, first heard at the Globe Theatre, Depot Royal Marines, Deal on 1st March 1961 only serves to enhance the Japanese setting of the play. Sir Vivian, who conducted this first performance, deleted the part for an orchestral gong presumably because there wasn't one available.

One has to go on to the more lengthy works to appreciate a composer's development, though one can see something of this in the various wedding music pieces Sir Vivian wrote for his family weddings.

The *Wedding Music for Patrick and Ann* (March 1968) draws on the tunes of *Carmen Carthusianum* and *Annie Laurie* in a setting reminiscent of Brahms, and although originally first performed by an ensemble of oboe, strings and organ, there is also a most effective version for string quartet; there is a passage allotted to the violincello until the rest of the quartet provides gossamer-like harmony. Here, this writer feels, this must have been meant for one particular cellist.

Influence and self-borrowings are very prevalent in the *Processional Music for John and Rosey*, written for the couple's wedding on 1st October 1966, and it was for this occasion that, appropriately, Elgar's *Salut d'Amour* was one of the pieces played by the Orchestra of the Royal Marines School of Music during the signing of the register. The *Processional Music for John and Rosey* opens in Waltonesque fashion. Trumpets, horns and timpani herald the piece with a fanfare, not dissimilar to the introductory bars of a section used in the overture to *The Young Elizabeth*, in 4/4 time:

Example 6

After the development of this theme, the second subject is introduced. Like J.S. Bach, two hundred and fifty years earlier and who constantly re-used, even recycled much of his own compositions, so too Sir Vivian did, for there is a variation on a self-borrowed theme first heard ten years earlier at the Empire Theatre, Leicester Square. It is no less than the heroic theme, the cantabile section, from the *Cockleshell Heroes* concert march. In place of a crotchet and two quavers of the theme, Sir Vivian wrote an even four bar melody, and whilst retaining the patriotic essence of the piece he skilfully produced a better overall effect by broadening out the crotchet and two quavers, and shortly before the end there is a musical quotation played by wind instruments of the *Praise to the Holiest* motif:

Example 7: Elgar

In almost everything Sir Vivian wrote there is some Elgarian element. When Roy Plomley cast him away on that famous Desert Island, Sir Vivian singled out *Praise to the Holiest* from *The Dream of Gerontius*, reflecting the time when he had conducted the Portsmouth Bach Society, while he was stationed there.

The overture to *The Young Elizabeth* opens with a good firm 'kick start' in a setting that is clearly a busy courtyard within the noble environs of the Tower of London. It is redolent of a twentieth century composer depicting a 16th century picture. Sir Vivian was doing what Walton did when depicting Portsmouth Harbour in his overture *Portsmouth Point*. But hardly a moment has gone by when we find one of those uncanny coincidences that sometimes happens in music for suddenly we are confronted by the tune of *Bridge Over Troubled Waters;* this is comparable to the inclusion of a theme very like the hymn tune *Abide With Me* in Mahler's *Symphony No 9*, and *Ba, Ba Black Sheep* in Rachmaninov's *Piano Concerto No 4*.

Serenity is the keynote in the contrasting, second section in which the cello has a particularly fine part against the rest of the strings. There is a Waltonesque character about this, reminiscent of the style of the *Touch her soft lips and part* movement for strings in Walton's music for *Henry V*; Tudor music characteristics at the cadences abound, especially at the progress from the second to the third movement, heralded by trumpets and horns. This gives way to a scherzo, structured as a question and answer affair being played by high and middle-registered woodwind, the main theme, here being introduced by low stringed instruments.

Sir Vivian frequently developed his diatonic melodies a stage further from Elgar and Hubert Parry by splitting strong beats of the bar introducing triple crotchets in common time, a device which enhances freedom and majesty, and to be found in the music of Brahms and J.S. Bach, though Bach usually set his triplet crotchets over groups of two, in a bar of 4/4. So, at the beginning of Sir Vivian's *Mountbatten March*, clarinets, horns, trumpets, trombones and strings declare a rhythmically and ingenious variation, thus:

Example 8

This breaks the rigidity of the familiar discipline usually associated with *A Life on the Ocean Wave*; the same rhythmic device, but not a variation of Henry Russell's song, occurs again in the 13th bar of *Man of Action*.

From this, it is easy to understand what influenced much of Sir Vivian's compositions. It is a reminder of the debt he owed to Elgar, for, as he said to Roy Plomley[2] about *The Dream of Gerontius:*

> '... It is not only an emotional, but a great religious and musical experience, and I remember because I had the privilege of performing under Sir Edward Elgar and taking part in the marvellous performances at the Queen's Hall and the Royal Albert Hall, and also, when I was the conductor of the Portsmouth Bach Society, and later in east Kent with the Deal and Walmer Handelian Society. I recall conducting this and feeling the sort of tremendous influence of the work ...'

Notes:

1 Sleeve note by Sir Vivian Dunn to his LP record *'The World's Greatest Marches'* (EMI Records CSD 3637, 1967)

2 *Desert Island Discs*, 6th November 1971

I must acknowledge help for the preparation of this appreciation to Mr John Ambler of the Royal Marines Historical Society, and to Ms Verity Steele, Deputy Chief Librarian of the Royal Marines School of Music Central Library who allowed me to consult various of the scores mentioned.

A.M.
West London and Okehampton, Devon, December 1998

Alastair Mitchell is a conductor, lecturer and musicologist who trained at the Guildhall School of Music. He is the author of several books and his Chronicle of First Broadcast Musical Performances in the United Kingdom, 1923-1996 *will be published in 1999 by Ashgate Publishing Ltd.*

APPENDIX B

The Military Music of F Vivian Dunn

An Appreciation by Major Gordon Turner MBE

Whilst on a visit to the Royal Military School of Music, Kneller Hall, Sir Vivian was asked to name the outstanding composers produced by the British services. Without hesitation he replied that two stood out above all others: Walton O'Donnell for his three major military/wind band works *Three Humoresques, Theme and Variations* and *Songs of the Gael*, and Kenneth Alford for his wonderful military marches. Risking a rebuff, the questioner asked how Sir Vivian thought his own marches compared with those of Alford. A smile came across Sir Vivian's face, and after a few moments he elaborated his previous statement that Alford was outstanding and really no other British service musician had risen to the same standard. Warming to the subject, he likened himself to the 18th century court musician, in that most of his marches had been written for a specific occasion or person, thus at times being a little restricted; Alford, on the other hand, had virtually a free hand in all that he wrote. Despite this, however, Sir Vivian was at pains to emphasise that, even if Alford had been restricted, he – like the great court composers of the past, and like the Russians writing under communism – would still have stood out.

When I was first appointed Professor of Orchestration at Kneller Hall, Sir Vivian advised me to have the students copy out Alford's marches as full scores so that they would learn not only how to construct a march but also how to orchestrate one. Like Alford, he was a great believer in writing interesting parts for the secondary players. 'If you see a 2nd or 3rd clarinet player looking happy at a concert, it is one of two things – either he has some interesting parts to play or he has a date afterwards', he once said: 'Whilst we can do little about the second, we can try to write interesting music.' He explained that in his very early works he had been content to write good melodies, counter subjects and harmonies, but had made little attempt to give the secondary players anything other than mundane rhythmic parts.

A march that has recently been discovered and recorded is ***Eastney***. Whilst there is no doubt that this march has a good melody line and well deserved an airing, the scoring is not as interesting as works written at a later date. The question and answer effect between melody and counter subject in the Trio is quite delightful – so simple and natural – but on the down side, the endings of the phrases in the bass line are in the main a sustained note, as opposed to little flourishes that can be found in later Dunn marches. It is always difficult to write 'accompaniment' parts such as horns in 6/8 time and here they tend to be a little uninteresting especially when compared with those in *Cannatex* (also in 6/8 time). Perhaps it was because of these slight defects that it was put away and did not emerge during Sir Vivian's lifetime, though the composer is not always the best judge of his own work. *Eastney* may not be of the same standard as *The Captain General* and the like, but it is still the equal of many published marches by well known writers.

Example 1

Most top flight composers have 'trade marks' – favourite idioms that frequently appear in their works and Sir Vivian was no exception. The following can be found used to great effect in his marches:

- octave leaps in the melodic line
- scalic passages to be found in the melodic line and also to great effect in the bass
- rhythmic figures in the bass at cadence points
- the rhythmic figure of three quarter notes (similar to the opening of Alford's *Eagle Squadron)*

These may appear to be run-of-the-mill devices but it takes a gifted writer to use scalic passages as successfully as we find here, and the use of the octave leap is inspired. Studying Alford's marches no doubt influenced the rhythmic bass cadence points

Under the White Ensign was written in 1949 and was dedicated to the Royal Naval Old Comrades Association (now the Royal Naval Association). It contains the naval bugle calls 'Alert' and 'Carry On', together with references to *Rule Britannia* and *The Sailor's Hornpipe*. The second subject has an excellent use of scalic passages in contrary motion with the melodic parts ascending and the tenor/bass descending.

Example 2a

Halfway through the same subject is a beautiful answering effect melody to counter subject.

Example 2b

Like Alford's *Great Little Army*, the first half of the march is in 2/2 time with the Trio in 6/8. A four bar unison passage (basically the descending scale of E♭ major) serves as an introduction to a melody which is the equal of most trio themes by any composer. The bridge passage is based on the descending scales and then comes the Grandioso. Powerfully scored, with unison tenor trombones doubling the melody an octave below the first cornet, there is a brilliant florid passage in the high woodwind. At salient points, the trombones leave the melody to reinforce the bass line, and at the halfway point the euphonium is given the opening phrase of *A Life on the Ocean Wave.*

In 1949, ***Cannatex*** was written for the Canadian National Exhibition. The opening has a strong similarity to Holzmann's *Blaze Away* in both rhythm and orchestration.

Example 3a: *Cannatex, opening bars*

Blaze Away, opening bars

As Sir Vivian rarely did anything without considering the implications, we can only assume that this had some particular significance to the Exhibition. The melody of the first subject is based on a scalic pattern and at bar nine the heavy brass had a wonderful descending scale.

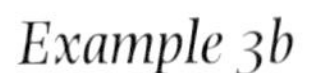

Example 3b

Four bars from the end of this subject we have a beautiful effect crested by a major chord on the flattened submediant. The second subject commences with a bass solo, again based on a descending scale with all instruments marked *ff* (very loud). Halfway through the melody, once more embracing the ascending scale, moves to the higher end of the band and the dynamic drops immediately to *p* (soft). There is a recapitulation of the first subject and then a four bar introduction into the trio tune. This theme, scored for the tenor section, commences with an octave leap (dominant to dominant) and is in fact a snippet taken from the Canadian National Song *The Maple Leaf for Ever.* The effect created is quite beautiful especially as the melody gradually descends for four bars and then the treble instruments enter with an ascending answer. In the bridge passage there are references to the opening but is more fully scored, whilst the Grandioso is a reprise of the trio tune, strongly scored with a bravuro style trombone counter subject.

Example 3c: *Cannatex, trio tune*

Maple Leaf Forever

In 1954 the film *The Dambusters* was released and was an immediate box office success. A march, specially composed by Eric Coates, was used whilst the credits were shown and references to it appeared in the background music composed by Leighton Lucas. Plans were already in hand for a similar film on the story of ***The Cockleshell Heroes*** with John Addison writing the music. Sir Vivian was invited to compose a march to be played at the film premiere and possibly used in the film. The producer strongly suggested that it be in the same vein as *The Dambusters* with a big, broad Coates tune. The march produced by Sir Vivian certainly has a hint of Coates about it and an examination of the two themes from each march show a passing resemblance.

Example 4a: *The Dambusters*

Cockleshell Heroes

The march does however quite clearly have a Dunn stamp about it, with an octave leap at bar five of the Trio, the descending scalic bass and the three reiterated notes (which are the basic musical germ in the opening and first subject). In this case the rhythm suggests the words 'Cock - le - shell Her - oes'.

Example 4b: *The Dambusters, 1st theme*

With his fine ear and superb academic training, Sir Vivian never needed a keyboard or any musical instrument to compose, and apparently composed this march whilst on a journey to Ascot. The following day he put it down on paper! When completed, an arrangement was made for theatre organ. The producer and director were to show film clips at the Empire, Leicester Square, and also demonstrate some of the proposed film music (including Sir Vivian's march) on the organ to representatives of the company backing the film. Bearing in mind the request for a big broad Coates tune, Sit Vivian gave the organist instructions to start halfway through where the tune started and then go back to the beginning. Various officials were late arriving and everything became a little rushed. Sitting in the back stalls Sir Vivian was dismayed to hear the march started from the very first note, and before the organist had arrived at the broad tune, the producer had said 'Enough!' and proceeded to the next item. Due to the organist's error, this splendid march never had the exposure in the film that it warranted.

Bill 'Dusty' Duthoit, resident band arranger at Chappell and Co, arranged the military band version. This was no reflection on Sir Vivian but merely an inflexible music publisher's rule and, as 'Dusty' explained at the proofing session, the composer had clearly indicated who should play what.

The Captain General was composed specially for the occasion when on 19th December 1949, HM King George VI, then the Captain General Royal Marines, dined with the officers of the Corps at the Savoy in London. The four bar introduction, which commences in unison leads to a strong but unfussy theme, contains several examples of the three reiterated rhythm figure. The second subject is worth studying in that the bass line for the first eight bars is exactly the same as the bass line of the second subject of *The Mountbatten March.*

The first two bars of the introduction to the Trio are the same as the opening and then comes the trio tune – one of the finest I have heard. It starts well though not spectacularly and then, in moving from bar two to three, the melody appears to overshoot its destination and slides down in semitones for two notes; it really is a wonderful effect. A bridge passage based on the rhythm of the introductions and also the reiterated three notes naturally lead into the Grandioso. Conventionally the melody is the same as before, but now there is a scalic counter subject on trombones and euphonium. Whereas in most of Sir Vivian's scoring he writes for two tenor trombones and a bass trombone, in this march he appears to be thinking more of three tenors. Most good composers avoid solo cymbal crashes, as they do in the main sound extremely 'corny'; here, however, in the bridge passage of the trio, the cymbal and bass drum fill in the second beat rest most effectively.

The Mountbatten March was dedicated to Admiral of the Fleet The Earl Mountbatten of Burma, Life Colonel Commandant of the Royal Marines. The introduction consists of, in immediate succession, melodic statements from *Rule Britannia, A Life on the Ocean Wave* and *The Slow March of the Life Guards.* The first subject commences with an ornamental quaver figure, which in true Dunn fashion, leaps an octave, and a few bars later the three-note rhythm appears. (As previously stated, the bass line of the second subject is identical to that of *The Captain General.*) At bar nine the tenor and bass sections state the opening of *Rule Britannia* followed immediately a minor third higher by the treble instruments. After a recapitulation of the first subject a four bar introduction based on *The Preobrajensky March* leads to the trio tune.

In addition to the numerous totally original marches, there are also ones that comprise mainly of folk tunes and the like. ***The Globe & Laurel*** is an excellent example. In 1935 each of the Corps' Directors of Music was asked to write a work that might be adopted as the Corps' official slow march. The committee failed to agree but favoured one by Ricketts (later to become *By Land and Sea)* and Lieutenant Dunn's march, based on the old English air *Early One Morning* and titled *The Globe and Laurel*. Arranged as a slow march, it commences with a strong four bar introduction with the instructions 'Molto marcato e pesante' (very heavy and marked). All instruments have the same rhythm. At bar five there is a complete change in style and dynamics when the folk tune enters. The players are instructed to play smoothly and only moderately loud. The music swells and dies away in each phrase. There is no attempt to use any chromatic chords or counter melody and the arranger relies entirely on a perfect balance and nicely moving inner parts. The tune is repeated with the volume dropping lower. With very little warning, a fierce bass and tenor passage follows. Whilst this work cannot be claimed as an original composition, it is much more than an arrangement.

An arrangement often heard at naval displays is ***Westering Home***. Unlike most 3/4 (waltz time) troops, there are no off beats in the band parts and thus a smooth silky sound is achieved. The side drum provides rhythm, which becomes a strong feature and, as in *The Globe and Laurel*, there are no counter melodies. There are several instances of the scalic passage 'feature' to be found in the bass line.

Example 6: Westering Home, bars 5 - 8

The fanfare ***Salute for Heroes*** written for band and bugles is only nine bars in length and lasts less than 30 seconds. It is, however, extremely effective with the majority of the band merely emphasising the first note of bars one, three and five and joining in the last chord. The brass section fills in from bar six. Whilst this is an original fanfare it is interesting to note that the first four bars are virtually identical to the opening of the quick march *Mechanised Infantry* composed in the 1930s by David McBain. From 1906-27 Sir Vivian's father, William James Dunn, was bandmaster of the 2nd Battalion The King's Royal Rifle Corps and on moving to the Blues he was replaced by David McBain. Although this is not the regimental call of the KRRC, I believe that it had some connection which had possibly lodged in Sir Vivian's subconscious mind. Whatever the explanation, *Salute for Heroes* is a fine bugle fanfare.

Example 7: Mechanised Infantry

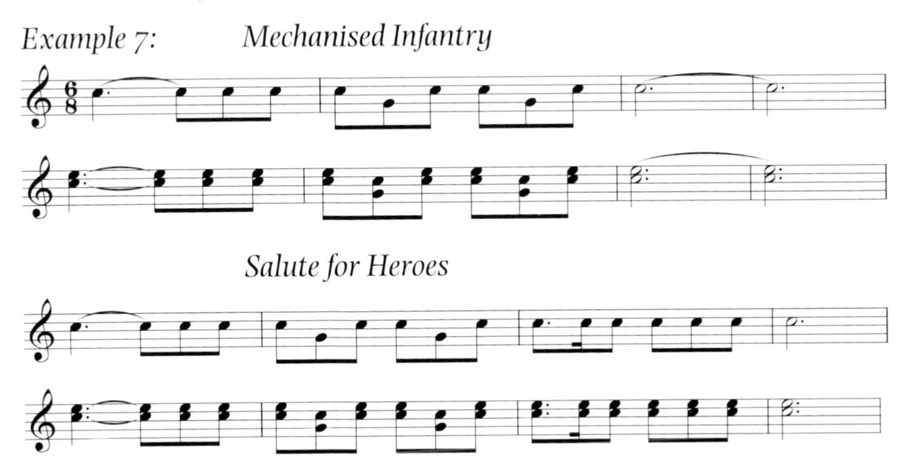

A more elaborate fanfare is ***Supreme Command*** scored for two groups of seven fanfare trumpets or one group plus band. It is intended that the two groups should be used antiphonally. A two bar unison statement (marked 96 beats per minute) opens the fanfare, there is a short break and then team one launches into a four bar rhythmic phrase at a slightly faster speed.

Example 8a: Supreme Command, opening

Team two answers with the same phrase a minor third lower. Back to team one, who now split up, with the four treble instruments making a statement answered by three trombones - this continues for four bars when the other team takes over with completely new material. At bar 23 the opening two bars in the quick time.

Example 8b: Supreme Command, bars 23 - 24

Bar 31 brings a change in tempo to piu lento and then five bars from the end the tempo slows once more, and all forces combine for a majestic end. Just as the end appears, there is a break followed by a bass note and then the remainder enter. Although in many ways a conventional fanfare, this is one of the few ever written that work successfully as an antiphonal work. No attempt has been made to describe the exotic chromaticisms and modulations that are used but it is perhaps worth noting that whilst the fanfare commences in C major it ends very convincingly on the chord of G major.

Jorrock's Chase is a musical novelty written for three post horns and three coach horns with military band accompaniment. Always aware of and appreciating the problems that small bands have, the composer cross-cues parts and on the front cover of the manuscript score wrote 'The coach horn parts can be played on B♭ Cornets or Trumpets and can be performed by instruments numbering from 1 Post Horn and 1 Coach Horn (Cornet or Trumpet) upwards. The Coach Horns are specific instruments pitched in C and convertible to B♭ manufactured by Messrs Boosey & Hawkes Ltd'. The work commences with a four note statement from the band followed by a 'call' on the Post Horn pitched in A♭. The same procedure is followed with the B♭ Coach Horn substituting the Post Horn, and then a third time using the C Coach Horn. Four bars on the band bring us the first subject played in harmony on three Coach Horns in C. A skilful modulation introduces the second subject, which features Post Horns in unison. Modulating back, there is a recapitulation of the first subject. This leads to *D'ye ken John Peel* in the key of F Major in which the Coach Horns are featured. The same tune falls a third to A♭ major and the Post Horns come into their own. A five bar codetta featuring all soloists rounds the work off. Mention should be made of the skilful use of temple blocks to create a horse hoof effect.

Example 9: Jorrock's Chase

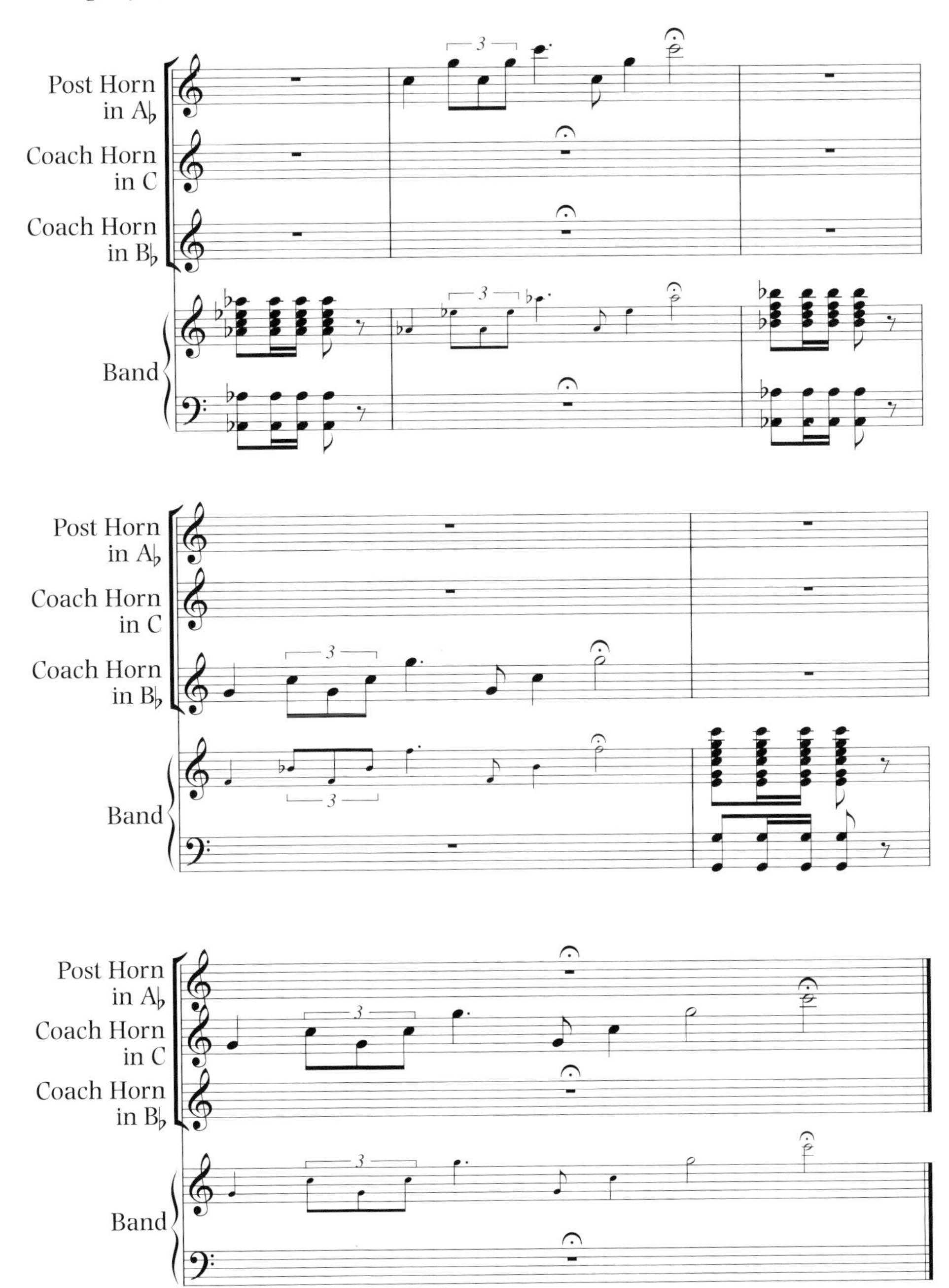

There is no doubt that almost without exception all these works show the craftsmanship and originality of an exceptional musician. Where extracts from folk songs, etc., have been used, they are skilfully woven into the original material; the harmonic structure is at all times solid, with chromatic chords being used sparingly in order to create the greatest effect; the orchestration using the instruments in a sensible and carefully balanced way.

Why then are we faced with a situation where, apart from the Bands of the Royal Marines, few others play any of these marches; and why have so few pieces been published? There are several contributory factors to this state of affairs; the titles are mainly naval, which has tended to discourage the bands of the Army and Royal Air Force, whilst there is no doubt that many of the older army bandmasters never forgave the man or the system for the way in which the extremely young Vivian Dunn became a director of music. Perhaps it was partly because of this early success that Sir Vivian, unlike some more pushing and unscrupulous directors, never felt the need to force his work on others, whether publishers or conductors.

Major Gordon Turner was taught at the age of ten to play the cornet in a Salvation Army band. He joined the Corps of Royal Engineers as a junior musician at sixteen and in 1958 became the youngest bandmaster in the British Army. He served as Bandmaster with the 15th/19th Kings Royal Hussars and with the Royal Green Jackets and was later Director of Music of the Royal Tank Regiment and the Royal Corps of Signals. He was for many years Professor of Orchestration at the Royal Military School of Music, Kneller Hall. In 1988 he became editor of Band International, *the journal of the International Military Music Society and now serves as a member of the Society's UK branch committee. He also became editor of* Fanfare, *the journal of Kneller Hall in 1990 and later began writing regular columns for* Legion *the magazine of the Royal British Legion. Since 1994 he has written, with his son Alwyn, a three volume work entitled* The History of British Military Bands *as well as the history of Kneller Hall,* The Trumpets Shall Sound.

Music excerpts reproduced by Captain Ted Whealing

APPENDIX C

Do's and Don'ts for Conductors

Vivian Dunn was probably best known for his conducting. The following manuscript was found, carefully corrected, but as far as is known never appeared in printed form.

Do's and Don'ts for Conductors

Hints designed to assist the approach and practice of their art.

Do's

1. Insist on punctuality at rehearsal and be there yourself at assembly.

2. Ensure the correct number of music stands, stands and percussion instruments are in position and arranged in a neat formation to allow easy room for each player, but without gaps

3. Seating sections is a matter of the conductor's preference and there can be licence in this, but positioning must be carefully calculated to enhance a balanced result.

4. Assembly must be orderly and, once tuning has commenced, all talking must cease and will not be permitted throughout the rehearsal. Questions may be asked by the players and should be answered precisely.

5. Prepare tuning thoroughly, section by section, and then the full band.

6. Discuss the programme with the Librarian well beforehand, and ensure a full complement of band parts are available and in good condition with nothing missing.

7. Give clear directions as to which work the rehearsal will commence and expect each piece to be found quickly and without fuss.

8. Create an atmosphere of eager, cheerful expectancy to engender immediate enthusiastic response from the players. Respect them and they will respect you. A sense of good humour helps the rapport.

9. Study the scores thoroughly, preferably at the piano, and be master of their interpretation so that they know that you know, and are working for their benefit rather than yours.

10. Train the band to react to whatever you say or do, so that when you stop, they stop at once; and are ready to recommence when you resume.

11. Speak clearly and distinctly and ensure the players listen attentively to every point you make. Do not allow inattention or slovenliness, as the secret of any musical combination is that it looks as alert and as well as it sounds. The highest standard is the minimum expectancy.

12. Rehearse meticulously and repeat passages to iron out difficulties - sometimes at half speed to inspire confidence and improve performance. Be patient and never lose your temper no matter what frustrations are encountered.

13. Listen critically to intonation and balance. Create a true sense of style in all sections aiming at professionalism and distinction. Nothing should be too much trouble.

14. Always look directly at the players as communication through the eyes is total.

15. Above all be severely critical of yourself as it is the key to your musicianship, technique, manner, appearance and the gift of creating a

polished performance through power, sensitivity and musical expressiveness. Too often the conductor is the last to know of his own indiscretions and faults by just not thinking and preparing himself thoroughly. Conducting is an art only to be practised by those who respect and aim to be worthy of it

Don'ts

1. Do not adopt an air of condescension so that the players are unwilling to respond or communicate with you.

2. Do not participate or talk at too great length to risk the players becoming bored. Remember they are more interested in the immediate playing of the notes rather than the musicology of the work under rehearsal.

3. Never address the band with your arms in the conducting position. Let them be relaxed at the side and then raise when you wish to resume.

4. Carefully study your technique to ensure it is the acme of clarity with the point visible at all times, shaping and phrasing the music.

5. Never get into the habit of merely duplicating the beats with the left hand. It is better to keep it balanced and used to indicate leads and assist marks of expression and climaxes.

6. A conductor must constantly practice his art by concentration and depth of thought. He can be guilty of as many 'wrong notes' as any of his players and his errors are easily detected.

7. Some points to avoid:
   a. An unclear beat especially when starting any part in the score.
   b. Lack of preparation where anacruses are concerned.
   c. Hurrying or flicking the beat leading to inaccurate rhythm in the tempo.
   d. Never be afraid to refer to a metronome as an infallible sense of accurate tempo is paramount.

e. Failing to conduct with expression. Slow movements are the most difficult and require special care on your part to make the music 'live'. Practice on your own and think out what you will do before attempting anything with the band. An ill-prepared conductor is a dull conductor and produces dull music.
f. Erratic movements of the arms and body, giving an impression of fidgetiness. Stand perfectly still with the legs slightly apart. Change of posture comes with the demands in the music - it should be natural and add to the expectation.
g. Never conduct with your eyes glued to the score. memorise passages (if not the complete score) and always look at the players for co-ordination. This can never be over-emphasised.

F. V. D.

APPENDIX D

The Compositions and Arrangements of F Vivian Dunn

Compiled by John Ambler

Chairman, UK Branch of the International Military Music Society

KEY:
(C) = Composition
(A) = Arrangement
MB = for Military Band
Orch = for Orchestra
SmOrch = for Small Orchestra
B & Dr = for Bugles and Drums
Orc/Pipe = for Orchestra and Pipes
Wind En = for Wind Ensemble.

NOTE 1: Many pieces of Sir Vivian Dunn's music were transcribed for orchestra, band, small ensemble etc. In such instances the most common form has been noted.

NOTE 2: In some cases it is difficult to differentiate between a composition and an arrangement. The music score, or parts, have been used as the indicator wherever possible. RMBS classifications have also been used.

DATE	TITLE		
1939	*Eastney*	(C)	MB
1940	*Heroes of the River Plate*	(C)	MB
1940	*A Life on the Ocean Wave*	(A)	Orch
1944	*O England My Country*	(A)	Choral
1945	*The Globe and Laurel* *	(C)	MB
1945	*Song of the Sea*	(A)	Orch

* *The Globe and Laurel* was originally written in 1935 for a march competition but was revised in 1945 as the march we now know.

DATE	TITLE		
1947	*The Springbok*	(C)	MB
1947	*Royal Vanguard*	(C)	MB
1947	*N'Kosi Sikelele*	(A)	SmOrch
1948	*Bolero*	(A)	MB
1948	*Mine Eyes Have Seen the Glory*	(A)	MB
1948	*Prelude to the Morning*	(C)	MB
1948	*Camberley*	(C)	MB
1949	*The Captain General*	(C)	MB
1949	*Show Business*	(A)	MB
1949	*Introduction to God Save the King*	(A)	Orch
1949	*Canadian National Exhibition (Cannatex)*	(C)	MB
1949	*The Tudor Maiden*	(A)	MB
1949	*The Pompey Chimes*	(C)	MB
1951	*Under the White Ensign*	(C)	MB
1951	*Enthronement Fanfare*	(C)	Fanfare
1953	*The Royal Marines Band Service*	(C)	Fanfare
1953	*Isa Lei*	(A)	MB
1954	*A Life on the Ocean Wave*	(A)	
1954	*Where the Blue of the Night*	(A)	MB
1955	*Cockleshell Heroes*	(C)	MB
1955	*Cockleshell Heroes Fanfare*	(C)	Fanfare
1956	*Combined Services*	(C)	Fanfare
1956	*Heroic Fanfare*	(C)	Fanfare
1957	*For an Ecclesiastical Jubilee*	(C)	Fanfare
1957	*For an Anniversary*	(C)	Fanfare
1957	*(The) Amethyst March*	(A)	MB
1957	*Salute for Heroes*	(C)	Fanfare
1957	*Brass Buttons*	(A)	MB
1957	*Commando Patrol*	(C)	MB
1958	*Crimond*	(A)	MB
1958	*Where e'er You Walk*	(A)	MB
1958	*Sarie Marais*	(A)	MB
1958	*For a Royal Occasion*	(C)	Fanfare
1959	*Pony Tail*	(A)	MB
1959	*The Young Elizabeth*	(C)	Orch
1960	*Soldiers of the Sea*	(C)	MB
1960	*Freedom of the City*	(C)	Fanfare
1960	*Shenandoah*	(A)	MB
1960	*Passing By (The WRNS March)*	(C)	MB
1960	*Navy Lark*	(A)	MB

DATE	TITLE		
1960	*Crown Imperial*	(A)	MB
1960	*Silver Bugles*	(C)	Fanfare
1960	*March & Air*	(A)	MB
1960	*Ceremonial Ruffle of Drums*	(C)	Drums
1960	*Emblazoned Drums*	(C)	Drums
1960	*Ceremonial Parade*	(C)	Fanfare
1961	*Teahouse of the August Moon*	(A)	Orch
1961	*Portrait of a Lovely Lady*	(C)	Orch
1962	*Edinburgh Tattoo (Scottish March Selection)*	(A)	MB
1962	*Sailor Boy*	(C)	
1962	*Gaelic Airs*	(A)	MB
1962	*Royal Tournament 1962*	(C)	Fanfare
1964	*Royal Flourish*	(C)	Fanfare
1964	*Orb & Sceptre*	(A)	MB
1964	*Salute to the Colours*	(C)	Fanfare
1964	*The Admiral's Regiment*	(C)	MB
1964	*The Preobrajensky March*	(A)	MB
1964	*For a Distinguished Assembly*	(C)	Fanfare
1964	*Songs for Male Chorus/Traditional Sea Songs*	(A)	Choral
1964	*Here's A Health Unto Her Majesty*	(A)	Orch
1965	*Eightsome Reel (Kate Dalrymple/High Road to Linton)*	(A)	
1965	*Drum & Fife Music (Spanish Peninsular March & Lilliburlero)*	(A)	
1965	*Will Ye Nae Come Back Again?*	(A)	MB
1965	*Glockenspiel & Xylophone Ensemble*	(C)	
1965	*Britain's Sea Soldiers*	(C)	Dr&B
1965	*Wedding Music – Andrew & Helen**	(C)	Orch
1965	*For a Royal Birthday*	(C)	Fanfare
1965	*Bugle Bells*	(C)	Bugles
1965	*Famous Songs of the British Isles*	(A)	MB
1965	*Jorrock's Chase*	(C)	MB
1965	*Hamilton House – Scottish Country Dances*	(A)	
1965	*The Meeting of the Waters*	(A)	MB
1965	*Green Hills of Tyrol*	(A)	
1965	*Journey into the New World*	(A)	Orc/Pipe
1965	*Aida (Insert to selection)*	(A)	MB
1965	*Pomp and Circumstance No 4*	(A)	
1965	*Symphony No 6 (Tchaikovsky)*	(A)	

* Classed by RMBS Central Music Library as a composition.

DATE	TITLE		
1965	*We're Nae Awa Tae Bide Awa*	(A)	Orch
1966	*A Life on the Ocean Wave/Heart of Oak*	(A)	MB
1966	RAH - BBC TV *(Moon River/Two Brothers/Mountain Greenery)*	(A)	MB
1966	*Processional March – Rosemary & John**	(C)	Orch
1967	*For a Royal Birthday*	(C)	Fanfare
1967	*Freedom of the City*	(C)	Fanfare
1967	*Processional Bridal March – Veryan & David**	(C)	Orch
1967	*Homage to the Queen*	(A)	MB
1968	*Beating Retreat*	(C)	Drums
1968	*Bugles & Drums*	(C)	B & Dr
1968	*The Royal Tournament*	(C)	Fanfare
1968	*Bugle Call Swing*	(C)	Bugles
1968	*Wedding Music for Patrick and Ann**	(C)	Orch
1968	*Holbrook*	(C)	MB
1968	*A Tribute to Alford*	(A)	MB
1969	*Salutation – Tribute to Sir Malcolm Sargent*	(C)	Fanfare
1971	*Processional Bridal March – Jeanne & Randy**	(C)	Orch
1972	*Flourish of Trumpets*	(C)	Fanfare
1972	*The Mountbatten March*	(C)	MB
1972	*Supreme Command*	(C)	Fanfare
1977	*Royal Naval Reserve March*	(C)	MB
1978	*The Royal Regiment*	(C)	MB
1979	*Man of Action (Mountbatten Suite,* 3rd Movement)	(C)	MB
1980	*Broadlands (Mountbatten Suite,* 2nd Movement)	(C)	Orch
1989	*Selection of English Songs*	(A)	Orch
1990	*In Praise of Gifford House*	(C)	Choral

* Classed by RMBS Central Music Library as compositions.

* * * * *

In addition to the above, Sir Vivian Dunn composed and arranged other music which cannot be accurately dated. This music is given below in alphabetical order, by type.

Ae Fond Kiss	(A)
Abide With Me	(A)
Finlandia	(A)
Light Cavalry	(A)

The Lost Chord	(A)	
Purchasers Song	(A)	
A Safe Stronghold	(A)	
Trumpet Voluntary	(A)	
Yeoman of the Guard	(A)	
Jerusalem	(A)	Choral
A Life on the Ocean Wave Fanfare	(C)	Fanfare
Carillon of Thanksgiving	(C)	Fanfare
*Celebration**	(C)	Fanfare
Fanfare	(C)	Fanfare
Fanfare Ending to Fleets in Port	(C)	Fanfare
Fanfare Parts to 1812 Overture	(A)	Fanfare
Fanfare for King Henry IV	(C)	Fanfare
Fanfare for a Display	(C)	Fanfare
Fanfare for a Festival	(C)	Fanfare
Fanfares for Bugles *(untitled)*	(C)	Fanfare
Fanfare with Concert Band	(C)	Fanfare
For a Celebration	(C)	Fanfare
For a Festival	(C)	Fanfare
For a Gala Occasion	(C)	Fanfare
For a Première	(C)	Fanfare
High Command	(C)	Fanfare
Lords Taverners, Corps Of Drums	(C)	Fanfare
Man of Action Fanfare	(C)	Fanfare
Modulation for God Save the Queen	(A)	Fanfare
The Mountbatten March Fanfare	(C)	Fanfare
Orb & Sceptre Fanfare	(C)	Fanfare
Pageant Music	(A)	F'fare/Orch
Royal Flourish No 1	(C)	Fanfare
Royal Flourish No 2	(C)	Fanfare
Royal Flourish No 3	(C)	Fanfare
Royal Flush	(A)	Fanfare
Royal Naval Association Fanfare	(C)	Fanfare
Torches Fanfare	(C)	Fanfare
Trumpets	(C)	Fanfare
Yuletide Festival	(C)	Fanfare
Bring Back My Golf Ball	(A)	Humour
The Chalkies Lament	(A)	Humour
Rule Britannia (Link to Abide With Me)	(A)	Link
A Merry Christmas	(A)	MB

* Composed for the Royal Regiment of Wales.

Army, Navy and Air Force	(A)	MB
Churchill March	(A)	MB
Heart of Oak	(A)	MB
Lord Lovat's Lament	(A)	MB
Marching Through Georgia	(A)	MB
The Marines Hymn (USMC)	(Tr)	MB
Singing With the Services (Medley)	(A)	MB
Westering Home	(A)	MB
Valse Marilyn	(A)	MB
Blow the Man Down	(A)	Orch
Incidental Music to Henry VIII	(A)	Orch
Lullaby (Brahms)	(A)	Orch
Rule Britannia (as a salute)	(A)	Orch
When Johnny Comes Down to Hilo	(A)	Orch
*Bridal March**	(C)	Religious
Carols, various	(A)	Religious
Eternal Father (Hymn 540)	(A)	Religious
Fight the Good Fight	(A)	Religious
*For a Processional Occasion – Charles & Verena**	(C)	Religious
Guide Me O Thy Great Redeemer (Hymn 397)	(A)	Religious
Immortal, Invisible	(A)	Religious
It is a Thing Most Wonderful	(A)	Religious
Lest We Forget	(A)	Religious
Lift Up Your Hearts	(A)	Religious
Love Divine, All Loves Excelling	(A)	Religious
O Worship the King	(A)	Religious
Onward Christian Soldiers	(A)	Religious
Praise to the Lord	(A)	Religious
Soldiers of Christ, Arise	(A)	Religious
There is a Green Hill	(A)	Religious
Thy Hand, O God, Has Guided	(A)	Religious
Traditional English Airs	(A)	Wind En

* Classed by RMBS Central Music Library as a composition.

* * * * *

Sir Vivian Dunn also composed and arranged other pieces of music which were either for a specific occasion or were re-cycled into other music. He also transcribed some of his music from orchestra to military band and vice-versa.

APPENDIX E

The Commercial Royal Marines Recordings of F Vivian Dunn

Compiled by John Ambler

Chairman, UK Branch of the International Military Music Society

KEY: (R) = Re-release, or taken from long playing records
(C) = Compilation

NOTE: Details are as given on the recording sleeves

1940	*Amporita Roca, La Belle Pense Op 98*	Capt Dunn, Orchestra of RM Portsmouth Div
1940	*Temple Bells, Less Than The Dust*	"
1940	*Kashmiri Song, Till I Awake*	"
1940	*A Life on the Ocean Wave, Hearts of Oak*	"
1941	*Grasshoppers Dance, Turkish Patrol Opus 83*	"
1941	*A! Frangesa, El Abanico*	"
1941	*Merry Widow Selection Pts 1 & 2*	"
1941	*La Caprice De Nanette, Demande et Réponse*	"
1941	*Un Sonnet d'Amour, Tarantelle Fretillante*	"
1942	*Skaters Waltz, Estudiantina Waltz*	"
1942	*Dance of the Comedians, Perpetuum Mobile*	"
1942	*Gypsy Love Selection Pts 1 & 2*	"
1950	*Salute to Amethyst, Pompey Chimes*	Maj Dunn, Band of RM Portsmouth Div
1950	*Royal Vanguard March, The Springbok March*	"
1950	*Prelude to the Morning, Sunset*	Maj Dunn, Band & Bugles of HM Royal Marines

1953	*A Life on the Ocean Wave, Hearts of Oak* (45rpm)	Capt Dunn, Orchestra of RM Portsmouth Div	(R)
1953	**'*Music by the Band of HM Royal Marines Portsmouth*'** – Lt Col F V Dunn *A Life on the Ocean Wave, The Globe and Laurel, The Captain General, The Sailors Holiday, Three Jolly Sailormen, March No 3 from Suite No 1 in Eb Major, Under the White Ensign, Cannatex, Waltzing Matilda, The Huntsmen, With Sword and Lance, Washington Post, Semper Fidelis, Blaze Away, Army of the Nile*		HMV
1953	*The Globe and Laurel, A Life on the Ocean Wave*	Major F V Dunn, Band of RM Portsmouth	(R)
1954	**'*Marching With the Marines*'** – Lt Col F V Dunn and RM Portsmouth *Army of the Nile, Washington Post, Under the White Ensign, With Sword and Lance, Semper Fidelis, Waltzing Matilda, Blaze Away, A Life on the Ocean Wave.*		(R) Gramophone Co Ltd (Aust)
1954	*The Huntsmen/Waltzing Matilda*	Lt Col F V Dunn, Band of RM Portsmouth	(R)
1954	*The Sailors Holiday/Army of the Nile*	"	
1954	*Under the White Ensign/The Captain General*	"	
1954	*Waltzing Matilda, March from Suite No 3*	"	
1954	*Washington Post/Blaze Away*	"	
1954	*Washington Post/Blaze Away* (45rpm)	"	
1955	*Cockleshell Heroes/Royal Review*	Lt Col F V Dunn, Band of RM School of Music	
1956	**'*White City Searchlight Tattoo 1956*'** – Lt Col F V Dunn & RM Massed Bands *Combined Services Fanfare, Sunset Ceremony*		EMI
1954	*Brass Buttons, Amethyst March*	Lt Col F V Dunn, Band of RM School of Music	
1957	**'*Royal Tournament 1957*'** – Lt Col F V Dunn & RM Massed Bands *Fanfare, Under the White Ensign, Trumpet Voluntary, The Little Bugler, Beating Retreat Ceremony, Brass Buttons, Commando Patrol, Ave Maria, Sunset, Salute for Heroes, Rule Britannia, National Anthem, A Life on the Ocean Wave*		EMI
1958	**'*Listen to the Royal Marines Band*'** – Lt Col F V Dunn & Band of RM School of Music *Commando Patrol, The Tudor Maiden, Tamboo, Cornet Carillon, Jesu, joy of man's desiring, Hungarian March, The Medallion, Serenata, Two Little Finches, Sandpaper Ballet, Pomp & Circumstance March No 5 Op 39.* (Also released as **'*Band of the Royal Marines*'** by HMV)		EMI
1958	**'*Band of HM Royal Marines*'** (EP) – Lt Col F V Dunn & Band of RM School of Music *Commando Patrol, The Medallion, March No 6 from Music for a Festival, The Tudor Maiden*		EMI
1959	**'*Colonel Bogey Marches On*'** – Lt Col F V Dunn & Band of RM School of Music *Colonel Bogey, Holyrood, The Thin Red Line, The Two Imps, The Voice of the Guns, The Great Little Army, Eagle Squadron, Dunedin, By Land and Sea, On the Quarterdeck, The Vanished Army, Thoughts, The Standard of St George*		HMV

1959 **'Marching With the Royal Marines, No 1'** (EP) – Lt Col F V Dunn & Band of RM School of Music (R) EMI
The Thin Red Line, The Voice of the Guns, The Great Little Army, The Standard of St George

1959 **'Marching With the Royal Marines, No 3'** (EP) – Lt Col F V Dunn & Band of RM School of Music (R) EMI
Holyrood, Eagle Squadron, The Vanished Army, By Land and Sea

1961 **'Music of the Sea'** – Lt Col F V Dunn, Band of RM School of Music EMI
Sink the Bismark, HM Jollies, Drake's Drum, The Old Superb*, Shenandoah, Viscount Nelson, Soldiers of the Sea, The Shanghai Sailor, Tradewinds*, Drake Goes West*, Sea Songs, Anchors Aweigh* (* with Frederick Harvey, Baritone)

1961 **'Music from the Ceremonies of Beating Retreat & Tattoo'** – Lt Col F V Dunn & Band of RM School of Music EMI
The Captain General, Where e'er You Walk, Mechanised Infantry, Ceremonial Parade Fanfare, Emblazoned Drums, The British Grenadiers, Hearts of Oak, Land of Hope and Glory, Cockaigne, Crimond, Sunset, Salute for Heroes Fanfare, The Middy, March and Air, Sambre et Meuse, Ceremonial Ruffle of Drums, Lilliburlero, Passing By, Crown Imperial, Royal Flourish No 2, Nightfall in Camp, Jerusalem, A Life on the Ocean Wave.

1961 **'Nightfall in Camp'** (EP) – Lt Col F V Dunn & Band of RM School of Music EMI
Crown Imperial, Royal Flourish No 2, Nightfall in Camp, Land of Hope & Glory, Cockaigne, Evening Hymn, Salute for Heroes, Rule Britannia.

1961 **'Marching On With the Royal Navy'** (EP) – Lt Col F V Dunn & Band of RM School of Music (R) EMI
Soldiers of the Sea, Viscount Nelson, HM Jollies, Anchors Aweigh

1961 **'Tchaikovsky'** – Lt Col F V Dunn & Band of RM School of Music. With the Philharmonia Orchestra EMI
1812 Overture

1961 **'Songs of the Sea'** (EP) – Lt Col F V Dunn & Band of RM School of Music (R) HMV
Drake's Drum, The Old Superb, Tradewinds, Drake Goes West
(All with Frederick Harvey, Baritone)

1962 **'On Land & Sea'** – Lt Col F V Dunn & Band of RM School of Music EMI
Cockleshell Heroes, Scherzo from Music for a Festival, Country Gardens, The Little Admiral, The Fishermen of England*, March from Suite No 2 in F Major, Derby Day, Night Flight to Madrid, The New Colonial, Up from Somerset*, Glorious Devon*, Bugler's Holiday, Pomp & Circumstance March No 4 in G Major Opus 39.*
(* = With Frederick Harvey, Baritone)

1962 **'Edinburgh Tattoo 1962'** – Lt Col F V Dunn & Band of RM School of Music Waverley
Musical Tribute to Scotland, All the Nice Girls love a Sailor

1963 **'Splendour of the March'** – Lt Col F V Dunn & Band of RM School of Music EMI
Grand March from Tannhäuser, Alla Marcia from 'Karelia' Suite, March from Little Suite Op 53, Entrance and March of the Peers from Iolanthe, Marche Militaire Française, Under the White Ensign, L'Entente Cordiale, Semper Fidelis, On the Square, No Hiding Place, España, Army of the Nile.
(US version was **'The Sound of HM Royal Marines Vol II'** – Liberty)

1963	**'1812 Overture'** – Lt Col F V Dunn & Band of RM School of Music with the Philharmonia Orchestra *1812 Overture.*		
1964	**'300 Glorious Years'** – Lt Col F V Dunn & Band of RM School of Music *Royal Tournament Fanfare, A Life on the Ocean Wave, Spanish March, Lilliburlero, The British Grenadiers, The Dashing White Sergeant, Southerly Wind and a Cloudy Sky, Braganza, Soldiers Chorus from Faust, Marching Through Georgia, The Globe and Laurel, Under the Banner of Victory, Sarie Marais, The Admiral's Regiment, The Preobrajensky March, Silver Bugles, Glorious Victory, Barcelona, Cavalry of the Clouds, Salute to the Colours, I Vow to Thee My Country, Orb and Sceptre.*		EMI
1964	**'The Finest Hours'** (EP) – Lt Col F V Dunn & Band of RM School of Music *The Churchill March, The Finest Hours, Call to Adventure, Welcome the Queen*		HMV
1964	*The Finest Hours/The Longest Day* (45)	Lt Col F V Dunn & Band of RM School of Music	(R) HMV
1964	*The Churchill March/March of the Victors* (45)	Lt Col F V Dunn & the RM Band	HMV
1964	**'Marching To Victory'** (EP) – Lt Col F V Dunn & Band of RM School of Music *March of the Victors, The Contemptibles, The Longest Day, The Churchill March*		HMV
1965	**'Edinburgh Tattoo 1965'** – Lt Col F V Dunn & Band of RM School of Music *Heroes of Vittoria, Loch Maree, The Admiral's Regiment, High Road to Linton, Kate Dalrymple, Here's A Health Unto Her Majesty, Minstrel Boy, Annie Laurie, Men of Harlech, Click Go The Shears, Jorrock's Chase, Hello Dolly, Rule Britannia, Will Ye Nae Come Back Again*		Monitor
1965	**'The Great War'** (EP) – Lt Col F V Dunn & Band of RM School of Music *Theme from the Great War, March Glorious from The Great War, The Fleet Air Arm March, Cockleshell Heroes*		HMV
1966	**'Both Sides of the Globe'** – Lt Col F V Dunn & Band of RM School of Music *Famous Songs of the British Isles, The Vedette, The Champion, Blue Devils, Here Comes the Band, Namur, A Life on the Ocean Wave, America the Beautiful, Battle Hymn of the Republic, Manhattan Beach, Ponderoso, The Black Horse Troop, The Pride of the Wolverines, The Alfafa Club March, The United States Marine Corps Hymn*		EMI
1966	**'The Art of the Military Band'** – Lt Col F V Dunn & Band of RM School of Music *Music for a Festival: 1st mvt – Intrada, 2nd mvt – Overture, 3rd mvt – Round of Seven Parts, 4th mvt Air, 5th mvt – Interlude, 6th mvt – March, 8th mvt – Scherzo, 11th mvt – Finale, English Folk Song Suite, No 1 March – Seventeen Come Sunday, No 2 Intermezzo – My Bonny Boy, No 3 March – Folk Songs from Somerset, Suite Française: 1st mvt – Normandie, 2nd mvt – Ile de France, 4th mvt – Alsace Lorraine, 5th mvt - Provence*		EMI
1966	**'1812'** – Lt Col F V Dunn & Band of RM School of Music with Bournemouth Symphony Orchestra *1812 Overture*		EMI
1967	**'Worlds Great Marches'** – Lt Col F V Dunn & Band of RM School of Music *Old Panama, The Contemptibles, Army and Marine, La Père de La Victoire, Belphegor, Marches Des Parachutistes Belges, La Ritirata Italiana, El Abanico, National Emblem, Hands Across the Sea, The Invincible Eagle, Cavalry of the Steppes, Old Comrades, Under the Double Eagle, The Gladiators' Farewell*		HMV

1968	***'Royal Tournament 1968'*** – Lt Col F V Dunn & Massed Bands of the Royal Marines *Bugles & Drums, Ceremonial Tattoo, Bugle Bells, Finale from 'New World Symphony', How About You, Girl from Ipanema, Zorba's Dance, A Tribute to Alford, Cavalry of the Steppes, Fanfare for a Royal Birthday, Sunset, Rule Britannia, National Anthem, A Life on the Ocean Wave, Sarie Marais*	EMI
1968	***'The Royal Marines Play Sousa'*** – Lt Col F V Dunn & Band of RM School of Music *El Capitan, Solid Men to the Front, Hail to the Spirit of Liberty, The Belle of Chicago, The National Game, Sound Off, The Gladiator, The Thunderer, The Gridiron Club, New York Hippodrome, Daughters of Texas, The Diplomat, Kansas Wildcats, King Cotton*	EMI
1969	***'Music of Pomp & Circumstance'*** – Lt Col F V Dunn & Band of RM School of Music *Finale from Carillon Op 75, Sursum Corda Op 11, Pomp & Circumstance March No 2 Op 39, Nimrod Op 36, Pomp & Circumstance March No 1 Op 39, Royal Wedding Fanfare No 1, Jupiter, Crown Imperial, Homage to the Queen*	EMI
1969	***'Men O' Brass and Voices'*** – Sir Vivian Dunn (Guest Conductor) *Salutation: Tribute to Sir Malcolm Sargent, Fantasy on British Sea Songs, The Old Superb From 'Songs of the Sea'*, 1812 Overture* (* = Owen Brannigan, bass, and the London Philharmonic Choir)	EMI
1972	***'Festival of Brass 1972'*** – Sir Vivian Dunn (Guest Conductor) *The Mountbatten March.* (Also featured *Supreme Command*)	EMI
?	***'West Country Songs'*** (EP) – Lt Col F V Dunn & Band of RM School of Music *Up From Somerset, Linden Lea, The Little Admiral, Glorious Devon*	EMI
?	***'Band of HM Royal Marines'*** (Portsmouth) (EP) – Lt Col F V Dunn & Band of RM Portsmouth *Three Jolly Sailormen, March No 3 from Suite No 1 in E Flat Major, The Huntsmen, Waltzing Matilda*	(R) EMI
?	***'Marching With The Royal Marines'*** (No 2) (EP) – Lt Col F V Dunn & Band of RM Portsmouth *With Sword and Lance, Washington Post, Blaze Away, Semper Fidelis*	(R) EMI
?	***'Band of HM Royal Marines'*** (Portsmouth) (EP) – Lt Col F V Dunn & Band of RM Portsmouth *The Globe and Laurel, Under the White Ensign, Cannatex, Army of the Nile*	(R) EMI
?	***'Mountbatten TV Music'*** (EP) – Lt Col F V Dunn & Band of RM School of Music *Life and Times of Lord Mountbatten Theme, The Preobrajensky March, Cockleshell Heroes*	HMV
?	**'Band, Bugles & Orchestra of HM Royal Marines'** (EP) – Major F V Dunn & Band of RM Portsmouth *Sunset, Prelude to the Morning, A Life on the Ocean Wave, Hearts of Oak*	(R) Columbia
?	***'Band of HM Royal Marines'*** (EP) – Lt Col F V Dunn & Band of RM School of Music *Colonel Bogey, Dunedin, On the Quarterdeck, Sarie Marais*	(R) EMI
?	***'On Parade'*** – Lt Col F V Dunn & Band of RM School of Music *The Captain General, Where e'er You Walk, Mechanised Infantry, Ceremonial Parade, Emblazoned Drums, The British Grenadiers, Hearts of Oak, Land of Hope and Glory, Cockaigne, Crimond, Sunset, Salute for Heroes, The Middy, March & Air, Sambre et Meuse, Ceremonial Ruffle of Drums, Lilliburlero, Passing By, Crown Imperial, Royal Flourish No 2, Nightfall in Camp, Jerusalem, A Life on the Ocean Wave, Colonel Bogey, Holyrood, The Thin Red Line, The Two Imps, The Voice of the Guns, The Great Little Army, Eagle Squadron, Dunedin, By Land and Sea, On the Quarterdeck, The Vanished Army, Thoughts, The Standard of St George*	(R) EMI

? **'Come Listen to the Band'** – Lt Col F V Dunn & Band of RM School of Music (R) EMI
Anchors Aweigh, Shenandoah, The Thunderer, Hail to the Spirit of Liberty, Bugler's Holiday, Cockleshell Heroes, Grand March from Tannhäuser, Old Panama, Hands Across the Sea, The Shanghai Sailor, The Thin Red Line, The Great Little Army, The Pride of the Wolverines, A Life on the Ocean Wave

? **'Come Listen to the Band'** (Vol III) – Lt Col F V Dunn & Band of RM School of Music (Also Lt Col Neville) (R) EMI
FVD track: *Troika from the 'Lieutenant Kijé Suite'*

? **'Marching With the Royal Marines Band'** – Lt Col F V Dunn & Band of RM School of Music (R) EMI
A Life on the Ocean Wave, Anchors Aweigh, Manhattan Beach, Blue Devils, Army of the Nile, HM Jollies, Cockleshell Heroes, March from Suite No 2 in F Major, March from Little Suite Op 53, Semper Fidelis, Under the White Ensign, The Champion, The Pride of the Wolverines

? **'Very Best of Military Bands'** – Lt Col F V Dunn & Band of RM School of Music (Also Lt Col Neville and others) (R) EMI
FVD Tracks: *King Cotton, Cavalry of the Steppes, On the Quarterdeck*

Compilations

1970 **'Marching With the Marines'** – Lt Col F V Dunn & Band of RM School of Music (C) EMI
A Life on the Ocean Wave, Anchors Aweigh, Army of the Nile/March from Suite No 2 in F Major, Under the White Ensign, Manhattan Beach, Semper Fidelis, HM Jollies, Cockleshell Heroes, The Champion, Blue Devils, The Pride of the Wolverines
(Also re-issued post 1970)

1976 **'Sunset'** – Lt Col F V Dunn & Band of RM School of Music (Also Lt Col Neville) (C) EMI
FVD Tracks: *The Preobrajensky March, El Capitan, King Cotton, Cavalry of the Steppes*

1977 **'Crown Imperial'** – Lt Col F V Dunn & Band of RM School of Music (Also Lt Col Neville) (C) EMI
FVD Tracks: *Royal Wedding Fanfare No 1, Homage to the Queen, Hearts of Oak, Land of Hope & Glory, Cockaigne, Crimond, Sunset, Salute to the Colours, I Vow to Thee My Country, Orb & Sceptre, Crown Imperial*

1977 **'Very Best of the Band of the Royal Marines'** – Lt Col F V Dunn & Band of RM School of Music (Also Lt Col Neville)
FVD Tracks: *Colonel Bogey, The Standard of St George, The Great Little Army, El Abanico, National Emblem, Anchors Aweigh, Semper Fidelis, Cockleshell Heroes, España, A Life on the Ocean Wave*

1978 **'The Very Best of the Royal Marines'** – Lt Col F V Dunn & Band of RM School of Music (Lt Col Neville) (C) EMI
FVD Tracks: *Colonel Bogey, The Standard of St George, The Great Little Army, El Abanico, National Emblem, Anchors Aweigh, Semper Fidelis, Cockleshell Heroes, España, A Life on the Ocean Wave*

1978 **'Songs of Land and Sea'** (By Frederick Harvey with various bands and orchestras) (C) EMI
The following tracks feature Lt Col F V Dunn & the Band of RM School of Music:
The Fishermen of England, The Little Admiral, Drake's Drum, The Old Superb, Up from Somerset, Glorious Devon, Tradewinds, Drake Goes West

1980 **'This is the Royal Marines Band'** – Lt Col F V Dunn & Band of RM School of Music (Also Lt Col Neville and Lt Col Mason) (C) EMI
FVD Track: *Cavalry of the Steppes*

1980 **'The Royal Marines'** – Lt Col F V Dunn & Band of RM School of Music (Also Lt Col Neville and Lt Col Mason) (C) EMI
FVD Tracks: *Anchors Aweigh, Semper Fidelis, Colonel Bogey, King Cotton, The Preobrajensky March*

1981 **'The Spectacular Royal Marines'** – Lt Col F V Dunn & Band of RM School of Music (Also Lt Col Neville) (C) EMI
FVD Tracks: *Alla Marcia ('Karelia' Suite), Grand March (Tannhäuser), Jupiter, Crown Imperial*

1983 **'Here Comes the Band'** – Lt Col F V Dunn & Band of RM School of Music (C) EMI
A Life on the Ocean Wave, The Vedette, The Contemptibles, Old Comrades, Sarie Marais, Viscount Nelson, The Belle of Chicago, The Gladiator, Cavalry of the Steppes, Barcelona, English Folk Song Suite, Country Gardens, March from Suite No 2 in F, Here Comes the Band, Pomp & Circumstance March No 1 Op 39

1983 **'Music of the British Isles'** – Lt Col F V Dunn & Band of RM School of Music (Also other bands) (C) EMI
FVD Tracks: *Famous Songs of the British Isles, Glorious Devon*

1987 ***'Under the White Ensign'*** – Lt Col F V Dunn & Band of RM School of Music (C) EMI
(Also Lt Col Neville)
FVD Tracks: *Emblazoned Drums, The British Grenadiers, Sambre et Meuse, The Standard of St George, Land of Hope & Glory, Cockaigne, Rule Britannia, Under the White Ensign, Dashing White Sergeant, Marching Through Georgia, The Preobrajensky March, Famous Songs of the British Isles, America the Beautiful, The United States Marine Corps Hymn, Entry of the Gladiators, Sussex by the Sea*

1989 ***'Best of the Royal Marines'*** – Lt Col F V Dunn & Band of RM School of Music (C) EMI
(Also Lt Col Neville)
FVD Tracks: *Pomp & Circumstance No 1, El Capitan, Solid Men to the Front, The Thunderer, King Cotton, Army & Marine, La Père de La Victoire, National Emblem, Hands Across the Sea, Invincible Eagle, Old Comrades, Under the Double Eagle, L'Entente Cordiale, Semper Fidelis, Bugler's Holiday, Anchors Aweigh, Colonel Bogey, On the Quarterdeck, Derby Day, Old Panama, The Contemptibles*

? ***'Here Comes the Band'*** – Lt Col F V Dunn & Band of RM School of Music (C) HMV
A Life on the Ocean Wave, The Vedette, Old Comrades, The Contemptibles, Sarie Marais, Viscount Nelson, Belle of Chicago, The Gladiator, Cavalry of the Steppes, Barcelona, Country Gardens, Here Comes the Band, Pomp & Circumstance March No 1, March (Holst), English Folk Song Suite

? ***'Military Band Favourites'*** – Lt Col F V Dunn & Band of RM School of Music (C) EMI
(Also other bands and DoMs)
Old Panama, Army of the Nile, El Abanico, The New Colonial, Under the Double Eagle, The Black Horse Troop, King Cotton, Sarie Marais, Seventeen Come Sunday, Blue Devils, The Globe and Laurel, Glorious Victory, On the Square, Cockleshell Heroes

? ***'Best of the Royal Marines'*** – Lt Col F V Dunn & Band of RM School of Music (C) EMI
(Also Lt Col Neville)
FVD Tracks: *Pomp & Circumstance No 1, El Capitan, Solid Men to the Front, The Thunderer, King Cotton, Army and Marine, La Père de la Victoire, National Emblem, Hands Across the Sea, Invincible Eagle, Old Comrades, Under the Double Eagle, L'Entente Cordiale, Semper Fidelis, Bugler's Holiday, Anchors Aweigh, Colonel Bogey, On the Quarterdeck, Derby Day, Old Panama, The Contemptibles.*

Note: Whilst reissues, particularly EPs and singles taken from Long Playing records, have been prevalent since the early 1950s, the compilation recordings of the Royal Marines became prolific during the 1970s and 1980s. Out of 85 recordings featuring bands and orchestras conducted by Sir Vivian Dunn only 46 were original – the remainder being either reissues or compilations.

Editorial Additions

In 1994 the Band of HM Royal Marines Plymouth, conducted by Captain J R Perkins LRAM ARCM LGSM RM, produced the following CD devoted entirely to Sir Vivian Dunn's marches:

'The Martial Music of Sir Vivian Dunn' Clovelly
(A musical salute to the Doyen of British Military Music)
Supreme Command, Cockleshell Heroes, Cannatex, The Globe and Laurel, Royal Vanguard, Man of Action, Westering Home, Sarie Marais, The Admiral's Regiment, The Preobrajensky March, The Captain General, Salute For Heroes, Commando Patrol, Where e'er You Walk, Soldiers of the Sea, Passing By (The WRNS March), March and Air, Under The White Ensign, The Mountbatten March, The Tudor Maiden, Famous Song of the British Isles

In 1998 the Royal Marines Historical Society released the following CD of re-mastered recordings, originally produced during WWII by the orchestra of Portsmouth Division (conducted by Captain F Vivian Dunn MVO ARAM RM) for the Overseas Recorded Broadcast Service:

'Concert Classics' Vol 1,
Capt F Vivian Dunn and the RM Portsmouth Division orchestra Eastney Collection
Montmartre from 'The Paris Suite', Trepak from 'The Nutcracker Suite', The Arcadians Overture, The Swan from 'Carnival des Animaux', Spring, 'Petite Suite de Concert', 1st mvt - La Caprice de Nanette', 2nd mvt - Demande et Réponse, 3rd mvt - Un Sonnet d'Amour, Bells Across the Meadow, Grenadiers Waltz, Dainty Lady Intermezzo, Bohemian Girl, By the Sleepy Lagoon, Waldteufel Memories, Perpetuum Mobile

* * * * *

Below are listed the LP recordings of orchestras conducted by Sir Vivian Dunn which were produced following his retirement from the Royal Marines:

'A Festival of British Light Music' EMI 1970
The Orchestra of the Light Music Society
Also released as **'Britain's Choice'**, The Orchestra of the Light Music Society Studio 2 Stereo 1970
March from 'The Colour Suite', À La Claire Fontaine, Suite of English Folk-Dances, 1st mvt - Jenny Plucks Pears, 2nd mvt - Ten Pound Lass, 3rd mvt - Dick's Maggot, 4th mvt – Nonesuch, 5th mvt - Hunt the Squirrel, 6th mvt - Woodicock, March from 'A Little Suite', The Boulevardier, The Watermill, Tabarinage, Suite: 'The Ring of Kerry', 1st mvt - Jaunting Car, 2nd mvt - Lough Leane, 3rd mvt - Killorglin Fair

'Percy Grainger'
The Orchestra of the Light Music Society Studio 2 Stereo 1970
Country Gardens, Molly on the Shore, Londonderry Air, Handel in the Strand, Mock Morris, Shepherd's Hey, Children's Overture Op. 17, The Haunted Ballroom, Dusk, Shepherd Fennel's Dance

'The Music of Percy Grainger' EMI 1970
The Orchestra of the Light Music Society
Country Gardens, Molly on the Shore, Irish tune from County Derry (The Londonderry Air), Handel in the Strand, Mock Morris, Shepherd's Hey

'Arthur Sullivan' EMI 1972
City of Birmingham Symphony Orchestra
The Tempest , No 1 – Introduction, No 4 - Prelude Act III, No 6 - Banquet Dance, No 7 - Overture Act IV, No 10 - Dance of Nymphs and Reapers, No 11 - Prelude Act V, No 12c - Epilogue, Merchant of Venice Suite, No 1 – Introduction, No 3 – Bourée, No 5 - à la Valse, No 7 - Finale, 'In Memoriam' Overture in C

'1812 Overture' Polydor 1975
The Scottish National Orchestra
Polovtsian Dances from 'Prince Igor', Waltz from 'Eugene Onegin', Polonaise from 'Eugene Onegin', Russlan and Ludmilla Overture, 1812 Overture

'Music of England' Polydor 1974; Chalfont 1977
The Bournemoth Symphony Orchestra
Trumpet Voluntary, When I am laid in earth 'Dido and Aeneas', Yeomen of the Guard Overture, Minuet 'Berenice', Nimrod 'Enigma Variations', March 'Things to Come', Greensleeves, Jupiter (extract) from The Planets Suite, Rosamund 'Where the Rainbow Ends', Crown Imperial

'Sounds of the Desert' State Records 1978
London Symphonic Concert Orchestra
The Arab Horse - Dance, Jarma - Waltz, Understanding - Serenade, Dedicated to my Mother's Soul - Lament, Nahed - Dance, The Autumn Dance – Dance, The Voice of Salah Addin Al Aubi – March, Tripoli's Beauty – Dance, The Whisper of the Breeze – Romantic, Sunset in the Desert – Serenade, The Bride of the Nomad Bedouin – Dance

'Music for a Country Garden' (C) CD, EMI1992
The Orchestra of the Light Music Society
The Watermill, Shepherd Fenne;'s Dance, À La Claire Fontaine, Suite of English Folk Dances, Dusk

* * * * *

In 1971 Sir Vivian Dunn also recorded an LP in honour of the 1900th anniversary of the founding of York, with the York Celebration Choir, the Grimethorpe Colliery Brass Band and the Hammond Sauce Works Brass Band:

'Stars on Sunday – A Choral Celebration' York Records 1971
Dies Irae, Hallelujah Amen from Judas Maccabeus, Battle Hymn of the Republic, Ave Maria, Jerusalem, O God our help in ages past, Onward Christian Soldiers, Easter Hymn from 'Cavalleria Rusticana', Abide with me, Unfold ye Portals, The Holy City, Hallelujah Chorus from 'The Messiah'

APPENDIX F

Major Appointments of Directors of Music mentioned

PDM - Principal Director of Music, Royal Marines
DOM - Director of Music

Lieutenant Colonel Paul Neville (PJ) OBE MVO FRAM RM
PDM 1968-1978. DOM Plymouth 1960-1961;
DOM Portsmouth 1961-1966

Lieutenant Colonel Jim Mason (JR) OBE MVO LRAM ARCM LGSM RM
PDM 1978-1982, DOM Portsmouth 1970-78

Lieutenant Colonel Graham Hoskins (GAC) OBE MVO LRAM RM
PDM 1982-1989, DOM Portsmouth 1978-1982

Lieutenant Colonel John Ware, (JM) BA OBE FRAM RM
PDM 1989-1994. DOM Commando Forces 1982-1987

Lieutenant Colonel Richard Waterer (RA) OBE MMus LRAM RM
PDM 1994 onwards

Major J F Ricketts RM (Kenneth Alford)
DOM Depot Deal 1927-1930, DOM Plymouth 1930-1944

Major P S G O'Donnell MVO MusBac(Oxon) LRAM RM
DOM Plymouth 1916-1928; DOM Chatham 1928-1937

Captain R P O'Donnell MVO FRAM RM
DOM Portsmouth 1919-1931

Lieutenant B W O'Donnell MVO FRAM RM
DOM Portsmouth 1917-1923: DOM RM Depot, Deal 1923-1927

Captain Tommy Francis (T) LRAM ARCM RM
DOM Chatham 1937-1950

Captain Dick Stoner (RH) LRAM RM
DOM Plymouth 1944-1950

Captain Ken McLean (KA) MVO MBE LRAM RM
DOM Portsmouth 1952-1961

Captain Tommy Lambert (LT) MVO LRAM RM
DOM Portsmouth 1966-1970

Captain Tommy Lang (W) MBE LRAM RM
DOM Plymouth 1950-1960

Captain Wally Shillitto (WW) LRAM RM
DOM Plymouth (Commando Forces) 1970-1977

Captain Peter Sumner (PAG) MBE LRAM ARCM RM
DOM Portsmouth 1966

Captain Ted Whealing (EP) MVO BA LRAM ARCM LTCL RM
DOM Portsmouth 1987-1991

Captain David Cole (DC) MVO MMus ARAM RM
DOM Portsmouth 1995-1998

Index

This index does not include Appendices, composers or compositions with a few exceptions. Neither does it include frequently recurring places such as Portsmouth, Plymouth, Chatham, Eastney, Deal, etc. References to photographs are in italic.

A

B

C

D

H

I

J

K

N

O

P

Q

R

S

T

U

V

W

Y

Z

THE ROYAL MARINES HISTORICAL SOCIETY

The Royal Marines Historical Society has been in existence for over 30 years. In addition to the publication of newsletters, journals and special booklets, meetings are held annually at Portsmouth and in the West County.

Its objectives are to carry out research into all aspects of the history of the Royal Marines, to work closely with the Royal Marines Museum and to carry out detailed research into particular historical projects.

At present the Society has nearly 250 active members, many of them retired Royal Marines, but welcomes others who are genuinely interested in particular facets of Royal Marines history and are prepared to contribute actively to the Society.

Further details may be obtained from:

Membership Secretary
Royal Marines Historical Society
c/o The Royal Marines Museum
Southsea
Hampshire PO4 9PX

EASTNEY COLLECTION

Eastney Collection was formed in 1998 primarily to oversee the restoration and marketing of the Royal Marines Historical Society's collection of historical recordings by the bands and orchestras of the Royal Marines. The first CDs and cassettes in a series of three volumes, entitled *Concert Classics*, were released in December 1998 to mark the 75th anniversary of the amalgamation of the Royal Marine Artillery with the Royal Marines Light Infantry in 1923. They comprise the wartime recordings made for the Overseas Recorded Broadcasting Service, by the Orchestra of Portsmouth Division Royal Marines conducted by Captain F Vivian Dunn MVO ARAM, as described in this biography.

The project is designed as a charitable venture with profits from sales being assigned to the Royal Marines Band Service Benevolent Fund.

Further information on this series of restored recordings may be obtained from:

Eastney Collection
60 Mayford Road
London SW12 8SN
Tel. 020 8673 6157 Fax 020 8772 9545
e-mail: eastneycol@aol.com